TRAVELING
THE CIRCUITS

TRAVELING THE CIRCUITS

By

Buck & Arlene Weimer

PREFACE

The motivation for sharing this story of love, travel, and adventure was because… well… we're getting old. Most of the events told in this tale happened over fifty years ago, a half a century. Memories grow dim and our ability to recall people, places, feelings, and experiences was slow and strained, but some memorable scenes remained imbedded and retain their vitality from the overall adventure. The facts may vary, but the experience of it all remains an integral truth of our two lives – forever.

The dimness of these memories does not make the events any less life changing, courageously uplifting, rewarding, and edifying; even though many experiences were sometimes terrifying, exasperating, and painfully difficult. Often, while recalling the details of our experiences, there was a tension in our relationship while trying to agree on the multitude of names, places and transportation choices. However, our together-memories remained clear enough providing the substance and opportunity to remember the life-changing events to write them down.

But together we were able to recall so much more than either of us alone. Collectively, our one plus one is greater than two as we learned and grew during this journey – at least as viewed from the present – for an autobiographical memory of events as remembered; some explicit, some implicit.

(If you really want to get to know someone, backpack with them around the world for a while.)

Verbally, we've told and retold this story many times to family, friends, and sometimes to acquaintances, but never in its entirety. A history of this length, depth, and breadth takes a very long time to share; and the average person begins to mentally drift away after the second or third part if the whole story.

So, we decided to commit the resources – the old passports, a few pictures that survived monsoon rains, several scratched artifacts from the discarded backpacks, and the myriad of memories in each other's head – to the written word in hopes that it will be read and enjoyed as a legacy to our loved ones; and communally held in digital form. An additional hope is to instill and inspire others with the significance of the travel imperative.

Our children and grandchildren are ultimately the benefactors of this enriched storied experience.

Before leaving the confines of our comfort zones, we were yearning for freedom, but from what, we didn't really know or give it much thought. Transcendence beckoned.

We were confident in knowing we would somehow, somewhere find a real identity, latch onto some meaning of why, the truths about the good life, and a value to call our own anchor to set us free. We were raw but fearless, opposite souls in so many ways, yet so full of child-like wonder, hoping for a fulfillment in the strangeness of the yet-to-be-experienced.

We wanted to again feel that breathless tonic of the adventure lure while reigniting the traveling often-overwhelming stimulus curiosity – a sincere spirit of investigation, the yearning of discovery; driven to exploration. Having lightly tasted the travel lure before meeting, could we again tap into those times of losing ourselves, expanding our consciousness, and connecting with humanity in return? Trust in each other, freeing ourselves from most social entanglements, we wanted more and felt responsible enough to corral the underlying fears; allowing a vision of the next horizon!!!

Love we had; albeit showing signs of needing growth. Arlene had some insecurity issues; being brought up over-protected by her parents whose first child died of polio at age 3. I had deep seated, and unresolved abandonment issue buried in my layered mind from being raised fatherless.

Such was our life by the end of 1969. I was the age of 30 and Arlene was 26.

FOREWORD

There are a thousand ways to get to where you want to go. It is simply a matter of choosing which circuit to ride. The hardest part of traveling is getting out the front door! Once on the doorstep and onto the circuit, travel anywhere in the world could be possible. What liberation!

We were two inter-connected and wondering souls adrift in a culture of clashing values and shifting mores in Venice Beach, CA. The late 60's was filled with wild and strangely exciting times of creative newness and comforting oldness everywhere. We wanted to escape the limitations of a mono-culture society while in search of a larger one. What does all of humankind have in common regardless of cultural upbringings?

Arlene was about to be awarded a Ph.D. in the Psychology of Aging from the University of Southern California. I was a factory worker at Bob Mitchell Designs supervising in the silk-screen wallpaper business and a wanna-be writer. While sketching early drafts of the Darien Jungle story, I played lots of paddle tennis by the beach across the street from our apartment. And, while not completely atheist, we strongly questioned religious dogma and every proselytizer. Most likely we would have been categorized agnostics.

The Beatles were big, (and had already been to India), Woodstock (unknown to us at the time) had attracted more than 350,000, Hendrix had just died of an overdose, and the first man had walked on the moon.

The Vietnam War, The Pentagon Papers, crooked politicians, flagrant marijuana users, long-hair, rock music, unique dress styles, and everything psychedelic (augmented by drugs) was the rage, creating a huge generational division bordering on sedition.

Memory is a funny thing! I remember when the first atomic bomb went off!

To avoid this inner and outer turmoil and return to the adrenalin-filled subculture and lifestyle of the international-traveler, we were poised and motivated to go <u>somewhere</u>; to go wherever and whenever directed by our excited hearts and minds. We were <u>travelers</u> and staunchly resisted any identification of being a mere <u>tourist</u>.

Inwardly there was a thirst for the untried and the unrevealed, though we sometimes identified with Dylan's "Like A Rolling Stone". Wanting to transcend our cultural history, we yearned to feel free and yet wanted to be a part of total humanity.

Our travel adventures lasted more than 2 years!

After having a typical "hippie wedding" in Sierra Madre Canyon, Ca., we drove an old '59 Chevy across the US. We got married again (2nd time) in Brooklyn, with Arlene's mother orchestrating a "proper" wedding; even finding an 80-year-old rabbi willing to marry a Jewish princess to an Irish-German *Goy*.

We crossed the Atlantic, docking near Athens on a creaky Greek freighter, after an exciting stopover in Tripoli, Libya. Then on to Israel for an indelible connection to history amid the Christian holiday spectacle. A Turkish train ride and we were off on the long chain of bus rides to Afghanistan into a backward glance in time, then quickly through Pakistan.

What can be said about India that has not already been said? A lot because it must be experienced! Kathmandu, Nepal was beyond superlatives, before landing in SE Asia, Bangkok, Penang, and Singapore. After Singapore our ride took a decidedly different route. Bali in 1971 was a dream fulfilled, but then…we joined as crew of a 40' sailboat crossing the Indian Ocean to the Seychelle Islands for our season in the sun.

Riding the circuits home from the Islands, we took a freighter to Pakistan, and a return to our glory days in Afghanistan. After a good bus ride to Istanbul, we somehow arrived in Milan and met a shady Italian guy who drove us to Amsterdam. In a manner unremembered, we managed to get on the passenger list of a chartered flight full of birdwatchers from London scheduled for New York. The flight was diverted to Philadelphia due to bad weather, barely affording the cost of transportation to New York.

Seems like a normal conclusion, right? But there was more riding to do!

Arlene artfully maneuvered her way into a one-year contract, teaching at Florida Technological University in Orlando. Our lifestyle and appearances were not a good fit for most Floridians, but during Arlene teaching courses we became friends with several locals and a few students from Costa Rica. After the end of Arlene's contract, we transformed a school bus into a camper and 9 of us drove it to Costa Rica and established a spiritual commune. (Out of breath yet?)

We had personal spiritual experiences there. Nine months later we were back in Venice Beach, CA where it all had begun; and soon gave birth to our lives anew in Pueblo, CO. where we are piecing together the fragmented events of this story. Forgive our untrained collective memories.

Memory is a funny thing. But…the question remains: does traveling (not tourism) serve a higher purpose; with all the personal gains, were <u>we</u> serving a higher purpose?

For most of the writing, the pronoun **_we_** was used, since the book is about both of us. In order to differentiate between our individual memories, **_I_** was used to refer to Buck (as the primary writer), and writings in italics were used to refer to Arlene's specific memories. However, this entire project was unequivocally a totally joint effort from beginning to end.

The use of the term _Circuits_ was unfamiliar to us during our travels, but when the writing started and the memories surged, we wanted to identify ourselves as such. As a noun the word _circuit_ has multifarious meanings and has changed over generations, so we are very specific here. In the old (1924 Edition) Merriam-Webster dictionary the definitions of _circuit_: <u>a regular or appointed journey from place to place in the pursuit of one's</u> calling…and…<u>journeys from place to place</u>. The new Merriam-Webster dictionary, while similar, has expanded the definition to include neuropathways of the brain and the omnipresent digital circuits.

We have accepted our travels as a part of the physical, intellectual, and spiritual circuits existing in and around us, and feel we were riding these circuits when traveling.

Granted, the surrogate traveler cannot be the same as the actual circuit rider. But, if you dare, please travel along with us through these pages and delight yourself in the in-depth particulars and nuances of this journey. Enjoy the ride as if you were along; and in many ways you were.

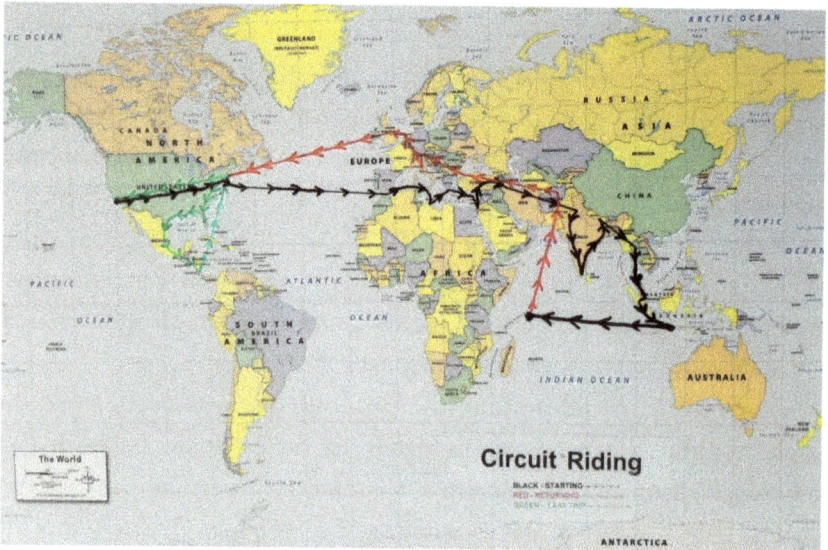

Circuit Riding

Contents

Chapter 1

THE FATEFULL $300 AND HOW WE FIRST MET

"And, ever since that night we've been together Lovers at first sight, in love forever…"

–Strangers in the Night – Frank Sinatra, Composed by Bert Kaempfert, lyrics by Charles Singleton and Eddie Snyder

Everyone travels, whether down the birthing canal, visiting a neighbor, or going abroad.

For us it seemed most appropriate to begin this travel-adventure story with the unusual and fortuitous circumstances surrounding how, when, and where we met. Especially, the Big $300 story.

Many differing circumstances of life allowed us to be in St. Thomas, the U.S. Virgin Islands at the same time. Arlene was a student on winter break from Brooklyn College graduate studies staying with her roommate's aunt somewhere on the island. As a seasoned sailor I was arriving on St. Thomas as a crewmember of a 96' ketch sailboat, the Iduna.

But since we have a friendly long-standing disagreement on some of the facts surrounding this serendipitous occurrence, we will tell the story as each of us remembered it.

My story begins with a very long back-story, and the significance of the BIG $300 DOLLARS! It feels a little selfish because it was rather long, but the importance of the $300 cannot be forgotten. With the interest of the reader in mind, attempts were made to minimizing by shorting some events while emphasizing others that fit into the overall history.

In the Spring of 1965, after driving a motorcycle from California to Panama, and having survived the several near-death experiences of walking solo through the Darien Jungle into South America (for which my 3 sons often express much gratitude, especially after reading my book about it: *"The Darien Jungle Shakedown Cruise"*).

I began island hopping up the Caribbean Islands with thoughts of returning to the pseudo-safety and gilded comfort of good ole USA. But, as fate would have it, I had this amazing and expanded good fortune of signing-on as a crew member of this big beautiful 116' sailboat, Panda by name.

The captain and a great mix male/female crew of 12 intrepids gathered for the wonderful thrill of sailing this square-rigged schooner from the Caribbean Island of British Antigua (where I boarded) up to Bermuda, and across the North Atlantic Ocean to the English port of Southampton. For me, the problem was…the captain required proof of *passport and money* by all in order to pass through immigration upon entering England. I had a passport but no money.

It all unfolded like this: The motorcycle used for the trip to the jungle I got from a good friend in Venice, CA by swapping my car, a 1955 English MG TF1500, in exchange for his motorcycle. But with the big caveat that he still owed me $300 because the car was worth more than the motorcycle. He didn't have the extra cash at the time; but vehemently promised to pay because he *really* wanted the MG. Accommodatingly, I said OK.

The captain, more impressed with my paratrooper experiences than my meager sail experience and upon hearing my story of potential funds, graciously agree to include me as a crew member sailing as far as Bermuda. He would discharge me from the Panda if I could produce the $300 once there.

So, I fired a letter off from Antigua to the friend in Venice owing me the $300, jokingly threatening him with severe punishing to sensitive body parts if, when I arrived in Bermuda there was no letter addressed to me at the general post office in Hamilton, the capital of Bermuda containing a cashier's check for $300.

It took about 3 weeks for the <u>Panda</u> to sail up to Bermuda and dock. I ran off immediately to Hamilton and the general post office and, sure enough, there was a letter for me there containing the check from my friend for $300. So, I was permitted to make the sail trip to England with the Panda and crew.

> (The true significance of this $300 story: had my letter been late getting to my friend in Venice, *or* had he not been there to receive it, *or* had he not sent it, *or* had his letter been late arriving in Bermuda...I obviously would not have been with the Panda sailing to England. The undeniable conclusion would have to be: Arlene and I would NEVER have had the opportunity to meet where and when we met. And the alternative courses for each of us are, disturbingly very different.)

Bumming around Europe that summer with the young gal I met on the <u>Panda</u> was enriching and enlightening! We watched painting Parisians along the Seine, ran with the bulls in Pamplona, and lived a creative life in a windmill on the Balearic Island of Formentera in the Mediterranean off the coast of Barcelona, Spain.

Alas, as the summer season waned and the Fall began, we separated; and I forged my way to the Canary Islands off the Western coast of Africa – specifically on the main Island of Tenerife; waiting and waiting for another sailboat to come along hoping to work my way across to the Western world. I was nearly broke, survived a shipwreck, lived off my wits, and wanted to return to the States.

A fortuitous opportunity finally arrived, when the 96-foot ketch <u>Iduna</u> under a Swiss flag dropped anchor just offshore in the Puerto Barco harbor, and the Norwegian captain came ashore asking around for an experienced seaman because the 1st mate had broken a thumb on the sail down from England.

Well, the sail across the South Atlantic on this beautiful boat was a delight – compared to the crossing of the always tumultuous North Atlantic. The setting or trimming the sails were required only a handful of times. The owner of the <u>Iduna</u> (a wealthy pharmaceutical mogul) and his entourage came onboard when we arrived on the Caribbean Island of Barbados, and soon we began island-hopping up the Caribbean vacation-style – stopping for a short while on most of the major islands. (The good news was the Norwegian captain convinced the owner to actually pay me for my time as a crew member – like all the regular crew members. He did, and I felt suddenly rich = 50 French francs per month (about $250 per) + free room and board. WOWIE!!!)

I (Arlene) was 21 years old, burned out from going to school for all but the first 5 years of my life. I was first generation Ashkenazi Jew, my parents immigrating to New York from Poland/Ukraine in 1921, to escape the pogroms, when Jews were being massacred by the Russians. My mother, who had a 7th grade education, was economically dependent on my father. She strongly encouraged me, her youngest and only surviving daughter, to be educated and independent. My parents' first child (a girl) died of polio at age 3.

Consequently, from age 3 on I recognized my mother's grief and became her comfort and confidant.

I conformed to her wishes until I turned 20 years when I moved into an apartment with my girlfriend and started to sow my wild oats. I was less interested in school than in proving that I was an attractive young woman. As a child, I was overweight and had a hook nose which I remedied at 13 years by losing weight and at 16 years by having rhinoplasty surgery straightening my nose. Years of being harassed by young schoolboys and by my brother, Ted, who was 7 years older, told me that I was "fat and ugly and would never get married." Fortunately, my brother Marty, who was 12 years my senior, was there to cuddle and comfort me.

At the time I met Buck, I had given up on men. I was being pursued by several men and was feeling guilty since I knew I was rejecting them. I was ready for a change. But the last thing I thought I wanted was a relationship with yet another young man.

The <u>Iduna</u> was moored at the St. Thomas Island dock, and the entire crew was soon given 24-hour shore-leave. (Again, WOWIE!!! my first <u>free</u> time since leaving The Canary Islands nearly a month and a half ago.) I promptly went to a nearby restaurant and ate some enchanting conch chowder with spicy rice and beans. My next inclination was to have a beer. Seeing blinking red neon "BAR" sign, I walked up the outside stairs to the second floor, went in, and ordered a beer. They didn't have any! So, I got a traditional rum and coke instead.

Sitting on a barstool, listening to oldies rock n' roll music ("Blue Velvet", "Sugar Shack" "P.S. I Love You"), and dance-watching, when in walked these two lovely American girls. I was immediately attracted to the one with long wavy blonde hair. It was Arlene!

After some insecure hesitation, and mumbling words, I asked her for a slow dance. Our bodies seemed to fit together well, and we responded perfectly to each other's every move. After exchanged pleasantries, I then said something very dumb! Because I knew the type of woman I preferred (smart and bright), and because Arlene was a blonde, I wanted to be sure she wasn't the "dumb blonde" type (my terrible stereotyping). Or, at least, that was my simplistic rationale.

So, I asked: "Have you ever read any of the writings of the Russian author Dostoevsky?" And I may have mentioned "Crime and Punishment" and/or "The Gambler" from my recent readings.

Well, it soon became obvious it was a complete turnoff for Arlene. She didn't say anymore after that and didn't look at me again after the dance. When asked to buy her a drink of some kind, she politely declined.

Oh well, "live and learn", I thought.

She and her girlfriend then left, going down the outside stairs; and I'm thinking I would never see her again. However, shortly thereafter, I heard a small commotion outside at the base of the stairs going down. Looking, it was Arlene and her girlfriend being harassed by three or four young American guys wanting them to attend a party.

I quietly walked down the stairs, intervened by separating the girls from the slightly booze-smelling guys, and helped them walk away. (I think, at that point, I became Arlene's "Knight in shining armor" and ultimately, Arlene became my "Guardian Angel".) The guys (Americans) could easily have collectively trampled me. But seeming surprised and slightly disoriented from the alcohol, they turned away; grumbling a few disquieting derogatory remarks.

Arlene's friend left and, instead of returning to the bar, we sat alone at an outdoor café by the dock and talked, and talked, and talked.

Never had I shared so much of my personal thoughts, feelings, hopes, dreams, and desires with another person. It was as if we had known each other our whole lives. We couldn't stop talking and didn't want to. We talked until the first rays of the morning light.

However, there were conspiring circumstances. With the new dawn, the <u>Iduna</u> and her crew were ready to make a 3-day trip to St. Croix, the next island in the Virgin Island group; then returning to St. Thomas.

We kissed a heavenly kiss. Arlene said she would be waiting for me on the dock when the boat returned. I hoped, upon hope. Realistically, I thought it was the last I would see of her.

The Iduna at Full Sail

Sure enough, as the <u>Iduna</u> returned into the St Thomas harbor and we began to tie her down, stern first, I looked up and there she was! I will __*always*__ remember that image of her standing alone, in a blue knit dress with the longing look in her eyes as she looked straight at me. Memory is a funny thing, and a fascinating part of the human experience. Some things can never be erased, indissolvable, always there, always a part of you. I can still see her standing there – full of loving hope. And I knew then I was in love with her. We were in love.

We were inseparable for the next twenty-four hours. But as the hours clicked away, we knew the circumstances of our different lives were continuing to move toward a separation, fulfilling our commitments and responsibilities. That tinge of doubt and fear invaded the feeling between us. Would we be able to sustain this loving bond after we went our committed ways? Or was it just another "summer love"?

Arlene and her girlfriend flew home, to Brooklyn, NY and returned to their studies, and I boarded the <u>Iduna</u> and remained with my crewmates for the sail up to Miami.

Separating, we made an anxiety-filled agreement to meet each other in Washington, DC in two months' time; during her Spring break.

In the meantime, I had to make a life-changing decision when the owner of the <u>Iduna</u> offered me a permanent full-time job, with potential for captaincy. I had to make the decision before arriving in Miami. Do I continue with the life as a seaman, **or** follow the heart with the emerging love for Arlene? The decision was clinched after remembering a line from a recently read book: "I always thought I loved the sea, but what I learned is the sea never loved me back."

I (Arlene) was socializing in the afternoon at the local bar where Buck and I later met. I returned in the evening to retrieve my sweater that I had left earlier that day, thinking I would immediately return home to my friend's aunt's home. As I walked up the stairs, I saw this handsome young blond guy and felt an immediate attraction. When he asked me to dance, I felt my heart pound with excitement, and agreed. Yes, I agree with Buck, about our bodies fitting together and gliding through the slow dance. When he asked me if I had read the great Russian authors, I was offended! I was an educated bright graduate student! Of course, looking back, I looked like a sexy "dumb blond". I did leave in a huff and was sitting outside the bar waiting for a taxi. Several young men began harassing my friend and I to go to a party, which triggered my burned-out feelings about men.

And then, Buck walked down the stairs and assertively told the young men to leave us alone. Whew! They left and I decided to give Buck another chance and agreed to sit at the outdoor café with him. He was now my knight in shining armor! (As I am writing this story, I realized that Buck reminded me of my brother Marty, who is 12 years my senior. He was my comforter when my brother Ted, who was 7 years old than me, would tease me. My early childhood unconsciously added to my attraction to Buck.)

We sat and talked from 10:00 P.M. to 7:00 A.M. when Buck was called back to the boat he was crewing on. We shared everything, from childhood memories to present feelings about life and relationships. I felt like we were soul mates. Two days later I was standing at the dock, hoping his boat would return and when I saw him on the deck sailing in, my heart was filled with joy and the thrill of a new romance that I had never felt before. Yes, we spent the next 24 hours together, sharing more of our life experiences and dreams, making love, and talking about how we wanted to continue our budding relationship.

We met in Washington, DC by way of the most unusual and fortuitous means, and guidance from unseen helpers.

I flew to D.C. from New York in December. The flight was delayed 4 hours due to a snowstorm. When I arrived at our designated meeting place in front of the Natural History Museum, Buck had long gone. I was quite anxious, (no cell phones back then to contact each other) being alone in a city without any friends or family. I decided to get a room at the nearest YWCA and then started searching for Buck by walking into every hotel in the area. After about 30 minutes, as I walked through the door of yet another hotel, a woman walking out of the hotel looked at me and asked, "Are you Arlene?" As fate, the angels would have it, Buck's sister-in law recognized me although we had never met. Truly no accidents when people meet!!!!!

Ah…together once again.

Constant in the memories of this time was a visit to the National Art Gallery where we stood mesmerized by the very large and great religious series of paintings by Salvador Dali; especially "The Sacrament of the Last Supper" and "The Christ of Saint John of the Cross". Even though, at that time, agnosticism pervaded our collective consciousness.

Having met my mother Ruth (Nan), sister Sheila, my brother Pete and wife Anna, we then traveled to Brooklyn where we met Arlene's family; mother Lilly, and father Louie; both immigrants from Poland/Russia. They were friendly and courteous enough, offering great food. But the awkwardness of being a non-Jew, a goy, and having a German last name, was undeniably projected; even if unconsciously.

We made a confidential pact to live together in California. I hitched a ride to Los Angeles and settled in an apartment on Venice Beach.

I (Arlene) remained in Brooklyn finishing the semester in graduate school, being a teaching assistant in an experimental psychology lab and doing learning experiments with rats (scars remain on my hands from rat bites to this day). It was an easy decision to drop out of school and move to California to live with the love of my life and start experiencing a new way of living. One of the influencing factors in me deciding to be with Buck, was a love letter he wrote to me while we were apart. Buck, even then, expressed his intense feelings so beautifully in writing.

I joined Buck in July and not wanting to feel the guilt of telling my overprotective Jewish mother that I was moving, told my family I was just going on a 3-week vacation. I stayed for 5 years living out of wedlock with a Goy while getting a PhD. in Psychology and Gerontology. My mother was able to overcome her hurt and disappointment and continued our relationship by phone and frequent visits. Years later, when my mother was in the early stages of Alzheimer's disease, she told me she was so hurt because I didn't tell her the truth about going to live permanently in California. She thought we had a closer more trusting relationship. My father, however, was concerned for my wellbeing, living with a Goy, and tried to pressure me into leaving Buck by disowning me for two years. TRADITION!!! When my father was 83 years old while recovering from major by-pass surgery, through tears of regret, he asked for forgiveness for disowning me saying: "How could a father ever disown his own child.?" Hugging with tear filled eyes, I replied that I had forgiven him even when we were going through our alienation, since I knew he just wanted me to be safe and marry a nice Jewish man.

Chapter 2

MARRIED – *TWICE*

"By all means, marry. If you get a good wife, you'll become happy; if you get a bad one, you'll become a philosopher."

–Socrates quote at the Delphi Oracle

Having previously lived in the Los Angeles area after a 3-year military stint in the paratroopers and before the Darien Jungle excursion, I was able to reconnect and continue the friendships and contacts there to help get reestablished, especially with an Army buddy Bill Hinkle, and his family. Seamlessly, I moved into a Venice Beach apartment as a friend was moving out, someone gave me an old used Plymouth car, and I returned to my previous job in Culver City with Bob Mitchell Designs printing silkscreened wallpaper.

While waiting, I wrote Arlene my most descriptive love letter ever, attempting to detail the full depth of my love – the first time I'd ever felt this – and how it was changing me into truly caring about another human being.

Arlene came to Venice Beach as soon as the Spring Semester was over; and we lived together for nearly five years.

I soon got a job counseling troubled teenage girls in an inpatient facility and quickly realized this was not to be my profession. The decision to leave was cinched when one of the teenage delinquent girls said" I hope you get killed driving home on the freeway." Thereafter, I had the great fortune to secure a fellowship in a PhD program at the University of Southern California in the psychology of aging (Gerontology) under the gentle tutelage of Professor James Birren. When Dr. Birren asked why I wanted to study gerontology, I spontaneously said "my maternal grandmother lived in our home for the first 17 years of my life. I truly had no real interest in aging except for the financial support.

But all was not peaches and cream in our Venice version of Paradise. I was diagnosed with Crohn's disease and took a leave of absence for a semester. The illness took over and both of us were overwhelmed. Buck withdrew spending most of his free time fixing his 30-foot sailboat (a yawl-rig). I needed more comfort and connection and became depressed.

Our relationship hit a rough patch, and we separated for 9 months. As was my relationship pattern, I would <u>run</u> at the first sign of conflict. (Or was the intimacy too close?) And run I did, crewing for 4 months on a sailboat going from Los Angeles to Puerto Vallarta and back. Coming back, I visited with Arlene and feelings stirred anew. We missed each other, but a tension remained!

I moved to San Francisco and rented a small apartment near the University of California, Berkley campus and enrolled in a writing course. My instructor was <u>Eric Hoffer</u>. It would have been impossible for me to have imagined a better teacher and of more good fortune! "The True Believer: Thoughts on the Nature of Mass Movements" (1951) I had already read and recently started "The Ordeal of Change" (1963).

Because the 60's were an obviously tumultuous time, not just in Berkley but everywhere, in class Mr. Hoffer restated in many ways: "<u>In a time of drastic change it is the learners who inherit the future. The learned usually find themselves equipped to live in a world that no longer exists.</u>"

Having met with him twice in his office, I remember he had the most penetrating glass-blue eyes and gruff voice but clear thoughts, when I told him of my desire to complete a book about my Darien Jungle experience.

He said: "<u>Write only what you know about – not anyone else's words – and sprinkle it with creative thought; no matter how different these thoughts may seem.</u>"

In the meantime, Arlene and I began having long conversations on the telephone in the evenings, long before cell phones. Soon she was taking the "Midnight Special" flights from Los Angeles to San Francisco, and we were spending more and more time together.

Eventually we were convinced of the importance of sticking together and learning to work things out; thereby expressing a willingness to confront my demons of using short-term relationships as a technique of avoiding true intimacy for fear of abandonment. For the first time in our relationship, I acknowledge that I loved Arlene and even said the forbidden "L" word. That was the true beginning of our lifetime commitment.

We resumed our lifestyle in Venice Beach and moved to an apartment on the canals; and then to West Hollywood because it was a closer drive to USC.

There was no formal marriage proposal, just a gradual acknowledgement to get married, and as soon as Arlene finished the requirements for her Ph.D., we would begin traveling. One superficial motive for marriage was to have the same name on the passports: making the travel circuits, in those days, a lot easier for getting into hotels, applying for visas, money-changing, etc.

I wanted to travel to find the truth about the good life and find more of my identity irrespective of the culture and environment in which I grew up.

(We still have those passports, both with the same issue and expiration date: September 16, 1970, to September 15, 1975. Flipping through the many pages and noting that every page is filled with either rubber stamped marks or real stamps, with languages and unknown hieroglyphics remains an incredible experience. Eliciting a nearly inexhaustible amount of nostalgia, memories, and a feeling of comfort I sometimes think it may be one of our greatest material treasures. It is also helpful when remembering dates and places. And to thin…we did all that!!!)

One of our reversion habits for getting away from the hustle and bustle of Los Angeles was to drive northwest to the small community of Sierra Madre, near Pasadena, about 35 miles or so, at the foothills of those mountains. Living there were our great friends Turtle and MT (having since forgotten their real names and last name) in an ideal and mostly secluded cabin-home with a garden-yard full of trees and flowers. We asked them, and they agreed, to be our best man and maid of honor and to have the wedding in their garden.

On June 6, 1970, we got married. Elvis was already married, so why not? It was a hippie wedding in every sense of the word, with an everything-goes atmosphere filled with all our friends, full of love, hope, and a knowingness that "we shall overcome"; as the Vietnam War raged on. (One of the great lessons I learned during this era "Your country right or wrong!" was no longer a part of my philosophy. My country was definitely <u>wrong</u> being there, on so many levels.)

We wrote our own marriage vows, of course, allowing us to feel each other's deep-seated commitment. The ceremony was presided over by a wonderfully soft-spoken all-faiths minister with whom we had previously met. It was mid-day with a slight breeze and rays of sunshine scrambled through the moving tree limbs. I will always remember the look on Arlene's face and in her eyes as: sooo sincere, so loving, drawing me in; being hypnotized, mesmerized. I wore a white Roman toga (sort of), she wore this most beautiful off-white, long, crocheted dress made with her own agile fingers and imagination, an amazing piece of art.

I completed the dress during my last year before graduating and found it was a great way to relieve stress and a vacation from my mental chatter.

The center piece of refreshments was the three-layered wedding cake; homemade chocolate-peanut butter with slices of bananas between the layers fashioned by my best friends' mother Vivian Hinkle. The smell of marijuana was pervasive. Laughter was bodacious and everywhere. We were on top of the world. And Turtle, even though he was an engineer in the aerospace industry at Jet Propulsion Laboratory, was well versed in popular music and became the DJ. So, we rocked and rolled all night long; to the old and to the new.

But all good things must come to an end. In the next two months we put into action our exit strategy for leaving and traveling cross-country to Brooklyn. Much to our glee, the glossy new passports arrived displaying the same last name. We sold the sailboat, had a garage sale, withdrew our savings, loaded what few possessions we wanted to keep into our old blue and white 1960 Chevy Bel Air, and began the long drive across to USA. A tube-tent and other light camping gear allowed us to save on hotel/motel expenses.

Again, to write about the entire trek across the USA could make a short story. But for brevity, we'll note only a few highlights.

Camping and trail hiking in Bryce Canyon and Zion National Park were exhilarating, and we stayed for several days. The ride through the Rocky Mountain on our way to Denver caused us to knowingly nod to each other: "Yeah, this looks like a place we could live!" And it was fairly easy to weasel our way into a biker "crash pad" in Denver; although we looked a little "straight" compared to them. They remained slightly suspicious during our stay.

Our longest and most memorable stop along the way was in St. Louis where we stayed with Arlene's eldest brother, Marty, his wife Esther, and their seven-year-old twin sons David and Aaron. Marty was a doctor and Esther was a social worker. The boys were a delight to be around, and we took them swimming at a local pool where I tried to teach them how to dive off the springboards; especially the high, three-meter board. Unfortunately, after I demonstrated the one-and-a-half forward somersault pike (dive) they repeated over and over and over "Do it again! Do it again!" It was hilarious, and we all enjoyed the time together.

Due to life's circumstances, Marty and Esther were unable to travel to Brooklyn for our second wedding, but they offered us a choice of gifts. It was a simple choice but not easy: to accept a signed pencil-sketch by Salvador Dali, or a hundred and fifty dollars in cash. Knowing our connection with Dali from our time at the Washington, DC National Art Museum, we were a little torn. But not for long. Knowing that a hundred and fifty dollars would carry us a long way in our travels – transportation, food, lodging, etc. – we opted for the cash. Still, we often think what the Dali sketch would be worth on today's art market.

Memory is a funny thing. **Same experience, different recollections.**

We walked under the St. Louis Gateway Arch, drove over the Mississippi River and headed straight for the Bensonhurst section of Brooklyn.

My mother, Lilly was a master at finding and getting what she wanted. She searched all over New York, and especially Brooklyn, until she found a rabbi that would marry a Jew and a goy. He was 80 years old, but with a clear mind and a soft voice; and today would probably be called a Conservative type of rabbi. And, story has it, he promised his wife, on her deathbed, to willingly marry any Jew to any goy so long as he could perceive they were in love — love being more important than tradition.

Both Weddings

It was a gala affair! Lilly and Louie found and rented a grand hall for the ceremony, many of Arlene's family and friends were there, a professional photographer was hired, a gorgeous chuppah (the altar under which we were married), a large three-layered white wedding cake was prominently displayed, I wore a yarmulke (yamaka) with a rented suit and Arlene again wore her beautiful, crocheted wedding dress with a fine white veil on her head.

Arlene's other brother Teddy (younger than Marty, but older than Arlene), was there with his then-wife Louise. My mother (Ruth), stepfather Milton ("Skidder") Scott, and my brother Pete were there; having the grace to travel all the way from Columbia, PA.

It was September 23, 1970.

After signing the legal papers, we were walked down the aisle by our parents to the flowery <u>chuppah</u>. The rabbi looked us in the eyes and read the marriage vows slowly, then told me to stomp on the linen-covered glass cup with my foot. Which I did! (Perhaps I stomped a bit <u>too</u> hard because: one, I wanted to be certain to break it, and two, I was trying to show my enthusiasm to everyone and my acceptance of their tradition.) We kissed, there was a short moment of silence, then a very loud and vigorous "<u>Mazel</u> <u>tov!</u>" was shouted by everyone (except my family who didn't understand the words or that tradition).

After more pictures, the celebration started! The dancing began with Arlene & me dancing to <u>our</u> song: "Strangers in the Night" (and is <u>still</u> our song); and each of us dancing with the others' parents. Then the loud and wonderful Jewish songs began blaring, and the Hora dancing began; led by Arlene's father, Louie. Wow! Could that guy dance! *My Dad's claim to fame was winning a Charleston Contest when he was 20 years old. When he danced joy filled his whole being. Dad passed the love of dance on to me as well as my brother Ted. A true form of self-forgetfulness!*

After the dancing, Arlene's brother, Teddy, called me to the side near the hallway and said: "If you ever hurt my sister I'll come after you and kill you." It was a full test of my pacifistic nature, my initial instinct was to punch him in the gut, but instead I quietly smirked and slowly walked away without saying a word.

My brother Ted, like my father, was protective of me, not trusting a Goy (non-Jew). Ted was diagnosed bipolar and at times impulsively expressed his anger. However, whenever I dance, I think of Ted with gratitude, since he taught me how to dance when I was 7 years old, and I know he loved me with all his heart. We both inherited the dancing gene from our dad.

We had a full meal, a wine toast, and cut the wedding cake. The music and harmonious atmosphere lingered long into the night.

The dream began exiting the front door!

Chapter 3

STONED IN LIBYA

"Courage is grace under pressure."

–Ernest Hemingway in a letter to F. Scott Fitzgerald, 1926

(A 50-year perspective offers a great advantage that only 50 years can offer when viewing the past, and when riding on the travel circuits of the world. Any time frame also offers the undeserved disadvantage because of the dissolved memories; more than remembered.)

What great unknowns and inner motivations cause individuals, families, even whole social groups to dream, bear the hardships, possible deaths, to experience the glory of traveling across oceans, plains, and mountains in search of a dream?

In the late nineteen-sixties and early seventies, riding the vibrant travel circuits from the US and Western Europe across Asia was wide open and expanding to individuals, couples, and groups; even with young entrepreneurs offering cheap, albeit often unreliable, bus trips from London to India; some to Nepal. It was a time of change! For the most part, these circuits were open to the adventurous because there was a modicum of political and religious peace. The hope of most circuit riders from the many cultures and countries was for these circuits to broaden, and new ones opened until the circuits of the world were open everywhere to everyone. But such was not to be the case! The thought of our children or our children's children traveling overland from Western Europe eastward today would be illusionary. But someday…

We booked passage from New York to Piraeus, Greece on a Greek freighter, "Angistri", by name. This was, by far and away, the cheapest mode of transportation for getting from the United States to that part of the world. Skipping Western Europe because it was too much like our culture, we both had been there, and wanted to explore non-Westernized worlds. And, of course, there was the always-present issue of wanting to make our dollars last as long as possible.

With backpacks filled with two changes of clothes, toiletries, odds and ends, a few softback books, and sundry items, we wore our newly tailored leather coats (bought for us by Lilly and manufactured by Arlene's uncle Max), a vintage black leather doctor's bag that became part of my persona, and a cheap Polaroid camera. Most importantly was the omnipresent leather pouch with strong cords around our necks keeping it about chest high and under all clothing containing money and passport; the two absolute essentials for any traveler. Initially, each pouch contained about $700 in American Express Travelers Checks and another $300 in cash and a passport. (American passports, in those days, were worth a *lot* of money on the black market and it was a difficult interruption and process to acquire a new one.

"Passport, money, and destination." became our official trifecta mantra when going out any front door.

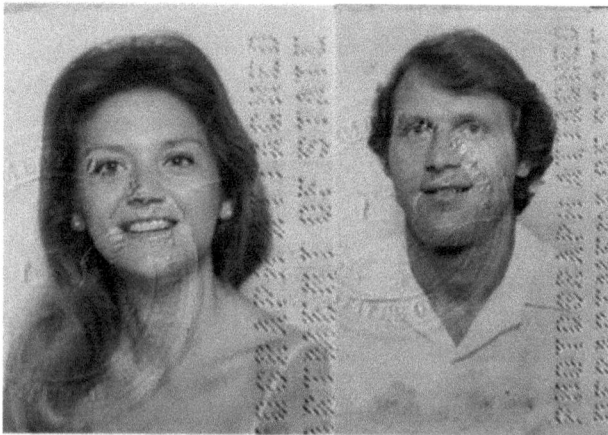

Passport photos - 1970

An agent of the Greek shipping company walked us up the gangplank and introduced us to the 1st mate who showed us to our cabin. The cabin was located close to the upper deck, was clean, and spacious with private shower and toilet. And we were much elated to be introduced to a young couple, traveling American hippie passengers much like ourselves, in a nearby cabin. Gerald and Casey spoke of mutual books of interest, styles of dressing, long hair, and the new thoughts, and distaste for the Vietnam War that made us feel like kindred spirits, and we "hit it off" immediately.

With the sound of whistles and loud horns the mooring lines were released, and we were heading to Greece! (WOWIE!!!) One of the young crew members told us Janice Joplin had just died, apparently of an overdose.

At sea we had three meals a day at the captain's table with him and any officers on duty at the time; and most of them spoke fairly good English. Sometimes we overslept and would miss breakfast. The bad news was the food which became repetitiously boring after the first week because the fresh foods eventually were depleted. We ate moussaka and pita almost every day, and occasionally some baklava followed by a usually unlimited amount of _ellinikos_ (Greek coffee); known for its strength.

We spent many hours of the day walking outside on the multi leveled grey painted decks and leaning on the rails pondering as we looked out to the rolling sea; talking and thinking of things to come. There was always an open invitation to the wheelhouse to watch the navigators slice the ship into the rolling waves, and for the most part, the seas were relatively calm, although we went through several uneventful and small storms.

But I was on the high seas again. I was again completely captivated by the enormity, complexity, and grandeur of it all; even though I had sworn it off after meeting Arlene. However, this time it wasn't a lifestyle.

Most of our time was spent in the cabins, Gerald & Casey's, or ours. But we came together daily. With the help of Gerald, I honed my backgammon skills; having recently learned this oldest known board-game from an Armenian elder, Ted's father-in-law, while in Brooklyn. The guys enjoyed backgammon more than the gals; while the gals were content to talk and plan about what to do after arriving in Greece. They liked to talk spirituality; but the guys tended to avoid those conversations.

So, we had discussions about music – rock music. Bob Dylan: "Lay Lady Lay" & "Blowin in the Wind"; Jefferson Airplane: "Somebody to Love"; BB King: "The thrill is Gone"; and they preferred the Beach Boys, we preferred the Beatles. And did they have their relationship theme song?

Ours was Sinatra's "Strangers in the Night", of course; they didn't have their favorite YET.

Then something unusual happened!

About ten days into the voyage when, the four of us sitting in one cabin, the omnipresent vibrating drone of the ship's engine suddenly fell silent. Knowing this to be unnatural, Gerald and I hurried up the stairwell steps to the wheelhouse, requiring us to go outside the confines of the cabins to validate the "Angistri" was no longer plowing forward. The captain said:

"We are having some minor engine difficulty. Please do not worry; it will be fixed very soon." We four were invited to go to the engine room where we spent time anxiously whispering among ourselves over the awesomeness of the gargantuan engines, while ignorantly watching the experts work on the engines.

Three or four hours later Gerald and I returned to the wheelhouse, and this time the captain said: "We will be underway shortly. But we will have to make a detour, unscheduled stop in Libya to get some new engine parts." And we all thought "Wow! This could be fun." Then sure enough the engine started, and the vibrating drone sound was once again all around us; albeit slightly less strong and consistent.

The "Angistri" passed through the Strait of Gibraltar, on a sunny day, and we could see dark shades of land on both sides; Morocco on our starboard and Gibraltar on the port side; only (approximately) 7.7 nautical miles wide. Three days later we were moored at the dock of

Tripoli, Libya. The captain said we were free to visit Tripoli during the sunlight hours the next day; and we did.

It wasn't long before we four were in the middle of a crowded Muslim marketplace, or bazaar. All things were so different; especially after having been at sea for several weeks. There were scores of hand-drawn carts and wooden stands with vendors hawking their goods; fresh or dried fruits and vegetables; old military boots and other footwear; prayer rugs; brightly woven cotton material; and lots of figs and dates.

Men dominated the population of the marketplace and appeared visibly intense. Their dress was a mixture of modern Western clothes to traditional wrap around (Jarid) cloth, while many wore the traditional brimless Kufi white skull cap. Of the few women we saw most were wearing the traditional Hijab. Most of the young people and energetic children were dressed in modern clothes; curiously staring at us for what seemed like a long time and not always smiling.

We passed under a long carved mysterious archway and walked to the front of a beautiful structure we thought could have been an old Christian fort perhaps used by the Crusaders. Gerald and Casey wanted to explore the building more and agreed to separate – with us heading down a narrow, less traveled street.

Big mistake!!!

A few blocks into our exploration, four young pre-teenage boys suddenly emerged from a shadowed doorway yelling at us in shrieking tones we knew to be unfamiliar but definitely threatening. Momentarily we glanced back at them, seeing the shadow of whispering adults behind them. Without provocation they began throwing stones at us, large smooth stones; some golf-ball sizes. The first one hit the brown stucco building to our right with a loud dull thud. So, we knew they were throwing with force and intention.

At this point we knew they were serious about doing some damage as more stones whizzed past us.

"BUMMER" I yelled, "Come on; let's get outta here, **FAST!**"

With hearts pounding with adrenaline pulsating through our veins, we ran straight down the middle of the sloping and uneven street, hoping for a business building or any safe haven. Observing our fear and running, the boys were emboldened to follow in pursuit.

The stones continued toward us, but with less accuracy because of the separating distance until we burst into an open central commercial area from where the docks were in sight. Ahh yes, we could see many other people around us and the welcoming site of many boats in the very near blue of the Mediterranean harbor. And the stoning stopped at the same time.

But the intense afternoon continued.

The "Angistri" was moored next to a very large Russian warship with their obvious large red flag with a yellow star and hammer and sickle flapping in the winds off the stern. Walking closer to the dock we could see two uniformed Russians men from the warship heading our way. About fifty yards from the dock, and as we walked in a straight line to the "Angistri", the two Russians headed toward us. They got within a few yards of us and stopped; directly in our path. We knew they were officers because of their peaked caps and large brass symbols and shiny buttons down the front of their dark blue coats.

In unison they yelled "Kopitolist pigs!" badly pronouncing "capitalist" (but did well with the pigs) several times and stood close together with smirking smiles and intimidating presence. We made a sharp walk around them continuing our hasty stride toward the "Angistri" without looking back. They were, however, successful in the attempt to intimidate us.

And again, as we walked closer toward the "Angistri" gangplank, we heard several shouting sailors leaning over near the stern of the warship:

"Kopitolist pigs!" with an even stronger mispronunciation of "capitalist". My first inclination was to give them the rude finger gesture, but our travels were just beginning and the last thing we wanted was to get involved in an international incident or sustain any physical damage. We were content to continue to the safety of our ship and solitude of our cabin.

Gerald and Casey returned an hour later, and ironically, experienced neither a stone-throwing incident nor an encounter with

Russian sailors. We shared our stories long into the night. Early the next day we were steaming our way toward the Greek seaport of Piraeus, near Athens.

(Before sharing about our time in Greece, let's take a pause to mention a small geo-political observation. At the time the "Angistri" had stopped its engines and the captain told us of engine problems, we had not yet passed through the Straights of Gibraltar. In retrospect, we ask: why did the captain choose to go the Tripoli, Libya for engine repairs or parts? Logically, Barcelona, Spain or Palermo, Italy offered closer seaports, and perhaps other ports as well.

New York to Tripoli is about 4,040 nautical miles; and Libya is/was a third world country. Whereas New York to Barcelona, Spain is 3,338 nautical miles, and to Palermo, Italy is 3,795; both first world countries. Each of these ports are well below the distance to Tripoli; and most likely to have emergency parts for a ship's engine. So why dock in Tripoli?

The political aspect was equally important. In 1969 Muammar (Colonel) Gaddafi led a coup d'état over King Idris; the ruling monarch and Western leaning leader at that time. Gaddafi quickly abolished the monarch and created the Libyan Arab Republic and put sharia law in place; and was committed to Arab Nationalism and Arab Socialism. Needless to say, he quickly became opposed to the international objectives of the United States. And he was presumed responsible for the Pam Am Lockerbie, Scotland bombing in1988 and the death of 243 passengers and 16 crew members.

Was the "Angistri" delivering an illegal shipment of goods to a US restricted country? We never knew.)

Chapter 4

ATHENS, MYKONOS, AND ONWARD

"Muse, tell me of a man who was made to wander far and long. …Many were the men whose lands he saw and came to know their thinking."

–Odyssey, Poem by Homer

When debarking in Piraeus, Gerald, Casey, Arlene, and I thanked the captain and said goodbye to the "Angistri" and several of the crew members toward whom we had grown close. Easily changing dollars for drachma by the Port Authority, we quickly jumped on a small, crowded bus heading to Athens. Once there, each couple secured cheap hotel rooms and then began the thrill of experiencing all the sights, sounds, smells, and people Athens had to offer, the cradle of modern civilization.

Floating through our consciousness as if in a dream, the great Greek goat's milk yogurt (soooo satisfying), and the inviting smell of vertical rotisserie of lamb and pork wrapped in pita filled the air, the nearby marketplace was bustling with people seeking bargains on fish, fruits, and vegetables. We sat down at a small outdoor café, and I drank a tiny cup of espresso and nibbled on some pastry while Arlene had some tea. "Ah", in a collective sharing, "We made it!" Our only concern, consciously and unconsciously, was to dissociate ourselves from any possibility of being identified a tourist. A stereotypical tourist flaunted wealth, wore their own clothing, while maintaining an air of superiority, among other irritations. We were the hoped-for opposite. We were travelers, damn it, and proud of it! We were circuit riders!

The next day, Arlene and I went off to explore the Acropolis! Gerald and Casey went their way, on a different track, for the day.

Stepping onto the marble stairs of the Parthenon my eyes flitted about as my excited neurons received a thousand stimulants a second, while trying to remain focused.

Searching for a word?

One word like <u>love</u> can mean so much: an idea, an ideal, a value, a person, a place, a thing, time, space, science, philosophy, religion. Ah, philosophy. Yes, Socrates, Plato, and Aristotle have tread upon these steps; their ghosts abound. And busts of goddess Athena were here and there, balancing the male energy.

Does the collective conscious retain the thoughts and quotes of these great men, and the many others? How about the collective memory?

Apostle Paul, after observing the Greek inscription "To An Unknown God" stood in the shadow of the Acropolis and delivered the Areopagus Sermon (named for a low hill by the Acropolis), ultimately kick-starting Christology in the West. (Wikipedia)

"Forasmuch then as we are the offspring of God, we ought not to think that the Godhead is like unto gold, or silver, or stone, graven by art and man's device." Acts 17:29

So, there we were standing on the steps of the Parthenon, looking over the Acropolis mesmerized by the ancient city of Athens below in the dimming light of day. What gives life meaning? Which way to go? Love is such a splendid thing. Experience the truth. Who are we? Going where? For now, and for an eternity?

The urge for food, and to reconnect with Gerald and Casey drove us back into some sense of reality and our hotel room. For dinner we had some yogurt, moussaka, and a little honey & baklava at a moderate priced restaurant; actually, Arlene had some <u>taramasalata</u> = yogurt, cucumber, and garlic. We shared travel stories with Casey and Gerald who had spent the day exploring the Temple of Zeus, Temple of Hephaestus, and the National Museum (being more spiritual).

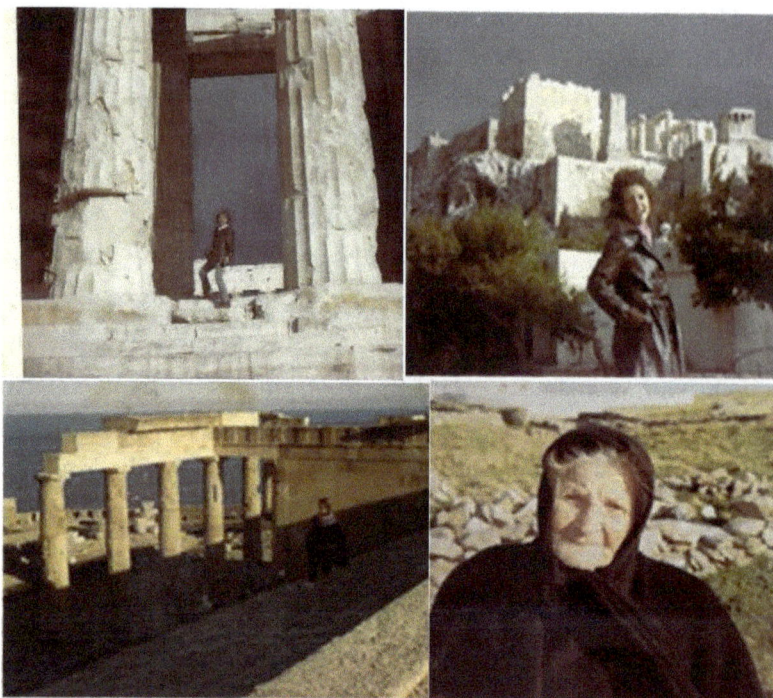

Old Greece

We had much discussion on wanting to travel to one of the islands; and which one. The three islands we researched were: Santorini, Mykonos, and Corfu. We all agreed on Mykonos as the Island to explore.

Ahhh...Mykonos, its beauty popping up from the brilliant blue Aegean Sea, was often the playland of royalty, movie stars, and famous artists, Jackie O, Maria Callas, Grace Kelly, Brigitte Bardot, Sophia Loren, Brando, and many more.

Petro the famous, great white Pelican was there to greet our incoming ferry boat, and most of the fisherman on the dock appeared occupied with the immediate tasks of cleaning fish and stripping squid, paying little attention to the newly arriving visitors. We unloaded our backpacks at an outside café near the water, sipped on some ouzo, ate cake, and began planning our next move.

Because it was at the end of the tourist season (WHOOPIE), it was fairly easy to get a cheap hotel for a few nights. We then went in search of a house to rent and found a large and ideal house approximately a kilometer from the bay area. It had 3 bedrooms, running water, a shower, and a propane stove for only a hundred US dollars a month; $50 each couple = vhat a deal!!

We did nothing for a few days but did manage to walk the path to town during the early evening to mingle with locals, tourists, and travelers – and, if we could, scope out an intellectual or bohemian-type: regardless of language or culture. And how enchanting it was! The newly whitewashed houses with balconies highlighted with bright red bougainvillea and freshly varnished brown doors, electric lights harmonizing them with the darkened sky, narrowing winding cobblestone streets gradually sloping toward the Old Port. It never grew old.

This was our first real rest since leaving California.

Some days we would explore the island with Gerald and Casey, while other times it was just the two of us. The windmills, about a dozen of them, were scattered on the hill tops just outside of town and were unique because of their 24-inch triangular canvas tips at the outstretched end of each arm; and mostly facing the prevailing north wind which was used as a driving force to mill wheat as the main ingredient of their historic diet for centuries. Donkeys were the beasts of burden.

One day, while walking back to our rented house, we passed the small farmhouse we'd passed several times previous. This time there was a group of about 15 Mykonosan farmers and wives seemingly celebrating and sitting around several wooden benches. They waved for us to join them, resolutely handing us small drinks (ouzo and frequently clinking our glasses all around) and food with pride (strange looking pink cheese, what was probably meatballs and a great honey desert). We didn't understand a word of Greek and they didn't understand a word of English, but we had a glorious time enjoying our common humanity; toasting, laughing, and eating as one family. An unforgettable time!

Mykonos

They were a hardy bunch, and most were much older than us with wrinkles abound and few children. We sensed a feeling of commonness and oneness, while sharing food, laughter, and an unspoken joy. The men dressed in dark pants and vests with white shirts, and the women wore plain cotton dresses and high boots; a few had head scarfs. We were dressed in jeans and t-shirts and light backpacks, and obviously not tourists. They probably didn't know from which culture we came – or care. And that was the beauty of it all.

I had a memory of walking along a path outside the city proper and passing an old woman with a scarf neatly tied over her hair. As we passed each other we looked deeply into each other's eyes and smiled. Without words, I asked her if I could take her picture and she generously agreed. I will never forget her face reflecting a life of hardships and a peaceful wise acceptance.

Then there were lazy days – no schedules, no pressure to be or go anywhere. We would walk to town or go an opposite direction to the hidden Panormos Beach with its few houses, and a great restaurant. We would eat fresh-baked bread, fruited yogurt, and drink some bubbly-gased water and just sit there watching the ocean tides and rippling surf. At the end of the day friendly fisherman would invite us to eat delicious freshly caught fish to be washed down with unlimited ouzo.

In the evening we would play backgammon and toke off a pipe with Gerald and Casey and talk a lot about movies. Although not exclusively, we all liked some of the arty foreign films; Ingmar Bergman's "The Seventh Seal" and "Wild Strawberries"; and, of course, Federico Fellini's stuff: "81/2" and "La Dolce Vita". We all loved "2001: A Space Odyssey", "Dr. Zhivago", and "Butch Cassidy and the Sundance Kid"; and my personal favorite "Lawrence of Arabia". We were surprised they had not seen the English film "Two for the Road" (Albert Finney & Audrey Hepburn) – which we loved and reminded us of ourselves.

It was already October, so the weather was beginning to chill. Our 30-day rental was nearing an end, so we spent thoughtful discussions on the next circuit to ride.

Arlene had a relative living in Tel Aviv, Israel, and we were encouraged to visit her by her mother and father when leaving the States. It was unanimous then – our next circuit ride was to Israel; and we became excited and felt the collective <u>desire</u> to ride! How we would get there we didn't yet know – only the cheapest way possible! We knew we could ride a series of cheap ferry boats to the eastern most Greek Island of Rhoades. But then getting to Cypress and on to Israel was an unknown. But we had faith in the circuits.

<u>Money, passport, destination and we're out the front door</u>!

A few days later, we boarded a small boat going to Rhodes for an uneventful trip. Pulling into the Mandrakes Harbor, we passed the two pillars on either side with a stone-carved deer (and where the original Colossus of Rhodes once stood).

Without hassle, we found a nice hotel, had some good eats, and began exploring. Arlene and I went straight to the Temple of Athena Lindia on the Acropolis of Lindos. And it was a mindblower! The pillared marble remains, some of which still had connecting blocks, retained their beauty in the late afternoon sun; contrasted by the pale blue sky and the deep blue of the nearby comfort of the Mediterranean waters. We were the only ones there! Walking slowly around, sitting on the edge of the high stepped terrace, wondering if this was what life was like during the Hellenistic period – 3rd and 2nd century before

Christ. Many historians believed Jesus had traveled to Rhodes.

But alas, our time on Rhodes was not long lasting. Within a few days we were on a boat bound for Cypress.

To say that Cypress has had a messy cultural and political history since recorded history would be a gross understatement. Because of its natural, critical location at the eastern end of the Mediterranean Sea, the 3,572 square mile island has been coveted by the dominant military power of every generation. Some written materials suggest the Garden of Eden/Atlantis was underwater near Cypress.

Subjected to the rule of the Ottoman Empire until 1914 when Britain took over, the population was alternatively dominated by Turks and Greeks – Greeks being the largest group in numbers; with a smattering of Armenian and Maronites (Catholics in union with Rome). They were granted independence in 1960, but the ongoing conflicts between the Turks and Greeks erupted, again, in 1964.

Because we were coming from a Greek island (Rhodes) and entering a Greek seaport (Limassol) on the geographically divided island we had no visa problems but were warned by the visa officials about an unrecognized "Green Line" separating the two territories, because the Turks may be hostile.

We didn't pay much attention to their words of caution, thinking if we had landed on the opposite side the Turks would have said the same thing about the Greeks. As usual with each new destination, we went about looking for a cheap hotel with a potentially warm shower, while making quiet inquiries of our desire to secure transportation to Israel.

Memory is a funny thing. It changes with time.

We spent 3 or 4 uneventful days there, mostly hanging out in our hotel rooms overlooking the busy harbor, when suddenly we heard a hard knocking at our door. A local youth, out of breath and in broken English, said an Israeli Cruise ship coming from Marseille, France had just docked for a few hours and would take passengers to Israel. We thanked him giving him a small tip.

Chapter 5

THE HOLY LANDS?

"To be homeward bound, no matter what tragic memories
you have harbored, is unlike any voyage a man
can ever make."

–Leon Uris, Redemption

Without considering the possibility of being denied passage or entry into Israel, we feverishly gathered our belongings and hastily marched to the boat dockings and were soon pointed to a large white passenger ship – of the Zim Lines, we discovered. After showing our passports, we were permitted onboard and escorted to the wheelhouse and introduced to the captain. He was pleasant enough, asked us a few incidental questions – but eyeballed us thoroughly, and said YES, he would take us to Haifa, Israel on the overnight voyage. We paid the Purser $40 each for the overnight trip to Haifa, and each couple was given separate cabins several decks below.

It was a first for each of us! And we were totally amazed!

The MS Molelet (?) was a passenger boat in which all the passengers and cabins were of the same, one class; and they were large, comfortable, and clean; and, with hot showers. We loved it. And we'd been on board less than 2 hours when the Molelet was tugged from the dock and was steaming on the open seas toward Israel – talk about good timing!!!

After settling in, Arlene and I went up to the main deck. It was a quiet sea giving us a smooth ride, the sky was clear, and we visited with several willing people – asking the usual superficial questions: where are you from, where are you going, etc. Most had embarked at

Marseille, France and felt as if they were "exiles" returning home. We often heard the Hebrew word "aliyah" = literally "going up" a true blessing to them. Soon all the passengers were beckoned to the dining hall for the last supper for everyone of the entire voyage.

And what a treat it turned out to be!!

It was a grand hall with a high ceiling, and everyone was in excited spirits, with some singing songs in Hebrew. We four sat at a large round table with 8 other passengers each having real silverware, several sized plates, and cloth napkins. A prayer could be heard in the background, as the servers carried the food to our table and gave each a fair portion. The four of us agreed that compared to the Greek freighter "Angistri" when crossing the Atlantic, this was **truly** first class. And the best was about to come!

After the used main dishes were removed, the lights in this large hall were dimmed, and a line of strong male servers walked out of the kitchen area carrying large trays of brightly flaming ***Baked Alaska*** on their shoulders to the tune of Hava Nagila. We thought we had died and gone to heaven. (Traditionally, Baked Alaska is made of ice cream and a cake topped with browned meringue; and the flames come from a lighted splash of dark rum.) Vat a deal!!! We had not eaten this well since our NY wedding 3 months before.

Needless to say, we ate with relish and fell in a minor state of gastric overdose and bliss.

We slept soundly that night to the gentle roll and pitch of the ship at sea.

The next morning, December 5, 1970, the ship's passengers were in a very high state of emerging enthusiasm. On deck could be seen dozens of people; smiling males, teary-eyed females, old and young, peering forward, leaning over the rails, watching as their homeland of Israel came into view; becoming larger and larger, clearer, and clearer, closer and closer. It would have seemed a state of collective hysteria, except for the controlled sentiment of joy coupled with a real infectious excitement – near impossible of description! The look in their eyes and sound of the voices conveyed a real sense of returning; homecoming and an indefinable sense of belonging within each and all. It was real to them, perceived by us.

Going through the Israeli customs and immigration was relatively easy; except we knew, as questions were asked, the interviewer was looking directly and deeply into the pupils of our eyes searching for signs of insincerity or deception. The only difference at this country's immigration was that the Israelis slid a blank white page into our passports to stamp (the page would be removed upon our departure). Necessary because, when entering an Arab country, if you had an Israeli stamp in your passport, they would refuse entry. (Keeping in mind…this was only 3 years after the Six Day War. The Six-Day War was a short but bloody campaign fought in June 1967 with the Arab states of Egypt, Syria, and Jordan.)

We were in their main seaport Haifa and felt totally elated. We ate one last lunch with Gerald and Casey; and somehow knew it was the last time we would see each other. And it was! Having spent a lot of time together, often in close quarters, and having zero conflicts with them, yet we never felt very close to them. They were good people, but more reactive to goodness rather than proactive.

We separated with hugs; they headed toward Jerusalem, and we headed toward Arlene's mother's cousin in eastern Tel Aviv, the capital, for a prearranged visit. We never saw Gerald and Casey again. But they remain a vivid part of our memories.

After we settled into Arlene's Cousin's apartment, I promptly got sick; ill with a digestive/bowel ailment. While laid up for 4 or 5 days, Arlene went shopping, helped cook, and comforted me with water, tea, and small amounts of food: gradually restoring me to health. Then we were ready to get out the front door.

With the blessing of Arlene's relative, we decided to head to Jerusalem; especially old-town Jerusalem.

Old Jerusalem was truly OLD!!! We had seen the ruins in Greece that were thousands of years old, but here was a whole TOWN that was even older!!! There was the Western Wall, the Church of the Holy Sepulcher and, of course, an infamous Temple Mount with the Dome of the Rock. The Temple Mount was a hill near the center of the Old City that for many thousands of years has been venerated as THE holy site for Judaism, Christianity, and Islam alike. It was the source of many religious wars. Each believing they have the God-given and eternal ownership.

The many narrow streets were jammed with small shops offering just about anything and everything – from food & drinks, trinkets, expensive rugs, and every sort of antique (supposedly) from the beginning of time.

Sabra became known to all as the unique key word, which meant any Jew born in Israel, and considered near royalty.

But everyone kept saying: "Now is the time to go to Bethlehem, go to Bethlehem!" We were so disoriented and out of it, we did not realize it was Christmas Eve - December 24th, 1970.

The short 30 minutes bus ride south via the Hebron Road got us to Bethlehem quickly and smoothly. The place was jammed with foreigners of every culture, of course! Christian pilgrims dominated and dressed in all sorts of robe styles and colors, and tourists too, all attempting to get into grotto under the Church of the Nativity – the believed birthplace of Jesus. It was way too crowded for us, so we just hung out at the nearby Manger Square observing the many lights and soaking in the feelings.

Crosses were everywhere! They were of every shape, color, and material; and everyone seemed in a festive mood; with many handshakes, hugs, and smiles, even though there were hundreds of armed Israeli soldiers on watch for Arab hostilities. It was quite uncomfortable for me; feeling saddened that during this celebration of Jesus' birth there was this horrible sense of fear and hate rather than peace and love. It suddenly hit us! There were <u>hundreds</u> of armed Israeli soldiers everywhere, on watch for Arab hostilities. I was somewhat irked by it all! Our spiritual needs had not yet been awakened. (Although in retrospect, we agreed this experience may have contributed to the beginning of the awakening of our spiritual journey.)

We were in the holiest city in the world during the holiest night of the year. But…somehow it didn't seem so holy.

Part of what stood in the way of being able to fully absorb the spiritual atmosphere, was the multi-military presences. Machine guns were mounted on top of most corner rooftops of the earthen colored buildings, for blocks around the Grotto. Active groups of Israeli soldier units patrolled the streets. There were half-track armored personnel carriers, and even a full tank nearby.

Our sense was that the soldiers were not just ensuring national sovereignty but also protecting pilgrims who came to celebrate a holy holiday.

It had been a tough year for Golda Meir (Israel's then Prime Minister). It was only 3 years after the brutal Six-Day War with Egypt, Jordan, and Syria, so tensions remained understandably high. And already this year there was heavy fighting on the Golan Heights, many terrorists' attacks (including one where multiple school children were killed near Avivim, in Northern Israel). While Israel was trying to get Egypt missiles withdrawn from the Suez, the Egyptian President Nasser died and was replaced with Anwar Sadat.

So, between the stunted religious activities and the politics of inertia, we wanted to get away from it all.

We opted for the kibbutz experience; the Jewish collective community traditionally based on agriculture. But first we took a bus trip to the Dead Sea and the ancient fortification and recently rediscovered site of the Masada.

We arrived at a youth hostel in Ein Gedi, a stone's throw from the Dead Sea beach. It was a beautiful site with not too many people. It was also the site of our first tiff, when Buck wanted to go up to the top of the Masada, and I didn't. Not being a risk taker and wanting to have a relaxing day, I didn't feel comfortable climbing all the way to the top because it was an unmarked path, we had no guide, it was very steep, and the weather was suffocatingly hot and dry.

But I was determined (an ego trip?)! And, except for a bottle of water, an extra shirt, and some snacks I emptied my backpack. Looking back at the scene of Arlene drinking a glass of tea, I began following hand-painted signs pointing out of town toward the Masada; visibly eastward.

Because of the excited archeological renovations, a lot of traffic was going that way; and I was lucky to hitch a ride in a military jeep to the Western base of the former fortress. Following the better prepared two male climbers, I persevered my way up what was known as the assault ramp – apparently used by the Romans to get men and materials to the top during their final assault. After a lot of sweat, burning leg muscles, and shortness of breath, the top was reached!

It was a very high mesa-like plateau – over 1800 feet on one side – with steep cliffs going nearly straight down: an obvious choice for a fortress.

Standing on the sun-drenched, ancient tiles, looking westward toward the Dead Sea, and beyond; a sense of history was overpowering. The ancient structures were remarkably well preserved, even with disjointed rooms without roofs, unevenly sheared pillars, broken rainwater cisterns, and stairs going nowhere. A hand-scribbled information board, written in Hebrew and English, said it was first built as a fortress about a century before the Roman client King Herod from Judea used it. He used it as a safe vacation getaway and built two palaces off the left or northern edge of the cliff in about 37 -31 BC; barely recognizable as such, now. The Jews took it over after Herod's death, and used it as their last-stand against the conquering Romans during the Jewish-Roman War about a hundred years AD; for which it is most famous. It was reputed that, 960 Jews jumped to their death rather than be captured; most of whom were Zealots.

The view was consuming, especially of the distant Dead Sea. I knew Arlene was there next to the water and tried to imagine her with me and me with her. Kings, statesman, historians, and commoners have absorbed this panoramic view into their consciousness.

(And yes, that was that <u>same</u> Herod, the Great that ordered the death of all baby boys in Bethlehem under the age of two; fearing a prophesy that a recently born baby in Bethlehem would take his place as "King of the Jews". This caused Mary and Joseph to hastily flee to Alexandria, Egypt with baby Jesus and stay with distant relatives until Herod's death. He died in 4 BC and his son, Herod Antipas, took over.)

In time, I slid and scrambled my way down the rocky path and was again fortunate to get a return ride to the Ein Gedi hostel and the patient Arlene. We were so happy to see each other the <u>tiff</u> was nearly forgotten after we kissed. Having shared each other's story of our time separated, it was agreed separating was not the best thing to do; even though we each had somewhat enriching experiences. Personally, I felt devastated because of the lesson I <u>thought</u> I had cemented into my brain after the Darien Jungle trip: I went through that jungle alone and had no one to share it with. I swore I would never do it again!

The only memories I have of that day is of sitting at the café and knowing me, possibly chatting with a few people and then being anxious regarding Buck's safety and angry, feeling abandoned. I'm sure I made up all kinds of danger filled scenarios. Not a fun day for me to say the least.

Memory is a funny thing! Anxiety inhibits recall.

A bus dropped us off at the unpaved driveway leading to the kibbutz, a kilometer or two from the city of Beersheba. We didn't know what to expect as we walked into the main doorway. A single uncolored picture of Golda Meir hung as the only decoration on the walls; and she was once a **kibbutznik**.

The kibbutz was often cited as being responsible for "turning the barren land into a garden" because there were several hundred kibbutzim throughout Israel. Politically they were based on socialism and Zionism; and it was because of this initial structure the Soviet Union voted in support of Israel as a potential socialist state at the UN in 1949.

After surrendering our passports, we were cordially accepted into the compound as official <u>kibbutzniks</u> (Having in my earlier years been identified as a <u>beatnik</u>, this had a familiar and pleasant ring to me!). We were given separate sleeping quarters (male/female), and Arlene was taken directly to the kitchen, and I to the fields to pick weeds from between the growing stalks of corn. It was communal living to the full – the permanent residents didn't own anything, even their clothes, all the tools belonged to the kibbutz, and nobody could own a radio/television unless everyone could have one.

On the upside, there was nothing materially to worry about! All your basic <u>needs</u> were taken care of by the communal setting; even clothing if you needed them. Of course, there were a lot of <u>wants</u> you may have wanted, but those could wait.

In the meantime, we just enjoyed the <u>kibbutzniks</u>. There were people there from, seemingly, all over the world: Ethiopia, Russia, both sides of the Mediterranean, Europe, the Middle East, and, of course, the United States. The vast majority was Jewish; but only the few administrators were <u>Sabras</u>.

We had long discussions with a young traveler, Jim, from Indiana, USA (actually younger than us) who repeatedly and encouragingly said: "You <u>must</u> go to India!"

He spoke of gurus who did strange and unusual things with their bodies, manifest material objects in their hands from thin air, and shared the secrets of their life after long and deep periods of meditation.

We didn't give much credence to what Jim was talking about, but it did reignite the desire to get moving again. (Before leaving California an old surfer buddy implanted the idea of going to the Seychelles Islands in the Indian Ocean; saying it was the last unspoiled islands in the world for travelers to hang out.) Jim said he was taking a day trip to Eilat, at the very southern tip of Israel which was the country's seaport to the Red Sea and to the Indian Ocean. So, we thought: "Why not?" (Perhaps we could obtain sea passage to an African country – ideally Kenya – and from there a boat to the Seychelles). Jim decided to leave for Eilat before us.

After slightly less than 3 weeks of total time there, we retrieved our passports, checked out of the kibbutz, and went to the bus station in Beersheba. Looking for passage to Eilat, we were hoping for a way over the 117-mile road straight south. We soon discovered, however, the bus service went only as far as Mitzp Ramon; about halfway down. But we were happy to get it!

From Mitzp Ramon we started hitchhiking early in the morning. It was interesting. The Negev covers about 55% of the total land mass of Israel; Beersheba being the capital. The western side of the Negev shares a border as part of the Sinai Peninsula. It was a rocky and dusty place, and almost devoid of life. But it was fun for us; with an occasional caravan of camel herders going in the opposite direction; warning us to be on the lookout for hungry Arabian leopards. Then we would go through patches of sand dunes; some over 80 or 90 feet high.

A Camel Sale and Hitchhiking in the Negev

But hitchhiking rides were not easy to come by – mainly because there just weren't that many vehicles on the road. Occasionally a train of Bedouins with camels would pass on our left, heading north. But we were lucky and got short rides in 10- or 12-mile increments; mostly by officially dressed males who spoke a little English and they all had some type of firearms available. As early nightfall descended, we could see the city lights of Eilat and were thrilled!

What can be said about Eilat to fill and intrigue the spirit? It has, or has had, everything, from an historical past dating from the times of the Egyptian Pharaohs through World War One (Lawrence of Arabia?), and to the time of Israel statehood. It is a seaport at the southernmost tip of Israel with ships embarking in the Gulf of Aqaba and draining into the Red Sea then opening to the entire Indian Ocean and the world; used by explorers, sailors, merchants, and pirates, and especially before the Suez Canal was built or during wartime when the Canal was closed. And, of course, the awesome Eilat Mountains off to the West gave a late afternoon shade and brilliant sunsets.

(Egypt blocked the Straits of Tiran, near the southern point of the Gulf of Aqaba and between the Island of Tiran and the city of Sharm El Sheikh. This blockade of Eilat was considered the initial event precipitating the countries into the Six-Day War.)

But Eilat was fascinating to experience! To walk along the shoreline remains memorable; with the clearest saltwater we'd ever seen to that point in our travels. And we could even see lots of multicolored small fish shooting about searching for food. The Jordan city of Aqaba had shown white and bright across the bay almost beckoning us to come. We bumped into Indiana Jim again, an obvious circuit rider, and had tea and lunch with him, talking of travel. He was thinking of going to Egypt, and again reinforced his suggestion we go to India. But we remained steady in the desire of getting to the islands of perfection (The Seychelles).

Much of the local populations were seamen and others somehow connected with the shipping industry. We asked and asked everyone and anybody we thought might have knowledge of ships going out of Eilat to Africa that would take us along as passengers. But nothing! We even went to the manager of the Port Authority; still nothing.

We spent several hours, just the two of us, at an outside café looking at each other, sometime in silence, sometime tossing out ideas on which circuit to ride next. Most of our American Express Travelers checks remained and we had no time constraints.

We loved each other with a deep soul resonance and wanted to keep going; continue our travel adventure. Simultaneously, a welling up began with each of us, as if fresh water from a sprouting spring. "Yes, yes, yes…let's go to India!" Perhaps we could find a boat passage from Bombay to the Seychelles!

Money, passport, and destination, and out the front door we went!

Chapter 6

INTO THE GREATER
UNCERTAINTY

"Sal, we gotta go and never stop going 'til we get there."
'Where we going, man?'
"I don't know but we gotta go."

–Jack Kerouac, <u>On the Road</u>

It all happened so quickly and smoothly neither of us had much memory of the events. We bused our way back to Haifa, were able to get another passenger boat to Cypress; and we booked a flight on the Turkish Airlines (one of the few times we actually flew); to Adana in southeastern Turkey. From there we bought train tickets to Erzurum; about 375 miles to the northeast.

And on our way, we went!

(Of course, going through Turkish immigration was interesting because they knew we were coming from Cypress and scrutinized our passports closely for any possible Israel stamps or markings! If there was an Israeli stamp in our passports, entry into Turkey would have been forbidden.)

The rapid change of cultures, from Jewish to Turkish, was startling and quite profound. In Israel it seemed as if everyone was trying very hard to be Jewish; in Turkey it seemed like everyone was just trying to be Western or…whatever! The Islam Sunni culture was there but wasn't very rigid as we had imagined. And the people dressed in many and varied styles from modern Western to classic looks of old-style or ancient cultures.

Somehow, we made it on a train heading north to Erzurum; with the thinking of crossing the border nearby then busing it across Iran and into Afghanistan. But we were in motion again! Truth be told…we had no idea what we were doing! We just knew there was an open circuit to India.

We called the train "The Erzurum Express" because it was slow and made many stops. But we didn't care. We were in a train-car that was seemingly large and warm; the seats were covered, cushioned, and semi-comfortable. Many of the passengers smoked cigarettes, but the windows opened easily. Spring was coming and it was still cold when going outside during stops, but warm inside the coaches.

We sat near a large family of four or five children, several women and men, and a few goats, all gathering in familial style at one end of the car; and chatting continuously. They dressed like gypsies. Unlike most of the other drab-dressed passengers, their clothes were wrinkled but brightly colored; jewelry sparkled but slightly tarnished, they wore thick woolen headgear difficult to describe. After noticing my stare, the woman who was the center of attention and probably the mother of most of them, waved for me to join them.

One of the younger family members spoke a little English and asked me where we were from and where we were going. I told them our immediate destination was Erzurum and a more distant destination was Afghanistan. After the young man translated, their eyes widened, and their faces smiled. They knew we weren't tourist, businesspeople, or spies – and dressed for travel. The mamma gave me a sugar cookie; I thanked her and the family and returned to my seat.

Meanwhile, I, was engaged in an unusual conversation with a well-dressed businessman to the right of us about – the usual stuff – where are you from, where are you going, and why are you here? We were enjoying getting to know each other. What was unique about this conversation was: the gentleman was speaking German while I was speaking my limited Yiddish. My maternal grandmother, who spoke mostly Yiddish, moved into our home after my grandpa died when I was four and stayed until I was 17 years. He was surprised when I told him I was speaking Yiddish and he said it sounded like a German dialect.

And although the outside of these passenger cars was of sheet metal, the insides were covered with stripes of hardwood, retaining smells, charcoal from burning candles, hair oil where human heads rested, and smears of old food!

Walking through the gently swaying cars the atmosphere was rollicking, mostly with young men. Without hesitation, one would stop me to ask where I was from, another asked where I was going; but mostly just to practice their English. I was able to ascertain they were going to Erzurum because of the relatively new and high-quality college there, which would afford them great opportunities in the future.

Memory is a funny thing! Same experience different recollections.

Same people, same place, and same happenings you remember others you don't; it's a complex and complete mystery! AND, when experiencing the same event, you may remember something your partner doesn't. In retrospect most of the <u>clear</u> memories involved meaningful interactions with other people. The train ride seemed like a memory capsule in time held by the circuits in our minds.

The city of Erzurum was like that. I can still see a tall thin dark-skinned man with an animal-fur hat handing us a kebob picked from an open fire with the night frost from the cold air coming out his jovial nearly toothless mouth; in the 6,000-foot altitude. It was obvious to us that the average person or business owner didn't get to see many of <u>our type</u> there, the true circuit rider. Though we saw few women on the street (it was already late dinner time when we got there), few were wearing the traditional Muslim <u>hijab</u> or <u>burka</u>; the men were very friendly and eager to help us find cheap lodging for the night and places to exchange money on the black market.

(It soon became a habit of ours to change our US dollars on the black market; usually choosing a person from an uneven line of men along some backstreet. Why? A person could always receive more local currency on the black market than at a large bank or upscale hotel; anywhere from 5 to 25 percent more. It's simple arithmetic. The exchange rates established by the national governments are purposefully kept low by 3rd world countries, thus insuring a great number of US foreign aid dollars. The black marketeer will always make more profit than the banks when selling US dollars. Of course, these governments threatened <u>harsh</u> laws against selling or buying on the black market; albeit seldom enforced.)

Though having never been to Russia, the atmosphere and culture seemed very Russian-like.

But it was time to get back on the circuit! Garnishing bus tickets to Tabriz, Iran in the early morning, we knew full well we were in for a long bus ride, about 8 hours (or 585 km), but…

When leaving (as when arriving) the Turkey customs and immigration offices, seeing our written German-appearing names, or hearing us pronounce it, we were generally treated with a friendly smile. Mostly, we presumed, because the Turks and the German have been cultural, military, and political allies historically.

As we stood together in the early morning chill, waiting for the passengers and buses to make the transition into Iran the mixed passengers, several circuit riders, were staring intently to the North.

It was Mount Ararat!!!

Because of the early morning mist, we could see only the snow-covered top.

But it was impressive; easily the highest mountain in the region (16,854'). There was a light snow covering the ground where we stood at the border, and it was a desolate and sparsely populated area with only an occasional one- or two-story building surrounding the official buildings. A handful of us, all strangers from several countries and cultures stood in silence looking at the mythical mountain: with many thoughts rambling through the channels of our minds.

Mt. Ararat near the Turkish-Iranian border.

One circuit rider with a northern Europe accent said: "It tis lovely." (And I wasn't sure if he was talking about the mountain or Arlene!)

Believed by many, especially Christians, to be the final resting place of Noah's Ark, it has taken on a sense of beauty, awe, and respect since Biblical times. The whole experience was forever imprinted in our consciousness. We wanted to stay, but knew we had to keeping moving with the bus; feeding the desire to get to India.

Despite being only 200 miles from the Turkish border, the trip to Tabriz was ruff, slow, and dusty. The roads, it seemed, were in less favorable condition than any in Turkey, the bus making many stops, (twice for prayers and food of kebob and flat bread). It was cold, but we kept close keeping each other warm; anticipating another 400 miles to the capital of Tehran. We found a cheap hotel near the bus terminal and got up early the next morning and boarded another bus; this one to Tehran after viewing some fabulously handwoven rugs and hand-made jewelry at the grand bazaar repudiated to be part of the old Silk Road.

Like the ride to Tabriz, the bus to Tehran was bumpy, slow, and dusty. But now, during the many stops we knew we could buy plenty of freshly roasted kebobs, even an occasional meatball, warm flat bread, and some saffron rice. Peanuts seemed omnipresent. We drank plenty of tea – always making certain it was very hot to kill bacteria and prevent intestinal problems.

Tehran was like most bustling capital cities full of energy with a feeling of excitement. The monarch Mohammad Reza Shah Pahlavi was in power, and a feeling of liberation was at hand; and many young men – mostly in their 20's – stopped us on the street to talk to us. Most were followers of the Shia Islam belief. They didn't want to talk religion, but talked about music, dressing, and other influences of Western lifestyle.

We saw a few Western businessmen and spoke excitedly with several circuit riders from France at the bus station; some going South to Esfahan or Shiraz in Iran; none going east to Afghanistan or India.

The trip to Mashad turned out to be our most difficult ride yet!

It was 450 miles of mostly barren land spotted by rare communities, although we did pass through a nice, wooded area. We stopped at 3 or 4 of these communities to refuel the bus, eat, and drink bottled soda.

There was a sordid memory that happened somewhere along this route. It seemed we were out in the middle of nowhere but stopped at a government checkpoint. Suddenly a heavily armed soldier with a stern look on his face came on the bus with a passive middle-aged man in a white medical coat. Quickly and without questioning the medical guy began jabbing shots into the arms of each passenger; even though many of them tried to dissent and seemed agitated. The medical man used the same needle for all passengers as we looked aghast.

We had no idea about what was going on – inoculating against a epidemic or what! When they got to us, I got up from the seat and loudly protested, saying "No" loudly and many times. Pulling out our passports **and** International Certificates of Vaccination shot records we received before leaving the States. After a long whispering consult between the armed guard and the medical person, they bypassed us and continued until everyone on the bus had been syringed with… what? We never knew but were told not to worry.

We were a bit unnerved by this incident until we got to a hotel room in Mashad. We were surprised, almost shocked, to see the large size and beauty of the city of Mashhad; with towering gold domes (the shrine of Imam Reza, the 8th Shia Imam), bright lights, and people everywhere; and good food. We decided to stay an extra day because we liked it there and needed the rest after so much monotonous and grueling bus riding all the way from Erzurum (about 1,300 miles).

But our anticipation of getting to Afghanistan was growing; and so, we kept riding the circuit. Surprisingly, we began meeting more and more circuit riders along the way heading to Afghanistan and India.

We caught the earliest morning bus to the Iranian border town of Qaderabad, in Taybad; about a 3-or-4-hour ride. From there it was about an hour bus trip to the Afghan border. After passing through the customs/immigrations in Iran and the same into Afghanistan, something **_very_** unique happened once inside the land of Afghanistan!

Two nonchalant Afghan soldiers apparently took notice that we were hippies and motioned for us to follow them. With uncertainty they led us into this small, almost tent-like room with little lighting; for it was nearly nightfall by then. In the center of the room was a 3-foot-tall hookah with a very large bowl on the top with glowing charcoal surrounded by 4 quiet but hospitable looking soldiers of various ages all wearing loosely wrapped turban on their heads. It became quickly obvious by the smell that the dark objects in the bowl of charcoal was hashish; large chunks of it!

Also, joining the soldiers and taking turns puffing on the leather and wire hoses of the hookah, were 4 young circuit rider – 3 men and 1 woman – with wide and welcoming smiles.

It wasn't until that moment, once inside Afghanistan and seeing other hippies, and feeling the same inexpressible joy, that we realized we were part of something bigger, something more than just our private travel experiences. We came to understand that hundreds, more likely thousands of circuit rider traveled along, what became fervently known as, the **Hippie Highway!!!** Collectively we were opening circuits on our way overland from North America and Western Europe traveling to…India and elsewhere with no particular mission or goal. All were just heading eastward – even as far as Southeast Asia.

And why?

Who knows? Some say it is for the adventure; some say it is for the hashish; some say because it was on the cheap; some say to see the sites; some say seeking enlightenment; some say it was a mindless wandering; some say it was for free love or sex; some say it was a pilgrimage; some say it was for the camaraderie; some say it was for liberty and freedom; some say it was to spread the hippie counterculture ideology; but most didn't know why. It was just an intuitive imperative! Something inside said we <u>had</u> to go!

The fact that the Hippie Highway was permanently closed in the mid-seventies when the Soviets invaded Afghanistan, the Shah was overthrown in Iran, and civil war started in Lebanon provided great room for more speculation. Had the Hippie Road continued unabated opening to the present time, who knows how much peace, growth, and advances civilization could have made.

Bullets, bombs, and bastards are what stopped it!!! They are all selfish bastards because they (the Soviets and Iranian clerics, American Military Industrial Complex, etc.) do not accept a Creator and the sovereignty of all humanity.

Enough ranting! Back to the story!

Chapter 7

THE MAGIC OF AFGHANISTAN

*"If anyone ask thee which is the pleasantest of cities, Thou
mayest answer him right that it is Herāt…The city of
Herāt being as the pearl in the middle of the oyster."*

–Rumi, 1207-11273 A.D.

We all got high (on their world class hashish) in the Afghan
Soldier compound, and quickly began sharing travel stories of
where we'd been, how we got there, and experiences we had; and
probably made up a few. One couple talked about the attraction of
Herāt, a good hotel, where to exchange money on the black market,
just a few hours away; and our next stop. So, we made an urgent
request to get there as soon as possible – even though it was already in
the dark of night.

Two or three hours later (we can't remember how we got there
or how long it took) we were lodged in the recommended hotel in
Herāt – actually, as we later discovered ANY hotel in Herāt would have
been okay, for they are all pretty much the same; cheap with great
hospitality.

Herāt was "rebuilt" by Alexander the Great (around 300 BC)
when it was known as the breadbasket of that region and was always a
great trading center on the trade routes between China, India, and on
to the Mediterranean; and well-known for their textile industry.

We woke up the next morning to the melodious sounds of
jingling bells. Standing on the small balcony on the second floor of our
hotel room we were completely dumbfounded at what we saw: a horse-
drawn carriage with bright, red, puffy toggles adorning their heads in

an unmanaged array. Most horses also had, what looked like a 12"
clump of white hair strung around their necks. Many of the toggles
stretched back to their carriage of 2 large wheels carrying a single male
Afghan in a white loosely wrapped head gear and a wooden horse whip
held high.

The toggles also were laced with small jingling bells – reminding us of the
Christmas Holidays. It all appeared otherworldly; standing there soaking it all in!!!
Everything was brown from the mud-brick buildings, and a bus with a red cabin
and painted mural, was loading with tons of personal belongings stacked on top.

Some of the carriages had make-shaft overhead roofs and carried
several passengers on the way to, or coming from, the market. Off to
the left was a young boy pulling a small wooden flatbed hauler with
rubber car wheels. A few women were in burkas: but not all. The faint
whiff of hashish was in the air. No buildings were taller than 2 stories:
with groups of men standing around in friendly conference. And even
though it was late winter, the weather was sunny and moderate.

After a light breakfast of milky tea, yogurt, fruit, and large pieces
of flat bread (Naan-e-Afghani), we then took a marvelous horse and
buggy taxi to the market. Everything was sooo cheap!

One of the grander experiences was feeling, smelling, and
touching the marvelous hand-made Afghan rugs (or carpets) - the best
we had ever seen. Typically, they were about 8' by 5' in size (and the
omnipresent smaller prayer rugs), often in a distinctive red color, with
unique patterns of multiple circles divided into four sections. Many of
the rug-makers placed one on the street in front of their tented
businesses for people, autos, and animals to walk on as they passed by;
thus, proving the rug's worthiness and longevity.

We felt as if we had stepped back in time a century or two, into
another worldly dimension!

Next, we had a typical Afghan meal; consisting of roasted lamb
kebab topped (sometimes) with raisins, rice, and tea; and they had a
sweet pastry like baklava. But it was the bread that lured the most
attention.

So, we went to a local bakery to watch. It was a most unique
process: the bakers would knead the dough (mostly wheat), shape it

into what could be called a large, elongated oval sometimes pointed at one end, placed on a wood board with a long handle, and then hand-slapping it to stick onto the inside wall of a wood-burning clay oven; until browned. Then, using two metal prongs, they would pull the finished bread out of the oven and place it on the pile of finished and slightly browned and curved Naan-e-Afghani for purchase and consumption: yummy! And guess what? Practically all the wheat used in making this naan was from the USA, and the state of <u>Kansas</u>!

An Overloaded Bus, Horse-drawn Carriage, and a Bakery

(Anyone ancient enough to remember Spiro Agnew, the disgraced one-time vice-president of the United States under Richard Nixon? On one of his few international diplomatic excursions, he was allowed – that was, of course, before his resignation – to visit Afghanistan and met with the then king Mohammed Zahir Shah and negotiated a wheat deal with the United States.

That was before Agnew's resignation in 1973 because of corruption.)

Then we discovered their Coke-Cola! To our delight a bottle of Coke cost only about 10 cents, and it tasted so good: reminding us of our youth. The taste of Coke in my later years – even in the Army – was very watered-down. So, whoever was making this stuff in Afghanistan was using the original formula or adding other unique ingredients.

But, to all this experienceable glory, there was a very definite **down-side** to our time in Herat, and Afghanistan as a whole!

First was tribalism. Most Afghans in Herāt were members of a well identified tribe; Pashtun being the most influential. As we know, tribal codes of living are very different from national codes, or even international codes. They had many codes of conduct; and two were especially good which were to always show hospitality, and respect of women. One that was especially brutal was their need for revenge. Public beheading by sword was their primary method; and we heard of two while there. We never witnessed it but spoke to a backpacker from Europe who had witnessed one from a distance.

Second, their sanitation habits were... very, very lax; to say the least. Of all the backpackers we met during out travels, (literally hundred) we never spoke with anyone who <u>didn't</u> get diarrhea! The water was undrinkable when it was actually available; especially for brushing your teeth and bathing. And, of course, the same water was used in cooking and in the iced drinks. The most difficult was disposing of human feces, for there were no toilets in all the land (exception maybe in foreign embassies). What they had in their WC "water closet" was long slots in the floor about 3 feet long and about 6 inches wide. The good ones were made of porcelain. So, you were always in a squatting position when moving your bowels. And worse yet, there was never toilet paper! We didn't see any the whole time we were there; anywhere, privately, or commercially.

Instead, they used their hand and water to clean themselves after emptying their bowels, from a small omnipresent tin can with the water. (It is the Muslim custom to use the left hand for cleaning themselves and their right hand for eating. And they stick with their belief that water is much cleaner on you bottom "bum" than using toilet paper.) We didn't know a muslin who was left-handed.

As much as we liked Herāt, it was time to keep moving and make our way to the capital, Kabul. We hopped on a very early morning bus; and were lucky enough to get our own uncushioned seats. However, like everyone else, we had to put our backpacks on top of the bus along with oil drums, large plastic wrapped packages, and sundry fruit. The bus was painted a bright red with a white trimmed top, many of the glass windows were broken or impossible to open. Several circuit riders were also on the bus.

As we got closer to Kabul, the Hindu Kush Mountains loomed larger and larger. Kabul itself was nestled in a large valley at 6,000 feet, and the tallest mountains reach 25,000 feet.

Once we got there, we headed straight to "Chicken Street" – the place all the backpackers said we could get a cheap hotel, descent food, and find the black market to change our money into afghanis'.

After checking into our hotel and taking a very cold bath, we went jaunting around Chicken Street. There were rugs in almost every store front, a lot of hookahs for sale (with or without hashish), and any number of clothing stores. We quickly changed our Western clothes for typical Afghan clothing; and I bought a light green set of pants and shirt (called _Khet partug_). The pants were somewhat tight around the ankles, reminding me of the "pegged" pants I wore as a teenager in the 50's. Arlene bought a "_Grande-Afghani_" with a brightly embroidered long top and a long, cream-colored, skirt.

But we were hungry! Surprisingly, there was no chicken to be bought on Chicken Street. As we followed our noses, we came upon this dingy looking bakery and some Naan-e-Afghani-bread-with-wheat-from-Kansas. This bakery had several large round ovens and produced larger pieces of bread; roughly about 20" long and maybe 10" inches at the widest. So, we sat there and ate one whole piece and drank a cold coke; heavenly. Another slab of bread returned to the hotel with us, along with some plain yogurt bought along the way.

It was a time of resting and communing with circuit riders. We lounged in the hotel common area, or at the many tea shops, openly smoking hashish. The hospitality of the Afghans was renowned as the world's ideal host for the traveler. One hotel owner offered us free room and board indefinitely.

He also gave us gifts of lapis lazuli and green and purple amethyst. It was hard for him to understand why we wanted to move on and not spend the rest of our life smoking hashish with free room and board.

Some circuit riders were heading westward and wanted to know what the transportation, lodging, and money value were like going through Iran and Turkey. Some were going southward to Kandahar as their route to get to India; some were going northwest to see the large 6th Century Buddha statues in Bamyan (learned of its destruction by the Taliban in 2001 and, of course, regretted not traveling the hundred or so miles to see them). But most riders, like us, were going to Jalalabad and on to the Torkham border crossing and on to Peshawar, Pakistan, as the immediate goal, then on the circuit to India.

Money, passport, and destination, and out the front door again!

Purchasing our bus tickets, we knew that by making our way to Jalalabad, it meant leaving Afghanistan. And we had many mixed feelings about it. On the one hand, we felt so good about all the wonderful amenities of Afghanistan and the Afghan people; being welcomed anytime, anywhere. Things were cheap, hashish free and available without lingering fear or guilt, an air of internationalism, and on and on and on. On the other side of the coin, this had internal drive, this feeling, this ineffable desire to be and see and experience more places and people kept us in motion.

The inner drive to continue won out (again) after having gained the feeling of a seasoned travelers.

The bus to Jalalabad was…like any old dilapidated 60's school bus from the States! The outside top was overloaded with sundry merchandise and luggage – including our 2 backpacks, and others belonging to circuit riders like us – and even a few straggling young Afghans who couldn't afford an inside seat. Most of the windows were either broken or stuck partway open. But the overall feeling of the passengers was one of excitement. A nearby Afghan man was nibbling on peanuts and raisins from a small plastic bag, a circuit riding couple was seriously chewing on some freshly baked naan, while we shared a cooled bottle of Coke. But we were going to Jalalabad and happy to be doing so; but not a single Afghan woman was on the bus.

The trip was scheduled to be three and a half hours, but due to engine resistance and one flat tire, it took us more than six hours to pass through the very dry and hot plains with almost no vegetation. Only a few camel caravans and some sheep herders were seen.

But as we drew close to Jalalabad, greenery began to appear more prominent. We were lucky! As it turned out the very large oranges grown were harvested only once every three years, so we ate a lot of orange when we got there. Many of the young men who attended the university in Jalalabad wanted to practice their English and spoke to us and we all tried our best to communicate. Most wanted to know what we did for a living, and how we were able to be free to do what we were doing. We asked about their courses of study and projected degree, family life, and the equality of women.

And then....

Uh oh... uh oh...uh oh...uh oh...no/yes it has begun!!! The Afghan crud, the drips, the runs, the diarrhea, the shits...whatever...hits us both about the same time, and it becomes a matter of self-mastery and preservation. The art of being able to "hold-it-in" until the bus stopped or until we could get to a suitable place to let it blast out became a very real and constant message in the channels of our bodies and minds. And the debate about using paper or water to clean afterward seemed moot. To say nothing about it being a major discomfort, it distracted from the whole experience of travel sights, sounds, and people (won't mention odorous <u>smells</u> at the time) along the way.

Jalalabad is the eastern most city of Afghanistan, but we don't remember too much about it because of our preoccupation with our churning and grumbling stomachs with the crud. It had a well-developed university and we do remember the confluence of the Kabul River and the Kunar River, and we learned it was only about 95 miles to Peshawar, Pakistan – out next destination.

We soon reached the border town of Torkham, got off the bus, openly smoked some hash, cleared the Afghanistan immigration, walked across the border, cleared immigration and custom offices, and got back on the same bus – all within an hour. And we were surprised how quickly we entered Torkham in Pakistan on the other side of the border.

Just after moving a little farther into Pakistan, we came to the small village of Landi Kotal and then we began the ascent into the legendary and mountainous <u>Khyber Pass</u>. And WOW what a ride!!! The ups and downs, the switchbacks, the tunnels, the stops to remove rocks and boulders, the infrequent attempts of 2 vehicles from opposite direction trying to pass each other on the narrowest of highway carved out of the stone flora-less brown rocks, and even went as high as 3,500 feet. Surprisingly there was an occasional and lonely petrol station that sold only gasoline or other items for vehicle emergencies.

Of course, the Khyber Pass historically was a vital link in the ancient Silk Road and has long been the primary route of commerce between Central Asia and the Indian subcontinent and the stop-or-go point in military excursions, and exploratory expeditions, from Genghis Khan to the colonialization by the British. Still, it was the only way of getting to Peshawar. So, in a way, we felt a tinge of danger coupled with the privilege of traversing such a storied circuit. And our diarrhea had somewhat abated due to the hash we'd smoked just before leaving Afghanistan.

Chapter 8

ACCOSTED IN PAKISTAN AND THE INDIAN BORDER

*We never know we go – when we are going We jest and shut
the door; Fate following behind us bolts it,
And we accost no more*

–Author, Emily Dickinson

Pulling into the bus station at Peshawar, as the passengers clamored to get off, I joined the others climbing onto the top of the bus to seek and secure personal belongings and luggage. Arlene remained on the bus because she was tired from consequences of diarrhea and the long arduous and bumpy trip.

And that was a mistake!

While on top of the bus working my way through the crowd of men rummaging through the stockpile of assorted containers while I hurriedly searched for our backpacks, the sound of Arlene screaming from the top of her voice pierced my ears. Alarmed, because it was the most desperate and unhealthy sound I'd ever heard from her!

As her long shrills continued, I awkwardly jumped off the top without safety-concerns for myself or others. As fast as my body would allow, I ran into the bus's open doorway nearly colliding with a tall Muslim man with a turban, scampering off into the crowd. The driver and I hurried to Arlene's seat – about halfway into the row – and she was crying and in an obvious state of near hysteria. We embraced as I sat down and, recognizing the driver, Arlene slowly began to calm down knowing she was safe.

Through the sobs she said: *When the passengers were off the bus a tall muscular man with a turban and a thick mustache, (apparently the same man Buck nearly bumped into getting off the bus), sat in the seat next to me. He put his arm around me and began groping my breasts. I was in shock and immediately began screaming for help, as if my life depended on it; and maybe it did! Buck and the bus driver soon came into the darkened bus and the man quickly got up and hurried off the bus. He was out of sight before I could tell Buck and the bus driver what had happed and what he looked like. I was sobbing and finally felt safe as I melted into Buck's arms overwhelmed with feelings of relief.*

To say Arlene was <u>rattled</u> would be a grand understatement, and it took quite some time for her to stop crying and be calm; while I excitedly exhibited and loudly let my anger be known to all within hearing distance. In the meantime, the driver chased after the assailant as if he knew him but returned a short time later shaking his head negatively to say he didn't see and could not follow the turbaned man. He intimated that the only image many of the tribal clansmen have of western women was what was seen in movies, and that it was usually of a sexually oriented and provocative nature.

That was our first impression of Pakistan, although it did get slightly better after that!

After spending the night in a cheap and dilapidated hotel room we caught the next scheduled 4-hour bus ride to Islamabad, the capital city, and, following the suggestion of fellow circuit riders, we found a clean hotel room close to the bus station. Part of our reason for going to Islamabad was to attempt to get a visa for India and thereby making the passage easy; also, because it was the shortest and most certain route to Lahore and onto the border crossing to India at Ganda Singh Wala.

The idea of getting a visa for India while in Pakistan was a complete fantasy! Since gaining its sovereign independence from India the 2 countries had been at near-perpetual war since – and most recently in 1967 - and were currently in diplomatic hostilities because of the liberation of Bangladesh on the Eastern side of India. War was brewing despite their many economic and cultural ties. Kashmir was always a hot button between them. So, the Indians were not issuing visas from Pakistan, and we calmly accepted the need to wait until the border-crossing for a visa.

The section of Islamabad where we spent most of our time was with narrow streets filled with loud-speaking vendors, electrical and other lines connecting buildings across the streets, smokey motorcycles, and hand drawn carts. Strangers smiled at us, but expressions seemed mostly insincere, an unhappy smile!

Except for food and ticket information for Lahore, we spent most of our time in the hotel interacting with a handful of other circuit riders; all of whom agreed to quickly move on from Islamabad in any direction.

The first half of our bus ride was rough and tedious because of the unattended road conditions, but the second half into Lahore seemed much better; maybe because the road was more kept, and the several stops were with more pleasant surroundings.

And, surprise, surprise, we actually liked the city of Lahore; despite being the second largest Pakistan city and very close to the Indian border. It was easy to notice the social and economic improvement compared to Islamabad and the cultural influence of other religions, especially the Sikh influence. Plenty of magazines and newspapers were freely available, showing pictures of a more liberal culture, especially movies.

The food was very good also. There was plenty of delicious chicken, mutton, some fish, and chapatti bread and rice everywhere; and all with yogurt. Our upset stomach's diarrhea had slowed down for now, so we ate most everything; but continued to drink the safe bottled water and soda.

But our excited anticipating of India was difficult to hide. There were 8 of us (circuit riders) queuing for good seats on the short bus ride to the border town of Ganda Singh Wala (later called Wagah) with feelings of lightheartedness and fun. The bus arrived there in little over an hour's ride, and we were all very chatty.

As it turned out, for us, getting into India was a potentially scary legal problem!

It was a long walk after clearing the Pakistani customs and

immigration office to the open-air tables on the Indian side of the border crossing. The customs station was first; unusual because the visa/immigration stations are typically first in line.

We were approached by an official-looking, tall, heavyset Indian woman who told us, in very good and firm English, to place our backpacks and my doctors' bag on this long table, and to empty all pockets. Then, with the assistance of a helper, they proceeded to carelessly open everything. The female border official then requested that all the women follow her to the lady's bathroom for a more intimate check for drugs or other contraband.

My (Arlene) heart began to race with a surge of panic since I had a small block of hashish hidden in my panties. Fortunately, when they arrived in the bathroom, I had a very urgent and real need to relieve my diarrhea-prone bowels, and showing great agitation told the woman I needed to go to the toilet. The customs' woman acquiesced when I completed the odorous deed; the woman had left the bathroom and returned to her table as a border official, being satisfied that my request to go to the WC was legitimate.

(Whereas the Afghans were super-friendly toward circuit riding hippies, the Indian officials seemed very suspicious and distant.)

The scary part was the full kilo of Afghan hashish I had strapped to my stomach area with a thin turban cloth! It was in 4 rectangular blocks wrapped in plastic and not visible because of my long Afghan shirt.

We were soooo lucky!!!

The female official cleared us and pointed all the hippie circuit riders to the immigration table further down the line where each of us was given a 90-day visa. We all expressed relief and joy! Several of us snickered to each other because we knew we all carried differing amounts of Afghan hash.

Soon, we were on a bus to Amritsar.

We were in India! Somehow everything, except for the customs official, was different – the people, the environment, everything – seemed so much more mellow. And, after getting to Amritsar, we traveled by train, soon on our way to New Delhi.

Chapter 9

THE BIG INDIA SCAM –
SOMETHING FOR NOTHING?

"If you tell a lie, you better have a good memory."

–Anonymous, Alcoholics Anonymous

Pulling into the New Delhi train station was like…nothing we'd ever seen! Scores of railroad tracking with a multitude of passenger coaches, commercial, and raw material box cars; all in various stages of ill repair, and hundreds of railroad tracks going in just about every direction. Scores of people were riding on top of the train cars; many just hanging off the sides. This coupled with a scattering of small wood burning fires, we saw human beings camped out arbitrarily inches away from tracks; mostly males with dark brown skin wearing skimpy white broadcloth (<u>dhoti</u>) hanging loosely like a loincloth. Several women could be seen carrying water pots on the heads cushioned by a rounded layered cloth material.

People everywhere!!!

Following the crowds exiting our coach we were, more or less, forced inside the main New Delhi Station. It was huge!! It had high vaulted ceilings with many pillars and large sized animal and human statues. There was a balcony high up going 360 degrees around the Station with small offices and a stream of well-dressed businessmen walking around portraying self-importance.

On the main promenade was a plethora of humanity: Westerners (hippies and non-hippies), Hindus of many class distinctions, soldiers carrying rifles, well-dressed Muslims, policemen, and an unending array of businessmen hawking their goods; from necklace flowers to clay pots to clothing of any style and size, and various forms and sizes of elephants; some real ivory, some plastic.

Though once colorful, time had reduced the many wall colors to dullness barely distinguishable from the light brown earthy dust. The Beatles had been there, around February-April 1968, at Rishikesh in northern India to study Transcendental Meditation with the Maharishi Mahesh. Preceding them in 1962 was the great beat poet Allen Ginsberg traveling all over India; wanting to reframe his cosmic obsessions toward the humanity around him, while learning compassion within the importance of the momentary present.

Learning from previous interactions at our hotel in Lahore and on the train ride to New Delhi, we were informed as to where to go for a hotel room and food; the Paharganj district of Delhi; fairly close from the train station.

Upon stepping outside the train station, we were hit by horrifying waves of humanity never experienced by us. As obvious Westerners, we came face-to-face with the real India!!! We were immediately surrounded by an unruly mob of beggars of the Untouchable class. Most of whom were disfigured in one manner or another, from missing eyes, twisted hands or feet, missing an arm or leg, unhealed scabs on various parts of their body, and worst of all were the beggars afflicted with *leprosy*. Most had missing fingers, hands, noses, eyes, ears. Cascading in unison, each beggar shouted baksheesh, baksheesh, the word for **alms**, inundating our senses into dullness.

These stunned, horrified, and frightened feelings caused us to literally burst through the crowd pushing away from the Train Station toward the Paharganj District. We wanted to feel compassion, but unable to do so because survival took charge. Hoping to minimize any physical contact, we hastily walked down the main street of the Paharganj district bazaar. It was a more familiar haven compared to what we'd just experienced, although beggars were omnipresent, but fewer. Shops were everywhere, the businessmen more friendly, the streets were narrow with overhanging wooden struts, noisy, dirty, and a little chaotic.

Another factor that required a great adjustment, and amongst all the humanity, were the COWS!!! Cows, cows, cows everywhere! Although not in large numbers, as the customary herds in the US herding community, they were usually singular and just aimlessly wondering unattended around and through the streets. There are millions of cows in India; the ones encountered in the city were homeless. They looked like the Brahmin type with flabby skin down the chests and large humps on their front shoulders, and usually of a dull white color. Some were with dye-colored horns, decorating beads, or other holy embellishments.

To the Hindu Indians, cows are sacred and represent the female aspect of deity and are therefore honored; not killed or eaten. They provide milk to eat, dung for fire, and, in extreme cases, urine drinking to cure diseases. Indian law usually issues the death penalty for killing a cow, and harsh punishment for eating their beef.

After chatting with 2 backpackers from Sweden, we bought some benign food to eat, and then found a suitable hotel with very slow and cold running water.

The next morning, we initiated the Big Scam! We bargained with an unshaven owner of a 3-wheel bicycle taxi to drive us to the business district of New Delhi and to the branch office of the American Express. Once inside we asked for the officer in charge of Travel Checks and were introduced to a short stout woman asking how she could help.

We told her we had lost our $600 set of American Express Travel Checks in Pakistan while in route to India and didn't discover the loss until we were on the train from Amritsar to New Delhi. We had the numbers to verify ownership.

While looking through our passports, she asked many penetrating questions about which hotel we were staying, our train travels, and where we might have lost the checks. Suspiciously, she assumed we were lying because she had gone through this same scenario often enough with other hippie sojourners and circuit riders. But she was resigned to accepting our misinformation and there was nothing to do about it; and her body-language showed it.

It worked like this: getting a renewed set of travelers' checks, we now had *two* sets of checks and in this case $600 each, an <u>old/bad</u> set and a <u>new/good</u> set. To anyone in the world, **other than** American Express officials, we had a cash asset of $1,200. All major countries in the world abide by the same travel rules pertaining to foreigners on tourist visas entering their country.

Everyone **must** show or have factual proof of the ability to return to their home country of origin; thereby avoiding becoming a ward of the host country.

Being in India, we were literally halfway around the world from the USA, and $600 was not going to take us through many immigrations check points; especially since we felt nowhere near the end of our travels. And so long as we didn't cash the <u>old</u> set of bad checks, we would not be considered lawbreakers; we never did cash them. We used the extra check only for <u>show,</u> no border guard or immigration official would ever know the difference!

We just had to remember which set of checks could legitimately be cashed.

The next day, and fresh off our successful check scam, we were on the noon train south to Agra to see the Taj Mahal; about 220 kilometers. It was supposed to be a 3-hour trip but took 6. The seats were wooden, and if you left your seat for the WC forget about getting it back, unless some authoritative person saved it.

We were with about 8 other circuit riders getting off the train and heading for a cheap hotel in Agra. We found a Guesthouse in the Sardar Bazaar area for ten rupees (about 75 cents) per night. We all decided to wait until the morning to see the Taj.

The entry fee was pennies. When walking through the arched Main Gateway, an impressive building in its own right, we could feel our rising emotions. Inscribed on the top of the structure was: "<u>O Soul, thou art at rest. Return to the Lord at peace with Him, and He at peace with you.</u>" as a reminder that the Taj was built in the early 1600 hundreds by the grieving Muslim Mughal Emperor Shah Jahan for the tomb of his favorite wife's body; and eventually his too. It was a monument to love.

At our first view we were blown away! Pictures are good, but the site of this structure far exceeded expectations. It could have been an optical illusion because the domed structure seemed gigantic and pure ivory white between the four tall minarets. As we slowly walked down the narrow reflective pool walkway meant to envision Paradise the Taj seemed to be getting smaller; but more beautiful.

Shoeless we went inside experiencing the symmetry and exactness of the vaulted dome and all the marble and stone fittings in each chamber gave us a feeling of quiet pleasure and sentimental contentment.

Arlene Inside the Taj

The visual pleasure of the mausoleum caused the channels of our minds to create visions of glory while physical inertia kept our feet planted on the marbled floor, as if in the grandest of art galleries. Time and space seemed intertwined. The wall reliefs of flora and fauna inlayed with intricate stones of yellow marble, some jasper, and a little jade were each perfect and symmetrically positioned. And though moderately crowded it was quiet and had a faint smell of an unknown but exotic aroma. A true wonder for all senses to experience; and remember!

We forced ourselves outside to do a 360 degree walk around this wonder. The backside was just as replete and perfectly inlaid as the front, and we sat on a low-marbled wall; mesmerized, as if in deep meditation, watching the placid Yamuna River drifting its way toward the sacred Ganges River, on to the Bay of Bengal, and into the Indian

Ocean.

Adding to this deified experience was the juncture of the full moon! We were two days late for the actual full moon but that was a good thing because, as we sat on the grass near the reflective pool leaning on a small tree, the moon slowly came up over our right shoulders full and bright as ever. We looked at the Taj and swore it appeared in light blue hue; maybe it was the dope we were on. We weren't sure and didn't care. But all our senses were alive and swooning together while our minds raced but remained focused, our bodies stuck together unable to move by the permeating love in us, between us, and around us. Being together against that small tree in the moonlight became a forever memory.

The train to Bombay…3rd class was, in our experience, what humanity is really like in India. Navigating our way to the train station, buying tickets to Bombay (now called Mumbai), and then getting an empty two-seater was a gauntlet; like running with the bulls in Pamplona! It seemed as if everyone was going to Bombay; but we soon accepted that the chaos at a train station was the norm.

We were, as always traveling the cheapest 3rd class; and lucky enough to get a wooden two-seater. Our coach was so crowded it was difficult sometimes impossible to see the doors at either end. Fortunately, there were overhead bins to hold our backpacks and the trusty doctors' bag allowing for a little more legroom. We sat across from two middle aged male Indians, both with slim mustaches and not very long black hair, while the isle was filled with standing passengers carrying personal belongings. The women were dressed in similar off-white saris and most of the men in similarly colored pants and shirts; some with green colored vests and white turbans, some without. Children were crying, children were smiling, but there was little semblance of a nuclear family, and no examples of a middle class.

The train to Bombay was scheduled to take about 24 hours, and actually took more like 60 hours; offering lots of time to think! Reviewing your life was a constant, easy for the good stuff, hard for the harsh. Hopes for the future tended to be over the top; and how far into the future can be seen? Trying to stay in the now presented fantastical thoughts. Like, wondering what it would be like to be somebody other than who you are. The somewhat painful travel conditions kept us gnarled in the present. The sound of the train whistles bringing back reality.

A rather well-known book in the 60's called "Europe on $5.00 A Day" (by Arthur Frommer, 1957) started us on the notion of traveling on-the-cheap. In doing so, little did we expect to experience the all-pervasive poverty in India! Difficult of description without the experience thereof, we knew the two of us could easily do India on $1.00 a day.

The English colonial imperialism ended in 1947, leaving India with16% literacy, a life expectancy of 27, and over 90% of the population living below poverty levels. And the English continued to acknowledge and promote the dreadful caste system which was solidified during the era of the sacred writing of the Bhagavad Gita – about 200 BCE – 200 CE; and are, generally, as follows:

Brahmin = priests
Kshatriya = warriors, kings
Vaishya = merchants, landowners
Sudra = commoners, peasant, servants
Untouchable = outcaste, out of any caste

Each caste was cemented into their own styles of marriage, meals, and worship. A Brahmin accepting a meal from any of the lower classes would be unthinkable. Any person from the upper 4 castes would be committing a horrible karma to even touch a person in the untouchable caste because of their impureness of blood, skin, etc. They were considered subhuman, less than a cow.

Upward social mobility within the system was unimaginable because of the karmic belief in reincarnation; accepting the belief that persons are born into the caste because of the previous life and consequent karmic fate of that life; even if an animal. You must fulfill the fate of the caste you are presently in before you have any hope to move to a higher state of karmic fulfillment in the next life.

Mahatma Gandhi sought to change this by calling the untouchables "Children of God". While calling them "Children of God", Gandhi certainly may have elevated their spiritual status in the eyes of some of their countrymen and the world, but...by many philosophers and sociologists, this could have been seen as a cheap moral and ethical rationalization for the inertia of helping millions of individuals out of the inhuman social spiral of starvation, disease, and the lack of housing.

The whole religious and political moral justification allowing the caste system remains unconscionable; especially when viewed from origins and destiny of civilization into a Golden Age.

Selfishness ruled (rules) the world!

Thoughts of 'why there is something instead of nothing' and our place in the world would briefly separate our consciousness from sore muscles and stiffened bone joints from sitting on the wooden seats; drifting in and out of consciousness as the noisy nights in the coach seemed endless.

The Bombay central train station, Victoria, was even more...filled with near unbelievable throngs of such a wide variety of humans as to stagger the imagination. And yet everyone seemed to know where they were going. From soldiers, sailors, priests, to foreigners from every race and creed to businessmen and hawkers of cheap trinkets were there, seemingly going in all direction. And we had no idea where _we_ were going, except needing to find a cheap hotel with running water and a bed!

(The name-change of Bombay to Mumbai didn't happen until 1995 and was done as a way to withdraw from the legacy of British colonialism, and by the then in-power political party; paying tribute to the Hindu Goddess Mumbadevi.)

Once outside the central station, we were again inundated by the throngs of untouchables begging for _baksheesh_, _baksheesh_, and _baksheesh_. As before, we were repulsed by the prevalence of leprosy afflicted on men, women, and children, and on various body parts. It presented a real moral dilemma for us; on the one hand we could see, feel, and sense that many or most of them needed whatever money they could get for the necessities of living, but on the other hand we could easily hand out all our money to them leaving nothing for self needs. So, we had to pick-and-choose to whom to give the gift of *baksheesh*.

We escaped the parasitic atmosphere by hiring a rickshaw driver to pull us (by human strength) through the maze of a variegated traffic of people, vehicles, and cows to find a cheap hotel. He seemed to know what we wanted, and after about a 30-minute ride he entered a long narrow street and stopped by a hotel with a hand painted sign "King Hotel". It was adequately clean and had running water (but not hot), and a rather large bed; and it was only about fifty cents per night. A very cheap deal, considering Bombay was India's largest city.

Memory is a funny thing. For you and against you.

The next morning, we headed straight to the harbor by the Indian Ocean.

And in doing so, we passed through the olden and glorious Gateway of India; constructed in 1924 to commemorate – who else – the British monarchy. But it was an impressive vista nonetheless – the archway itself being 85 feet high.

We were led by an official to the Harbor Masters Office building. There we talked to 5 or 6 persons of authority to inquire about possibly obtaining passage to our coveted and desired destination - the Seychelle Islands in the Indian Ocean – either on a freighter or passenger boat.

Each man was pleasant enough, but each said they knew of no way for us to get transportation to the Seychelles. One man, spoke softly, and acknowledged the possibility of a freighter from Karachi, Pakistan carrying passengers; but due to the very poor political conditions between the two countries he was not permitted to give more information. Not wanting to return to Pakistan, and wanting to see more of India, we essentially released the idea of ever getting to the Seychelle Islands.

We stayed an extra day in Bombay to rest and chat with other circuit riders; and were on a train to <u>Goa</u> the following day. We had spoken with <u>many</u> circuit riders in our travels and most of them spoke of Goa as their immediate destination; saying it was, basically, a hippie paradise because there was cheap living, freedom of activities, and friendly villagers; and, of course, there were the great beaches. So off we went.

As we boarded the coach, we were asked to show our tickets and passports to an unknown (to us) official, which local Indians were not required to do. And as in all 3rd class train rides in India, the coaches were filled <u>beyond</u> capacity, but we managed to get side-by-side seats of wooden slats with a window on our right and placed our backpacks under our seats and the trusty doctors' bag in the overhead bin. It was about 500 miles to Goa.

Chapter 10

LOOOONG TRAIN RIDES

"If you cannot feed a hundred people, then feed just one."

–Mother Teresa

There were so many small-town stops along the way it seemed as if the locomotive pulling the train was barely able to get up to full speed (40 miles per hour, if lucky) before again stopping. It took over 48 hours and we couldn't sleep much because at every stop, regardless of the time of day or night, young Indian boys would squeeze their way up and down the aisles yelling "chai, chai, chai" at the top of their sharp resounding voices. We occasionally bought a banana and one of these hot teas served in throwaway earthen cups because it was all we were able to get to drink; and were probably dehydrated and didn't know it. We could get bottled water if we had time to get off the train for a short while.

At one of the longer stops at one of the larger stations a very strange thing happened!

Three well-disciplined soldiers came on our coach, one with a rifle and 2 with holstered pistols, and came directly up to us. Suddenly and without provocation they confronted us; as obvious hippie-looking targets. The ranking soldier demanded permission to inspect our back packs. He peered into our eyes as we complied. Loudly and agitated we demanded to know why they were checking our bags, but they ignored us and clumsily continued rummaging through our belongings.

The frightening part came when the youngest of the 3 soldiers wanted to look in the doctors' bag. My gut churned in panic since we had hidden under the false bottom of the doctor's bag a kilo of Afghani hashish. I held my breath as Buck lifted it down from the overhead bin and held it open at about chest high. The soldier stuck his arm inside, reaching about shoulder height on him. He haphazardly scrambled his hand around on the inside of the half-filled bag shuffling things around and, fortunately, quickly removed his arm; seemingly satisfied there were no contraband, or drugs, inside. Once again, we could have ended up in a third world country jail, this time in a dilapidated Indian prison. I guess our angels were working overtime having a more value filled life in store for us. With a huge sigh of relief, my gut calmed down and the train began to move. Life on the Hippie Highway!

The travels continued south flowing through a beautifully greened countryside with rolling hills with men tilling the fields, women carrying pots of liquids on their heads, and children scampering about. India's railway system had been embedded into the consciousness of the population since the 1850's when the British built the first steamed locomotive rails out of Bombay. And, except for expanding the rails over most of the Indian continent, it hasn't changed much since; easily outpacing a very stodgy busing system.

An occasional whiff of burning coal producing engine power drifted through the coach with little or no notice of anyone. Just the rhythmic sounds of the metal wheels turning on the steel rails: clickity clack, clickity clack…creating a meditative state while staring at the dim overhead lights. The punctuated sounds of the train whistles were not disturbing because our coach was far back from the trains' leading engine; somehow reassuring.

Memory is a funny thing. A conscious first memory?

As a wannabe writer, I thought about story plots, character strengths and flaws, conflicts, love stories, and resolutions. But mostly I began to think more about larger questions for which we had no answers; but always searching. The usual: who am I, where did I come from and where am I going? And these questions usually led me to some sort of self-analysis and a review of my life thus far, and to transcend that I'd pondered thoughts like: how did it <u>all</u> begin and where was it <u>all</u> going? Was there such a thing as a beginning and/or an end? Are these leprosy-ridden untouchables and I related in some way of commonality? But please… <u>not</u> the cows!

I remember once when about 7 or 8 years old, I was walking in the countryside and came upon this very large rock. It was next to a spring of water and after I drank the cool water I stared at the rock. It had little bits of different colors sprinkled throughout making it a conglomerate whole, and I thought: what if, what if I was inside that rock, what if our world was inside that rock, what if our universe was inside that rock and there were thousands of universes inside the rock…

The history of travel was intriguing. How the first humans moved away from their lesser primates, and the various races spread out over the world; always moving, moving, moving. Discovering the world as round helped early circuit riders to solo trek, sail, and fly around the world; always opening new circuits. What enlightenment! Eventually this moving will carry us through the cosmos.

Eventually I fell asleep with my head full of fantastic meaningless thoughts, and a feeling of at-easement, despite the uncomfortableness of wooden seats and crowded conditions. After all, we were in India, heading toward another adventure on the beach; such is life for such travelers on the circuits.

My thoughts focused on the extreme physical discomfort and fears about my digestive problems which triggered memories of flares ups of Crohn's disease which started when I was 25 years old. I also looked at fellow travelers and exchanged courtesies, positively commenting about their children. I slept a lot!

As the train pulled into the Madgaon Station (sometimes called Vasco-daGama) we saw unusual things: 2 dogs marginally above the dying-by starvation level, and a nun dressed in all-white with a head scarf. Somehow (and I hope this is not an unconscious bias) the station seems a little cleaner and less crowded. We also saw their comforting State motto: "*<u>May everyone see goodness, may none suffer any pain.</u>*" We were bleary eyed but ready to get to our beach destination.

Chapter 11

GOA BEACH - A CIRCUIT RIDERS DREAM

*"Emancipate yourself from mental slavery, none but
ourselves can free our minds."*

–Bob Marley 1945-1981

Goa was a Portuguese settlement colony from the early 1500's. It remained that way until after India's independence from British rule and was annexed into becoming a territory in 1961, by invasion. Which was how it was when we were there (and later coming to full Indian statehood in 1987). To us it was always an amazingly wonderful mixture of Indian and Portuguese, Christian and Hindu, cultures.

Without letup we were accosted by baksheesh seekers outside the train station, but not as many or as aggressive, as we bartered with a rickshaw taxi to get us to the Margoa bus station. And surprise, there were fewer cows to avoid.

It was long before we were on our way to Colva Beach – the place we'd heard so much about as far back as Afghanistan. Some suggested Anjuna as one of the optional beaches but we rejected it because it most likely would be too crowded with other circuit riders.

The 5-mile bus ride to Colva Beach was cheap but bumpy. We were dropped off near the edge of the sandy beach and began immediately seeking our own living space, but available individual structures for rent were not plentiful. Luckily, we found a very small building near the owner's house and close to the beach. It had an 8 X 10-foot flooring and high enough for standing straight up – but just barely. A difficult to read sign, "TO LET" hung outside. It had a doorway at my eye level without a door and a window opening near the rear without anything covering it, and a small, short-legged chair, a kerosene stove, and a straw mattress.

Cost? About $15.00 a month! Current exchange rate was 12.50 rupees per dollar; but more if you went to the black market for exchanging cash rather than checks.

We considered ourselves lucky and were immensely pleased because not all the circuit riders had a private living space; unless you considered a canvas tarpaulin tied between two palm trees to be a private living space. But...anywhere near the beach was gloriously acceptable.

At a nearby small flea market Arlene bought several Indian saris with tops, and I bought a simple cloth with a string to tie around my waist and cover private parts. And that was pretty much the way we dressed most of our time in Goa, for more than a month's stay.

Off to the beach we went. An incredibly enticing beach, in width from the end of the palm trees and vegetation, it was nearly fifty yards to the salt water, depending on the tide. In length it was several miles up and down the coast, with pure white sand, occasional sea debris, and local fishermen with long boats tending their nets.

We were higher than kites (without drugs, too)!

Scores of circuit riders were all around; even though they may have had different hair lengths, skin color, clothing, multicolored necklace beads, shiny bracelets, or chillum pipes. We were alike; not by physical appearances, thought processes, or even of the multitude of ineffable experiences. We were a sub-culture, and we knew it for sure, but to us a glorious one! We had unity within our diversity, and a blissful collective consciousness that left us filled with joy, in the midst of less than comforting living conditions.

Conversations came easy: Do you have a place to stay? Where are you from? Where have you been? Were you in Afghanistan? Do you know where to find the black-market for money exchange in town? Do you have Afghani hashish? What of the latest music? Have you seen a guru? Are you going to Kathmandu? What of the Vietnam War resistance in the States? And of the India-Bangladesh conflict to the

East of us? Did you eat some water buffalo meat? Have you helped the fishermen pulling the nets?

Then there was the unspoken daily ritual of watching the early evening sunset.

At days end, most were loosely scattered about the beach sitting cross-legged looking westward to experience the sun setting into the Arabian Sea. Several intrepid ones would sit on the stiff sand near the incoming surf, but most were sitting in the soft warm sand near the palm trees. It was an awareness of time and space, and yet we felt apart from it. It was a consciousness uplifter.

Our Goa Hut

It was the dry season, so we practiced this ritual nearly every evening mesmerized until the last little speck of sun sank into the undifferentiated watery horizon; some staying until dark. Birds would fly in an imperfect formation, and some could be heard behind us in the wooded area. The smell of saltwater lingered with us until the night's sleep. Magnetically, each evening drew us to the Indian sunset.

Food was an interesting part of the Goan experience. We'd take the local bus to town (Margoa) and get off at the marketplace. A wide variety of fruit was usually easily available – such as pineapples, papaya, mangos (India's national fruit), coconuts, and of course, the omnipresent bananas. Our personal favorite, after papaya, was the pomelo fruit which was a large oval shaped citrus fruit and seemed to be a cross between an orange and a large grapefruit. Many referred to them as a *tarange*. The few vegetables were potatoes, tomatoes, onions, carrots, garlic, and lots of chili. Arlene made a delicious vegetable casserole with cheese. We did buy and eat a lot of rice, curried or otherwise, as a good stomach filler. And yes, the water buffalo meat was eaten.

Seafood was another story, and our primary source of protein. We could buy a small plate of deep-fried (in coconut oil) fish at the commercial stall operated by locals near the beach. But the greater experience came when helping the tribal fisherman fish by nets, which happened usually in the late afternoon just before sunset time.

There would be 20 or 30 men working together with long and large piles of fishing nets and using stakes to stabilize one end of the net, they loaded a single pile of the net on to their long boats. Several men would push the boat out into deeper water past the breakers and paddle it offshore for a hundred yards or so, all the while dropping off the netting into the water containing fist size pieces of cork tied to the top holding the net just above water. At a critical point from shore, the boat was steered southward and back toward the shore; forming a giant "U" with both ends of the single net on the beach. Once getting to shore and at the opposite ends of the netting, the hands of strong men began pulling the net toward the waiting tribesmen; occasionally verbalizing unknown sounds.

Then the work, and the fun, began. Groups of men at both ends slowly pulled the nets onto the sandy shore as the middle of the "U" got smaller and closer to shore. The fishermen were delighted with us (there were always 6 or more circuit riders helping) joining the brawny process of pulling in the nets because they usually were full of fish and other types of sea life (some very weird looking).

The ecstatic intensity of the growing crowd seemed almost chaotic, and yet quiet tribal leadership was understood and pervaded through the group. The male leaders were known and observed by what they wore! And each had a silver braided belt holding up their genital covering loin cloth. We found out later the number of silver braided strands on their belt, anywhere from 2 to 6, determined their position in the tribal hierarchy, the more strands the higher their position.

Hundreds, sometimes thousands of fish flipped flopped about in the shallow water and onto the wet sand as the barefooted men, women, and children filled their straw basket with fish and gleefully hurried inland; some for income, and family food satisfying for at least another day or two.

In addition, to the fish tribesmen gave us for helping, we could casually walk up or down the beach when at low tide (evenings or mornings) and dig for clams, taking as many as needed for the next meal.

Then we learned how to make the greatest of all foods – **dessert**!

To do this, first we'd buy some of the plentiful English graham crackers and finely crush them covering the inside of the pie pan already lined with *ghee*, a form of purified butter. Then came a handful of very ripe bananas mashed into a smooth paste filling the pie pan to the brim. Then, most important, we would buy several bars of British Cadbury chocolate, melt it, and pour it over the top of the entire banana filler. Finally, we would shred plenty of fresh coconut and sprinkle it all over the melted chocolate and let it cool. Then eat; waiting, IF possible, until it cooled!

Then we would pig-out, usually eating a whole pie at one sitting!!!

Speaking of pigs, we would be remiss in our storytelling if we didn't include the story of the pigs of Goa and how they affected our stay in Colva Beach.

Actually, it was a bit of a horror story for most.

Within dashing distance of our little cubicle home stood an all-cement structure about 5 feet high and 3 feet wide and 3 feet in width. On the inside were the sit-down portions of the stall with a hole, somewhat shaped like a normal Western toilet or potty seat. It was where many nearby circuit riders, and the Indian owners of our building, went to defecate. And defecate we did; often! Most of us had various stages of the *runs*; some form of diarrhea, very common for Westerners visiting that part of the world.

The thing was: there was no deep ditch or hole into which the feces would flow. Instead, at the back of the cement stall at ground level was a half rounded 1-foot opening where the 3 or 4 pigs would tussle with each other to see who would get their head into the opening first to **eat the feces**. We assumed the pigs knew the feces of the circuit riders because of the smell and it passed through our digestive system so quickly it was practically undigested food; and very nutritious for the animals. And, as mentioned previously, all methods of clean-up, after defecation in that part of the world, was water to cleanly wipe your bottom. (Gross, we know, but…)

We never ate any pork or pig products while there!

About halfway through our time in Colva Beach, Arlene contacted a parasite which added to the Afghani parasites and a Crohn's flare up. She experienced extreme diarrhea to the point of becoming very weak and was unable to keep any food down or sleep much. Urgently, we took a real autocab to the Victor Hospital in less than 30 minutes and Arlene was checked in promptly. Saddened and concerned, I returned to our beach shoebox-home, but lightened knowing Arlene was in the caring hands of the Nuns at the hospital.

Visiting the next day, Arlene looked and sounded better, saying she was able to get some restful sleep and keep a small amount of light food in her stomach. She said the Nun nurses had taken several stool samples and had a preliminary diagnosis of the parasite and started giving her the antidote to kill it. In just two days, Arlene was able to digest some food after 2 months of diarrhea. Our gratitude for the nuns at this Christian hospital has remained with us; even today. We went back to our tiny house in Colva Beach in time for the setting sun melting into the Arabian Sea with renewed energy and some peace of mind. And the hospital services were totally free.

I often visited the house of the family who owned our hut. The feeling of female connection was evident, expressed mostly nonverbally with smiles and gestures. They encouraged me to play with and hold their children. The common bond we had was love of family. On many occasion the mothers and daughters were observed picking lice out of each other's hair, and, yes eventually out of my hair. It was a true act of selflessness and kindness. Sadly, this technique did not help get rid of the lice, so we went to town and bought lice shampoo which got rid of the lice in my very thick, long curly hair.

Washing our hair and body was an interesting event. In the entire village of Colva Beach there was but a single water well; and it was fairly close to the beach. Twice a week we went to the well, waited our turn to use the clay pot tied to a rope and would pour the water over our heads and bodies, soap, and rinse. Several local women also used the well-water for various household reasons: like cleaning veggies, washing clothing, or cleaning their children. The thing was: all the cleaning done by us Circuit Riders and the locals was done within 10 to 20 feet from the well. Surely, much of our impurities must have seeped down to the water table and back into the well.

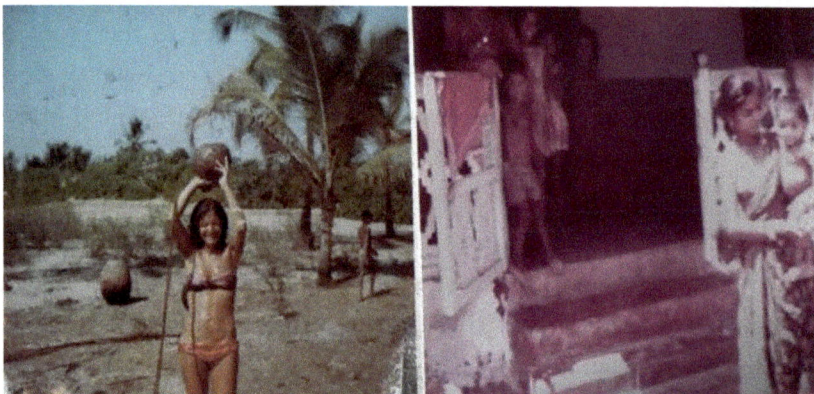

Community Well, and the Neighbors

We were befriended by 2 English guys, also Circuit Riders, living in a long thatch-roofed building nearby who were about our ages. Hinting, they may have been on the lam; for what they were never clear, but probably for drug dealing. Our primary reason for going to their hut, besides smoking their hookah and conversations about travel, life, and our personal experiences on LSD, was music. Teddy and Alfie had the only working turntable of the entire circuit rider population at the Beach; a 78-record player running on 6 batteries.

The thing about it: they had only one album, and the 78-rpm album was James Taylor's "*Sweet Baby James*"; and singing along without crying:

"With ten miles behind me, and ten thousand more to go, you know
There's a song that they sing when they take to the highway A song that they sing
when they take to the sea A song that they sing of their home in the sky
Maybe you can believe it if it helps you to sleep
But singing seemed to work fine for me
So goodnight, all you moonlight ladies
Rockabye, sweet baby James..."

We played it over and over and over and over and over and over and over again until we knew the music and lyrics practically by heart; and never got tired of listening. The batteries usually died after only a single night, maybe two, so we'd often buy new ones when we went shopping in town for food and other goodies.

Another interesting point, Teddy and I looked so much alike, that we were often mistaken for the other by many of the circuit riders whom we interacted with on or near the beach, and not just when high on hashish. We both had long blonde hair, blue eyes, and a reddish mustache; each other's *doppelgänger*. Once, on a lark, we exchanged passports and went to a bank in town separately to cash travel checks; Teddy changed my American checks, and I changed his British checks without a hitch. And we all had a big laugh!

Onlooking Women at the Well and My Doppelganger

Actually, it transcended just a laugh because it was a deep-seated belief most circuit riders had, an innate opposition to nationalities, international boundaries, different types of money systems, racial disparity, language, etc. Yes, we were dreamers, and many had already listened to and talked about the John Lennon "Imagine" masterpiece. We knew we were not alone!

While there was no actual go-to library to draw upon, many well-read and travel-worn paperback books – mostly novels – were easily passed around enriching our collective consciousness. Old ones like Salinger's "Catcher in the Rye", Hesse's "Siddhartha", Leon Uris's "Exodus"; and too many others to remember. Some of the more current ones I read were Vonnegut's "Slaughterhouse Five", Heller's "Catch 22", and was completely engrossed with Wolfe's nonfiction account of Ken Kesey and the Merry Pranksters in "Electric Kool-Aid Acid Test". The Bhagavad-Gita was always accessible; as were many books in foreign languages; mostly in French.

But all good things sooner or later end. Our evening crowd-gatherings for the glowing sunsets were growing smaller and smaller. Fewer hands were helping pull in the tribal fishing nets and fewer people came to listen to the "Sweet Baby James" music sessions at night. Sadly, the season, our season, in Colva Beach was about to end, and we were confronted with that wonderful and sometimes startling life determining position, once again, deciding where to travel next. The next adventure! We were literally halfway around the world from our starting point in California, and somehow felt as if we were only halfway through this time/space conundrum of our lives. Which circuit was next?

We listened to discussions about Riders leaving for Kabul, Kathmandu, and even as far away as Bali. Our friends Alfie and Teddy were heading to Kathmandu.

We decided to get out the front door and onto the circuit south to the island nation of Ceylon.

Chapter 12

INFINITE AND ETERNAL INDIA

"We had arrived at the armpit of the world; perhaps the universe!"

–Buck & Arlene Weimer, in Calcutta

Leaving Goa and our brotherhood community emoted feelings of loss and grief coupled with a renewed commitment to unity. But soon we were on a train with the destination of Jog Village to see the Jog Falls which was only about 215 kilometers from Colva Beach, another overnight train ride. But it was worth it!

Not many tourists were there and only 2 other circuit riders. And because we were there just before the start of the rainy season, the falls were not spectacular, but inspiring enough, being the second highest waterfalls in India at over 800 feet at its longest drop with 6 or 7 individual falls. Some local Indians were playing and bathing in the several pools at the base of the falls.

The circuit riders (both Swedish guys) were heading north to the Punjab and said the Ceylon circuit was rarely open because of the forever political unrest there. So, getting a visa was nearly impossible. But taking individual advice with a grain of salt, we doubted them and continued.

The next day we were on a train to Mangalore and onto Mysore City. Besides the long arduous train ride – the further south we traveled the slower and more difficult were the circuit rides.

Memory is a funny thing. Some cannot be forgotten.

2 events recalled.

First memory: On the station platform leaving Goa we met a young dark(orange hue) skinned Indian lad, probably in his early twenties, also on his way to Mangalore and we faced each other in our coach seats. Appearing obviously Western, and acknowledging we were from the US, he proudly displayed a small paperback New Testament Bible. Assuming we were Christians, he said he <u>too</u> was a Christian and quietly began reading short passages to us.

Not wanting to reflect the image of American arrogance (written succinctly about in the 1958 William J. Lederer and Eugene Burdick novel "<u>The Ugly American</u>" of an engineer sent to Southeast Asia), we displayed sincerity and patience while listening. Sharing our sense of being in a minority, we gave him some food as he talked about Christian theology compared to Hindu beliefs. And, wanting to show his generosity, he handed the Bible to Arlene to look at and read. Arlene was sitting on the window side of the seat with the window open. Somehow, she held the book in her right hand near the open window and just at that exact time the train turned sharply in the opposite direction. And POW, just like that! The Bible slipped out of her hand and into the darkened night; forever lost to our new Indian friend.

I have absolutely no memory of this event. Another memory blocked out because of anxiety and this time guilt!

Second memory: Following him for a short distance, we said a fond farewell to the Christian rendezvous; even as he continued to refuse any type of monetary compensation for the lost Bible. After which we had a sudden panic attack when unable to locate the connecting station platform for the train to Mysore City as we spurted around approaching any person looking official; and even some who weren't; asking for the train and/or platform number for Mysore City. People either looked bewildered, confused, disinterested, tired, or asked for money. But none gave a positive response.

Just then a slow train was pulling into the platform where we stood. The engineer released a large amount of hissing sound with a light-grey stream of thick air and…walking through the misty steam toward us came a tall smartly dressed man in a pressed grey suit and a very white turban on his head. He was obviously a Sikh, and asked with a distinctive clarity: "May I help you?" He led us onto platform 2 away from where we were, and, speaking perfect English, touching his greying beard said: "Here is you train. It leaves in 30 minutes, so hurry and be sure to get good seats." He guessed correctly we were travelling with 3rd class tickets.

We were flabbergasted and filled with gratitude, to say the least, and always remembered that selfless Sikh and the wonderful experience with him; and felt we could become friends. It was as if someone was watching over us.

Once in Mysore City we had 3 recalled memories.

#1: *I (Arlene) had a long-standing urge to call my mother in Brooklyn, NY and was directed to the Main Post Office in Mysore City. My first day there I spent several hours wading through the bureaucracy, just to get to a telephone with the potential of an international call. The second day there I succeeded in giving the attendee the long-distance number for my parent's home in Brooklyn, but the connection was quickly discontinued. Finally, on the third day I was able to speak with my mother, Lily, for a whopping 5 minutes. My Mom was audibly relieved to know we were safe after several months of not hearing from us. Our hearts were filled with gratitude and love.*

#2: This may seem a silly memory, but a memory none-the-less. We went food shopping the next day in the local outdoor market for some bottled water, peanuts, and fruit. By this time, our favorite fruit was papaya. We picked an exceptionally long and ripened one and returned to eat it at the hotel. It was at least 24" long, or longer, and when we cut it open lengthwise, we couldn't believe our eyes or luck! At the bottom of the long end was the normal small fist-size pocket of dark seeds, with the remainder of the papaya perfectly ripened, sweet tasting, thirst and appetite quenching, invigorating, stimulating, and a life sustaining fruit. (For whatever reason, we've always remembered this.) Unaware, we were probably dehydrated and malnourished!

I too have a vivid memory of that luscious papaya. When we brought it back to the hotel, we needed a knife to cut into it. The front desk clerk graciously helped us cut it opened. I still remember standing at the front desk in joyous disbelief, a most perfect papaya! Oh, the delight in small pleasures!

#3: On Arlene's third day at the Post Office in the effort to telephone her mother Lily, I went to the Main Train Station to inquire about tickets and departing times for trains to Coimbatore and on the Madurai; still hoping to get to Ceylon (Sri Lanka). Madurai to the southernmost tip of India (at least the closet to Ceylon) was a small town called Rameswaram; about 92 or 93 miles from Madurai.

Standing about 5th or 6th in line from the ticket seller when, without warning, the man in front of me fell suddenly to the ground and rolled onto his back with a solid thud; and after a few shaking jitters, the movements stopped. His clothing was traditional Tamil skirt (lungi) and a t-shirt.; clean but with holes from constant wearing. Some fluids seeped between his lips. He was balding and with a narrow faint mustache; probably of the *sudras*, or working, peasant, class. Only a few others surrounded the body, but nobody moved to touch him, and an official of the train station looked down at the body lying there, said something aloof in the Tamil language, and departed. Feeling awkward and uncertain, I watched the faces and body language of the men around their fallen comrade. Not one woman was present.

Soon his brown facial skin turned ashen, and everyone knew he was dead. It was weird for me, but it was as if those around the body had seen it happen hundreds of times before. They seemed unconcerned or didn't want to interfere with any Hindu karmic happenstance of the person who had just died. A nearby cow was given more attention.

The next day we were on a train to Coimbatore and on to Madurai. We had a layover of several hours in Coimbatore and we bought some cooked rice sprinkled with mushrooms served on a banana leaf which was unique and very tasty. Somehow, we seemed to have adjusted to the 3rd class train rides in India; and not many circuit riders, or <u>any</u> foreigners, were seen this far in the Southern India. The whitish ash-covered faces of some holy men, the ascetic sadhu renouncing the worldly life for the spiritual path, thin-as-a-rail with long braided hair and necks and arms filled with beads and bracelets, seemed omnipresent.

Madurai was as Indian as it got, with broad streets and numerous temples, and open-air markets everywhere. But still… we never did adjust to all of the untouchables! It was whispered: parents would purposefully disfigure a newborn child by breaking an arm or leg bone, gouge out an eye, or some other horrifically unimaginable ways of distorting and disabling their infant with the thinking that… they were doing the child a favorable service by insuring a likely more lucrative livelihood of begging. Otherwise, if they were born a healthy untouchable, they had little chance of survival and were doomed to another round of reincarnation. Many newborn girls were simply left to die.

It was at the Madurai train station that, when attempting to buy train tickets to Rameswaram, we were soundly confronted with the reality that travel to Ceylon (Sri Lanka) was currently impossible. Visas were not issued to *any* foreigners, Indians or otherwise. Apparently, a Marxist People's Liberation Front was trying to overthrow the current government; ultimately unsuccessfully. The rebellion was thwarted with the help of the British, Soviet, and Indian governments. Sri Lanka eventually became a constitutional republic.

So, the circuit to Ceylon was <u>short-circuited</u> because of another, and another and another blinded bolt of political and military misadventures. When will the leaders of this world learn? Unity fosters peace and prosperity.

Without thinking, we agreed to head north up the eastern coast toward the Bay of Bengal. Previously, we had heard from several circuit riders about Pondicherry and of the many gurus, ashrams, and temples. And soon we were on another train, going over 400 miles up the coast. We made several train changes in the deadening slow moving locomotives: belching dark smoke into our coaches and lungs. Always full, the coaches often contain farm animals, like goats and chickens, but never cows. Small children peering longingly into our faces hoping for a spark of attention from a foreigner to share with friends after returning home.

Finding an ashram in Pondicherry was easy. After warding off the <u>baksheesh</u> seekers outside the train station, we hired a hand-drawn rickshaw and asked to be taken to an ashram. Before long we were accepted inside the Sri Aurobindo Ashram and were encouraged to stay as long as we liked. In theory their yoga style was an integration of all types without renunciation of life in the material world.

After several days of sitting cross legged in silent mediation and eating a strict vegetarian diet, we were approached by a handsome, inquiring, Indian woman. Essentially, she wanted to know our financial situation, long term. Did we have an estate, inheritance, or any other financial status we might consider donating to the Ashram? We, of course, did not. But the whole process turned us off to the Ashram lifestyle, and we were back on a train continuing north to Madras (now called Chennai since 1996).

It was when buying our tickets for Madras in Pondicherry that the ticket master astutely noted that our Indian visas <u>were about to expire</u>! When we entered India, we were each granted a 90-day visa. We had become so enthralled and enveloped with all our travels in India - the people, culture, places, integrating ourselves, sometimes just surviving – we had completely forgotten such a (to us) mundane things like the particulars of a valid visa.

Madras is the capital of the southern state of Tamil Nadu and situated on the eastern coast of the Bay of Bengal, by the Indian Ocean. It was a large city, more cars than any city since New Delhi, and lots of paper handouts advertising Bollywood motion pictures, and there were many foreign embassies there. Still, Madras had its fair share of diseased untouchable beggars, and cow population. (<u>Madras is currently sister-cities with Denver, Colorado.</u>)

We went to a branch of the American Embassy, and they directed us to the correct office building for acquiring an Indian visa extension, which we did, and for no costs. A 30-day extension suited us just fine to get out of India, and we decided to continue the northern trek, hoping to go all the way to Kathmandu in Nepal. Whoopee!!!

(As a sidebar, and an interesting tidbit of history, we discovered something interesting about the history of Christianity in India. While in Madras we saw several non-ordinary Christian churches; most of which referred to Saint Thomas, the Apostle of Jesus in the New Testament, i.e., "Doubting Thomas". According to Wikipedia, Thomas sailed to India and landed in the southwestern state of Kerala, and eventually moved over to Madras where he established his ministry. He was eventually killed – martyred – by the sword of a Hindu Priest on 72 AD July 3rd. A contradiction in our research indicated the Apostle Thomas died at the hands of the Romans in Malta, off the coast of Sicily. And this, most likely, was the Apostle Nathaniel, son of Bartholomew, who set up that ministry and died in India.)

It was over a thousand grueling miles north from Madras to Calcutta (now Kolkata), and our third-class coach bodies were beginning to show the wear and tear. Plus, from the lack of proper nutrition, fluids, our bodies appeared emaciated. We had gotten skinny! We lost track of days and nights, were sleepy-eyed, and of dull minds. Still the monotonous clickity clack, clickity clack, clickity clack with the occasional tooting of the engine whistle barely penetrated our consciousness. It was as if we were the train, and the train was us. The chai tea sellers ran through the coaches, like thoughts in an endless stream of consciousness. The *baksheeshesers* were unheard at what seemed like a hundred tiny generic stations; names like: Nellore, Bapatia, Eluru, Annvaram, Naupada, Chatapur, Jaipur, and on and on. It was as if we were in another time, another sphere, and so far out of traditional awareness as to not be in a dream. Sights and sounds seemed as one; as our consciousness drifted in and out of the present; holding fast to each other as always.

(Another quick side bar: for those of you who are interested in the cinema, to get a very clear look at rural Bengali India in the 1950's we recommend viewing "**The Apu Trilogy**"; especially the first one: "Pather Penchali" or "Song of the Little Road". Directed by Satyajit

Ray, it was released in 1955 and considered by most world cinema critics to be one of the best films ever made. We totally agreed with the critics. The music was by the little-known Ravi Shankar, and completely captures the essence of all three films. Your cinematic history will be incomplete until this trilogy is seen. Certainly, these well-crafted films foreshadow the later mostly comical Bollywood genre.)

Finally, we pulled into Howrah Junction Train Station and Calcutta, and **nothing** in all our fantasies or travels could have prepared us for the shock we were about to experience! Stepping off the train coach, we both headed for the public rest rooms. What a shock! It was virtually impossible for me to forge my way near a standup or squatting stall without stepping into the piles of feces covering nearly every inch of the old, marbled floor, plus the slippery puddles of urine. And the stench… was…as an open sewer line. Other men were searching for barren spots of the floor to do their squatting. The sounds, sights, and stench were unbearably horrific. If there was a hell it could not be worse. Still, what was I to do; I <u>had</u> to relieve the bowels.

Choosing the first steps carefully over clumps of human defecation, some fresh, some old, in stockingless sandals, I soon gave up and walked in a natural gait to get to an open stall. Relieving myself, I then made my way to the outside of the station!

My (Arlene) experience was nearly identical. However, it was easier for me to get to a stall than Buck. There was a pathway though the feces and the woman were using the toilets to urinate and defecate rather than the floor. We woman are nesters even in these unimaginable unsanitary conditions.

Once outside the station, conditions were only marginally better, as we did the best to clean our feet and sandals. The gutters contained vast amounts of trash mixed with more human waste, and people everywhere! Whole families lived and called home each street corner at the end of the sidewalks, resting on makeshift cardboard beds while begging for anything they could get from passing strangers. This was their home, and their territory! No one dared encroach onto it, either out of fear or respect. The enormity of so much degraded indignity of humanity on one small corner was overpowering; to say the least. Each person, young or old was rail-thin, disfigured, dirty, and probably diseased; and seemed to have a strange orientation to their surroundings; unlike us and others passing bye.

They had only one <u>now</u> perspective, focused on air, food, and water, survival. I'm sure they used the restrooms inside the railway station to vacate their bowels. And yet, <u>something</u> held them together! What was it? Love seemed to be an abstract from an ancient relative.

Past the corners, the oppressive environment was…difficult to imagine how it all functioned without evisceration. Relentlessly, electric buses and smokey cars made a very unsynchronized and continuous unmelodic vibration into the atmosphere, in all directions. The air was saturated with multiple pollutants, limiting any worthwhile views. With shallow breathing, our noses and lungs burned from the toxic atmosphere. Cows of various colors and decoration clogged the side streets.

We had arrived in the armpit of the world, perhaps the universe!

This was it, we thought! We had arrived in hell!

After all the memories we've downloaded thus far, and all the beautiful places and wonderful people encountered, Calcutta was, without doubt, the worst! It'd been nearly a year since we got married and uprooted ourselves from our comfortable environment in Venice Beach, California. We had no home or a place in which to lay our heads, no familiar friends to embrace, and no anchors to hold onto; just each other. We held each other tight through the night! But Calcutta – NEVER!

So now what?

Consistent with our desire to go the Kathmandu, we somehow found the Nepalese Embassy in Calcutta and secured 15-day visas to "The Kingdom of Nepal"; and their visa stamp; maybe our favorite stamp. It was dated 05-05-71. And just as quickly we bought train tickets to the border town of Raxaul; a 500 miles journey north. We missed a hoped-for side-trip to Darjeeling, but…our train slowed to a near stop as we crossed the Ganges River as most passengers appeared in a prayer state and arrived at Raxaul station late the next night.

A restless night in a run-down hotel and we awoke early the next morning, caught a bus to the India/Nepal border, and cleared immigration and customs check post, and entered The Kingdom via the small trading town of Birgunj.

Passports, money, and destination, and out the beleaguered front door we went.

Chapter 13

KA, KA, KA, KATHMANDU

"...Up to the mountains, where I'm going to, If I ever get out of here, That's what I'm gonna do..."

–Kathmandu, Song by Bob Seger

Strange as it may seem, we hitched a ride on the back-bed of a truck going to Kathmandu; a hundred miles through very curvy and mostly unfinished rough road. But by this time, we were hardened travelers. Good thing, because the truck was transporting bags of dry cement, making our traveling circumstance <u>hard</u>; no pun intended. Despite the lovely mountainous impact, the cement made it very dusty for our eyes and nose, and we were constantly rearranging our bodies to distribute the muscle and bone pain. It was a looooong hundred miles, but we arrived in Kathmandu.

Debarking from the memorably hard cement-truck ride, we ran into several hipsters on the street who told us of a cheap hotel, where to get some food; and they were all smiles. Our hotel room in Kathmandu was cheaper, cleaner, and even had good running water, cold but clear and of all things a bidet.

I (Arlene) felt I had died and ended up in a Parisian hotel. We cleaned-up, rested, and went looking for food and drink.

We had struck nirvana! Our hotel, "Inn Eden" was smack dab in the middle of the famous "Freak Street" It was just off Durbar Square, where was located the government-run marijuana and hashish shops (and a crudely painted "HASHISH & MARIWANA" sign; obviously legal at that time), and restaurants serving western-style food. Our favorite was "The Chi & Pie" shop, with their lemon-meringue pies and sweet milky Darjeeling tea; and lots of good vibes from the owners and hippies from around the world. An especially good treat was the plain whole yogurt! It was creamy, rich, and flavored, and it quickly began healing our nearly ruined digestive systems from the long Indian abuse. When finished you were expected to just throw the earthen yogurt pots on the naked ground, a form of recycling. The pumpernickel bakery, yoga, transcendental meditation, shops full of rugs, burning incense, t-shirts, local clothing, and Tibetan masks initially overfilled our senses; and on and on.

Resting a lot, we just sauntered around the quiet street soaking in the cool, fresh, mountain oxygen. Somehow, we were consumed by the delirious feeling when thinking we had just gone from hell to heaven. Amazing, how the travel circuits carried us from the lowly depths to such great heights in only a few days. Traveling can do that!

Regaining strength and curiosity, we ventured out and had many enriching conversations with likeminded circuit riders; many wanting to hear about our time in Goa and how we got there and how we got to Kathmandu. Some trekkers fantasized about wanting to get to base camp of Mount Everest.

It was then we learned it was the annual time of Buddha's birthday festivities. His 2533rd birthday (563-480 BC) was celebrated on May 10, in 1971 with the birth name Siddhartha Gautama in Lumbini, Nepal; just 127 miles southeast of Kathmandu. His exact birthday varies from year to year based on the Asian lunar calendar, but usually around the same time of the year.

(Being a closed kingdom for most of its existence, Nepal was not opened to foreign travelers until 1951, and no roads led to Katmandu from the outside world until 1956. The US Peace Corps arrived in 1962 digging wells and providing vaccinations; and tourism started shortly thereafter along with the opening of the first western restaurant serving milk shakes and sweet pies.)

The Swayambhunath Buddhist Temple —usually called "The Monkey Temple" by visitors - was the place to be when we were there. It was a 60minute walk, or a 15-minute human taxi pull to get there from Freak Street. Freak Street became the renowned street where hippies gathered with locals sharing food, chai, hashish, and travel stories, and more. I (Arlene) recall sitting at an outside café for hours chatting with the locals who were always smiling. We were never in a hurry and connected with people culturally so different from us with comfort, acceptance, and a feeling of unity in our humanity.

Shortly after arriving at the bottom of the steep upward walkway, we had, what was termed by many, an <u>out-of-body experience</u>. Very long processions of Monks were meandering up the steps – sometimes called The Thousand Steps (in reality 350 steps) toward the top. There was a deep guttural calming chant and low tonal horns, not unlike the great jazz artist John Coltrane, and the higher pitched sounds of prayer wheels as their red hats bobbed in sync. Their golden clothing made them seem as one mystical glowing stream of light. And there was incense, too. All senses seemed magnified a hundredfold.

We, and a small group of circuit riders, followed them; stopping to stare at the painted meditating Buddha figures on either side and absorb the totality of the experience. We were gradually gaining a view of the large white dome <u>stupa</u>, or shrine, with a tall golden structure protruding from the middle. By the time we got to the top we were huffing and puffing mightily. Mental anticipation hastened our tiring body onward to the top and the main platform. And what a sight!

Monkeys clamored about everywhere. Dunghill pigeons fluttered around and to the top nearby structures. The unique cubicle tower rising from the <u>stupa</u> spiral had a face-like painting with 2 large eyes, (all-seeing?), eyebrows, and an unusual symbol that looked like a question mark or a nose (but was, in fact, a Nepalese figure symbolizing <u>unity</u>). Additionally, above and between the painted eyebrows was a small round red spot; apparently to emanate the cosmic rays of Buddha's third eye (all-seeing wisdom?). And, because the structure was cubicle in shape, there was a face painted on each side; 4 directions of the compass.

The Monkey Temple Stupa

Tied to the top and to the bottom of the <u>stupa</u> were long lines of small flags in a variety of bright colors; gently flapping in the constant wind. Then there was a slow walk along the line of cylindrical prayer wheels of faded brass; each about 10 inches in height but easily turning to the human touch. We said a silent prayer and purposefully turned those one by one; perhaps 20 wheels in all. There were many smaller shrines and ancient statues, shops selling anything Tibetan or Nepalese, and the panoramic view of Kathmandu Valley offered an ethereal feeling. The soft feel-good music was constant. The people, the place, and the entire experience was total rapture.

Time was still and in the moment. It was as if everything wanted to slowdown stop and last forever; to perceive eternity. We sat on a gray oval rock hearing the prayer wheels turn, looking into each other's eyes feeling the certainty of being guided and cared for by angelic hosts. That was our first imbedded personal faith experience; and so grateful we had it together.

Late that night, back at the hotel, we had long and deeply immersed discussions about God and our personal spiritual growth. I was raised a Christian Methodist, and after rejecting their dogma became an atheist. After reading a few of the world's great books – including the Bible, Koran, and Bhagavad Gita – I became a skeptic and grew into agnosticism.

I, (Arlene) was raised in an Orthodox Jewish household, going to Hebrew schools for 8 years, and had a bat-mitzvah. At 17 years old, I began questioning many of the laws and the image of God as, at times, wrathful which triggered fear and guilt. It didn't make sense that God loved me any less than my parents. It didn't make sense that in order to be considered a good person, I had to observe hundreds of Jewish laws. I too became an agnostic which was part of what drew us together. The transcendent experience at the temple triggered a realization that we were being guided by loving unseen beings. What was the likelihood of **accidentally** *being in Bethlehem for Jesus birthday and in Buddha's birthplace on his birthday?*

But after so many intense travel experiences thus far, especially with the experiences in Kathmandu, we were percolating into a newer and higher spiritual perspective. It was all unplanned and unexplained, beyond words; as William James said. We were in Bethlehem for the traditional Jesus birthday, now in Kathmandu for Buddha's birthday, we felt <u>something</u> grand and inexplicable was happening. And, we knew, we'd better start paying attention. Were the celestial organizers of the universe providing an open opportunity?

Thus, began a slow and gradual spiritual process of listening to our inner voices and evaluating outer experiences, with only the faintest flicker of faith<u>. Consequently, we began recognizing and accepting our spiritual DNA</u> <u>providing the passports to travel on the circuits, in this life and the next.</u>

Feeling rested and rejuvenated in all ways, we began to visualize the next move. Following our inner compass, we agreed to continue eastward, to Southeast Asia, and Thailand, a seemingly obvious destination. There were no overland circuits of transportation to

Bangkok or anywhere in Southeast Asia from Kathmandu, so we knew we had to fly the circuits; expensive, but the only choice.

Exploring options, the cheapest and obvious flight to Bangkok was via the Burmese Airlines, observing Mt. Everest on the way out. And, as an added bonus, for using this airline, we were granted a 7-day entry visa into Burma; a highly restricted country for ordinary tourists; especially longhaired hippies.

So out the front door we went!

Chapter 14

NOT JUST SOUTHEAST ASIA

"It is better to travel well than to arrive."

–Buddha

Landing in Rangoon, Burma (renamed Yangon, Myanmar) in the oppressive heat, we were guided to a hostel and what was believed to be their rendition of a YMCA (Young Men's Christian Association). An overnighter was so cheap as to be practically free. Fortunately, it was for only one night, as we came to understand why it was so cheap! After eating some really good fish and noodle soup, we went to our tiny dimly lighted room to prepare for sleep in the mattressless bunk beds.

But sleep would be difficult that night!

Cockroaches everywhere! **YIKES!!!** These legions of bugs moved over the floor like an agitated living rug. We didn't notice them until after we turned off the lights and turned them on again to go to the restroom. And not just small ones; they were huge and everywhere! We placed our backpacks and clothing as high as possible, and Arlene and I huddled together on the upper bunk; hoping not to feel them crawling while trying to sleep. We may have gotten a few winks that night.

In the morning we dressed and got out of there as quickly as possible.

As we left complaining to the desk clerk, he simply replied with a flat facial expression, in hard-to-understand English: "Vee understaan."

A few blocks away and dominating the skyline, was the gilded Shwedagon Pagoda (also called the Great Dragon Pagoda or the Golden Pagoda); the most sacred Buddhist pagoda in Burma. So, of course, we had to visit! Its beauty was astounding and somewhat overwhelming. A multitude of golden Buddha figures lined all around and a very large gonging bell resonated in periodic synchrony with our bodies. A large written inscription near the center of the main hall proclaimed to have 8 strands of hair from the head of the original Gautama of the Bodhi Tree. After the previous nightmarish night, this was a magnetic uplifting experience, and we felt as if enwrapped in the beauty of deity.

But we had only 6 days left on the visa. So, we decided to take the morning 500-mile train-ride on the north circuit to Mandalay to see the greatest <u>ruby</u> center of the world. The train ride was interestingly intense because at least a half dozen passenger, male and female, made a point to talk with us about their dissatisfaction with the government. They *really* liked Westerners, and Americans in particular and almost all asked if they could come to America and visit us with the intent of becoming U.S. citizens. We said "No" explaining that we were continuing our travels. It was as if it was rehearsed because they each pretty much repeated the same mantra.

<u>(Politically, Burma was then controlled by the military in the form of a one-party system call Burma Socialist Programme Party [BSPP] which placed too rapid an emphasis on industrialization at the expense of agriculture.)</u>

Mandalay, as the cultural center of Burma and second largest city, contained hundreds of Buddhist pagodas, and other structures of beauty; but we went straight to the gigantic warehouses where ruby merchants' stalls were everywhere hawking their goods; rubies of every color, quality, and shape.

It seemed like there were hundreds of vending tables with just about every form and cut of ruby imaginable; among other precious and semiprecious stones; like jade. The most famous ruby in the world was the 48,019 carat <u>Mandalay Ruby</u> because of its size and almost flawless color. Color usually determines the value of a ruby; called by gemologist <u>pigeon's blood</u>; too dark or too light subtracts from the value. And a ruby without flaws is not authentic, always artificially made by a manufacturer.

Most were way out of our price range, but we bought a few imperfect dark red ones, and left. We took everyone's recommendation and headed to the close <u>Hill Station</u> out of Mandalay. Hill Stations were an interesting phenomenon in Burma. Originally, they were built by the British Empire toward the end of the 18th Century to escape the "prickly heat" and with the thinking that the cool altitude made for better soldiers; additionally, there were many Hill Stations in northern Burma playing a part in World War II. The Burmese maintained them, and they were used by the affluent and tourists.

It was a pleasant 3-hour motorized taxi ride to the Maymyo Hill Station; with the taxi driver repeating hate-of-the-government mantra. The air was thin and had a slight chill as we entered the lodging. A small fire lit the main hall showing shadows on the high ceiling. Our room was clean, warm, and enticing; and, they had a hot bath – our first in many a month. Meals were served expertly, and with a server unobtrusively nearby; ready to open another beer or pour more tea.

We were beginning to feel human again. It couldn't have been better; except for zero circuit riders to visit with! But our 7-day visa was running out. Reluctantly, we formulated the exit plan and headed back to Rangoon for the connecting flight to Bangkok, Thailand.

The first thing I remember about Bangkok was buying a Thai ice-coffee from a street vendor. WOW!!! It was so good and refreshing! It was composed of strong coffee, concentrated milk, ice, and some other unrecognizable spice, or spices. I had a second one. And, for a fleeting moment, it felt as if we were back in the States.

Since I get jittery drinking coffee, I chose the luscious papaya and mango with milk drink, also sold by a street vendor.

Memory is a funny thing. Remembering to remember?

We found a cheap and somewhat rundown hotel, went out for some great Thai food (a noodle bowl with egg), and iced tea. After a good night's sleep, we sat briefly in the lobby and realized we were probably in a hotel of prostitution. We weren't a hundred percent certain, but there were way too many attractive Thai women wondering through the lobby and up the stairs dressed in clothes unlikely seen in public.

I can still remember opening our hotel room door and looking at a beautiful Thai woman dressed in nightclothes meandering through the hall. Our eyes greeted each other with a knowing smile.

Okay, we said to ourselves, let's see some of Thailand. Ching Mai was an easy choice.

The overnight 435-mile train ride north to Ching Mai was the best and clean train ride we'd had in a very long time; actually, having a space to lay in the supine position and sleep a little. Thank you, State Railway of Thailand.

Called the "New City" of Thailand, Ching Mai is an ancient city in the mountainous north on the west bank of the Ping River, and has over 300 Buddhist temples or *wats* in Thai. Also, there are 20 Christian Churches and 16 mosques about, as well as Sikh and Hindu communities. It was considered the "Northern Capital".

At a restaurant near the hotel, we ate some tantalizingly good curry noodles with fish, drank tea and a Thai coffee; and planned to visit some wats. But the friendly owner encouraged us to first visit the great Fabric District down by the river. We took a *tuk tuk* ride and the driver knew exactly where to drop us off. It was, perhaps, the most dazzling array of cloths, materials, and fabrics we'd ever seen in one place; and the shops and streets went on and on. So much beauty to absorb in a friendly atmosphere! The colors and combination of colors and the enchanting display of prints on some of the materials were so unusual and creative. (Is that being redundant?)

We didn't buy anything, but the memory persisted.

We were again ready to go onto the circuits. We set Bali, Indonesia as our next goal. But how do we get there from the hills of northern Thailand? Decisions had to be made! Decisions, decisions, and more decisions was the name of the game. How to do that? Can free will be really free? With so many intertwining factors, certainly we cannot freely choose for the sun to not come up tomorrow! A one-time thing? Does it determine our immediate destiny, and/or mortal destiny, eternal destiny? Of one thing we were learning, freedom and responsibility are inextricably linked. We were just trying to get to Singapore, then on to Bali. A right/wrong decision? Who knows if there is a connection between free will and the travel circuits? But we had a long circuit to ride; and we were arrogant dreamers. We could do anything!

Chapter 15

WHACKED OUT IN PENANG, AND THE PSYCHOTIC MONKEY

"Beating heroin is child's play compared to beating your childhood."

–Stephen King, The Waste Lands

Despite being repeatedly told about the dangers of hitchhiking, we decided to hitchhike from Ching Mai down to Bangkok, even though Arlene was under the weather with a cold. It seemed easy at first, with a series of small trucks taking us a few miles at a time, and soon we were literally, out in the middle of nowhere. The last truck dropped us off in the forested countryside, far from any businesses or populated areas; and few vehicles passed by.

The danger the local Thais warned about was caused by the uproar of the farming peasants in the area against the government because of the low price of rice; and the guerrilla rebels groups supporting it. In the mist of all this, I had a serious need to pee. The only realistic place to exercise this natural and immediate function was to cross the road to a weeded field. I went over and as I started to pee, I began to sink into the muddy marsh. I started crying and screamed for Buck to "help, help, help"!

Dashing across the dirt road and into the field, there was Arlene stuck and slowly sinking into the soft, muddy ground, already up to the top of her thighs. Crying and afraid, she was unable to get her body unstuck. It was a long hard pulling struggle for us working together, but she was eventually loosened from the suction of the soft soil. We made our way back to the original side of the road, huddling together.

AND it was my 28th birthday; June 7, 1971! I was having a giant pity party!

For a while we seemed lost, disoriented, and emotionally exhausted. Rudderless, with no place to call home and nobody to call friends, we wondered what would become of us, but tried to stay cheerful with the jittery Happy Birthday song.

At that exact moment, a shiny red American convertible car approached, and we quickly stuck out our arms and thumbs pointing in the southwardly direction. The driver, a young Thai male in his early twenties, spoke near perfect English, and after a short conversation invited us into his car and said he would take us to Bangkok. We warned him of our muddy clothing and shoes, but he strongly admonished us to jump into the sparkling red and white 1969 Chevy Corvette; backpacks, doctors' bag, and all!

We couldn't believe the luck! (Or was it divine providence, by this time?)

He said to call him "Charles" but admitted it wasn't his real Thai name.

Receiving a college degree in England, Charles was obviously not a usual Thai-guy for his age and was of the upper-upper class distinction. Well-dressed in silky-shiny clothes and black lacquered shoes set him apart. Coming from Ching Mai on business, he drove fast and with authority, but not recklessly. He liked Americans and wanted to be an international businessman. Somewhat naively, his dream was to someday create a simple product, perhaps a toy, and sell a million of them for $1.00 each; and hence become a millionaire.

Once in Bangkok, he bought us dinner at a classy restaurant and allowed us to stay at his apartment, which was consistently high style as with his food and automobile preferences. Our room was painted with bright colors with a large bed, beautiful Thai figurines of marble and brass, and a large modern English flag draped across the wall at the head of the bed. He obviously had maid service because everything appeared very clean and well-placed, for a single guy. He was keen to hear about all our travels, and said he hoped someday to do the same. We had a mutual affinity.

He shared a very self-revealing and intimate part of himself, which centered on "Why?" Why was it not possible for him to be like us? Be able to just buy a backpack and roam the world and be a circuit rider? Teary-eyed, he spoke of the many cultural, family, and personal restrictions; mostly fear based. His family was fairly wealthy, but he was not, and would have to wait for his inheritance. By then it would be too late because he would have his own family and be "locked in" to an all-encompassing cultural system he disliked, including marriage.

Thanking us repeatedly for sharing our admirable spark of circuit riding, he said he would always remember us.

The next day he drove us to the main Bangkok bus station, guided us (thankfully) through the process of purchasing tickets to Sadao, at the Southern border adjacent to Malaysia. Without Charles, it would have been a bit of a translation struggle for buying the correct ticket. Reluctantly, we watched him drive away from the bus station returning to his place in the city.

But we were on our way again.

It was not particularly difficult processing through customs and immigration leaving Thailand or getting into Malaysia. We easily sensed a changed attitude from the Thais to Malays going through the Bukit Kayu Hitam checkpoint. Whereas the Thais were open and accepting of "our kind", the Malays, while not hostile, gave off a suspicious vibe and were less friendly. Most of the population practiced the Islam religion.

Over the past few weeks, in our interaction with other circuit riders, we'd heard of the beautiful sandy beaches and accepting atmosphere on the Malaysian island of Penang; and soon we were busing the 90 miles through the thick wooded forest areas to get there.

And our brethren circuit riders were right! We quickly found a very cheap communal-like hotel that served food and was within walking distance from the beach, where we spent the first full day.

Late in the afternoon of the second day, and after returning from the beach, I was going through the medicine bag and found a piece of leftover Afghani <u>hash</u> about the size of a small candy bar. Thinking it was old and no longer potent, we first agreed to throw it away; and avoid any legal hassles. But after further consideration, we thought it best to try it first.

WRONG MOVE!!!

We each took a bite size chunk, chewed it and swallowed. We sat around the beds for a while discussing our move to Singapore, digesting the hash. It wasn't long before we looked at each other and realized we were so high we had to lie down in our separate beds.

And WOW!!! Eating the hash apparently increased severalfold the quantity of psychoactive THC (tetrahydrocannabinol) getting to our brains; and we were off – floating in our heads, into the universe, completely bodyless. Being so high was, at first, a little scary, but we relaxed and just went with it. We laughed, expressed amazement, felt connected to the unified whole, connected to the One, and experienced inherent love for each other and everyone in the world. We thought we would never come down.

A little scary? I fought off several panic attacks! I don't remember having the transcendent experience Buck describes. I did have moments of being in the moment and feeling a sense of awe and peace and for sure a deep loving connection with Buck.

Maybe the highest hash/marijuana trip we'd ever been on.

There was no time or space for the two of us, but a lot of colored visions. There was just a bigger larger picture before us, and the view was beyond glorious, no downers. We were intertwined as a single thread; even from across the beds where we laid there motionless. And for just a fleeting glimpse of a second in eternity we felt as if we had slide over those scourging limitations, yet fully accepting inherent capacities could not be exceeded (a pint could never hold a quart). The family and cultural childhood unconscious teachings imposed; some good, some bad.

But…thrilled we were in the moment, and we had no doubt that we were part of the cosmos reaching our potentials while knowing it would never end. Our love was <u>one</u> of that we were certain! And as that long timeless moment of resonance struck, our love was forever; knowing each other in body, mind, and soul. Our love thus grew.

The next day we were on our way to Kuala Lumpur; feeling a bit groggy and not very grounded, to say the least. From Kuala Lumpur, the train ride to the border entering Singapore was uneventful but pleasant. And getting into Singapore with an American passport was easy and obtaining a visa seemed automatic; albeit for 14 days only. We quickly learned all things – hotel, food, and transportation – were financially on the high end, quickly influencing the decision to spend a minimum time there. Also, we could feel and sense, it was a very <u>clean</u> city with stated written warnings about spitting on the pavement and sticking chewing gum anywhere, etc. were *forboden*! It seemed like the whole island was one big business district.

During our first full day in Singapore, we went straight to the harbor master building inquiring about cheap transportation to Indonesia. Fortunately, it was just near the Immigration & Checkpoints Authority; so, they told us where to go for the best information. As happenstance would have it, there were a bunch (probably 5 in all) of circuit riders at the same office seeking the same information; and (yeah!) heading to Bali.

An Indonesian shipping company carrying trade goods to Sumatra was willing to take all of us to the port of Palenbang; for $25 each. From there, we were told we could take a train to the southern tip of Sumatra, take a short ferry across to Java, go through Jakarta to the eastern end by train; after that there was a boat ride or plane to Bali. It sounded so easy, so we jumped at the $25 cost of the overnight freighter ride, which included sleeping quarters and a little food.

While not a rip-off, the sleeping quarters were exactly like the crews' and the food was of steamed rice, and maybe a few pieces of fish, although there was a whiff of peanut sauce in the taste. But the most memorable experience of the trip was all about the <u>monkey</u>! Monkey business?

The freighter was about 200 feet in length, very old, and greasy black in color; the Indonesian name, we couldn't understand nor tried to remember. The crew was very friendly, however, and wanted to spend as much time with us as possible; wanting to learn about the Western ways.

One of them, a small boisterous person with a dirty red handkerchief around his neck, had a monkey he seemed to be showing-off to us because he had the monkey with him each time we came on deck to get some fresh air. Disturbing to all of us was how he treated his monkey. The animal had a leather dog-like collar with a long chain leash connected to it and held by this owner. He often would slap the monkey on the head, pulling the chain to get the monkey's attention, or just generally mishandle the helpless little animal. It was as if this human was somehow exhibiting some type of superiority or mental/ego strength over the primate.

(We learned later it was a <u>long-tailed macaque</u> type of monkey (pronounced "muh-**kak**"), native to central Java; usually hunted and eaten by the local farmers because they tended to over-populate and feast on the farmers' crops.)

Finally, a circuit rider, a tall and thin frustrated Canadian guy, offered to buy the monkey as a humane gesture; with the hope of transporting the poor depleted-looking animal to the safety of the monkey sanctuary heard about in Bali.

As our freighter slowly crept up the Musi River toward the Palenbang seaport destination in Sumatra, the Canadian (Jacob) paid the monkey's owner $20 for the animal. As we all walk down the gangplank, we turned and heard shouts of despair. Looking around we saw the monkey biting anyone within contact. Buck and I walked back to see if we could help. Buck began talking to the monkey and the animal began to calm down. We then offered to take the monkey off the Canadian's hands which he readily agreed to.

Shortly thereafter, and as a group, we happily bought tickets and boarded the narrow-gauge train for the ride to Bandar Lampung, macaque monkey in tow.

The train coach was old, rickety, and very small; turn-of-the-century style. All 7 of us were in the same coach, the caboose, which gave us a wonderful view of the mountainous jungle as we passed through southern Sumatra. But with all the beauty and excitement of our shared travelling, a serious problem quickly erupted.

The monkey, whom we agreed to call Monkey-boy, had been sitting on Buck's lap tuned around and bit me and other passengers on the train!

Enough is enough!!! As the train slowed down adjacent to a lush forest Buck gently dropped Monkey boy off the back end of the coach hoping he would go into the forest and find his own.

To our unbelievable surprise, and with great irony, Monkey-boy was seen running in the middle of the tracks trying to catch up to the slow-moving train; and, we assumed, for a bit of safety from the potentially hostile jungle environment. The sight of the poor little animal gave rise to a slight and collective natural compassion amongst us. A few minutes later, we saw Monkey boy running up the aisle and, finding Buck, he stopped and promptly jumped into his lap.

Monkey-boy was now mine; err, <u>ours</u>. And, inexplicably, the monkey never bit me, and seemed to be comfortably attached to me; to everyone's amazement, my own included. Maybe it was the animal in me, but I never showed him fear. We had a strange connection. Arlene and I agreed to take the reins and accepted the mission of getting Monkey-boy to the Bali sanctuary; even though he had already bitten Arlene once.

Soon we arrived in Bandar Lampung, took a short bus ride (2 hours?) to Bakauheni, and waited on the next ferry boat to Mara on the main island of Java. The ferry rides were arriving and departing hourly.

Crossing the Sunda Strait on the way to Java, everyone's attention was called to a small island off to our right. It was the infamous volcanic Krakatoa! Krakatoa considered one of the most, if not <u>the</u> most violent eruption in recorded history, sank more than half the island into the sea. Rock and smoke went as high as 260,000 feet, several times stronger than any nuclear bomb, heard as far away as Alice Springs, Australia, and some say it clouded the sky in London for several days. The consequent tsunami killed an estimate of 100,000 people: depending on the various research records.

<u>(An interesting tidbit of useless trivia about filmmaking: the little known 1968 Hollywood film titled "Krakatoa, East of Java" received generally good reviews – mostly for the on-location cinematography in the Sunda Strait and the area – but made a huge propaganda blunder. Krakatoa is, in reality, **west** of Java; not east.)</u>

After the pleasant and smooth ferry crossing of the Sunda Strait, and arriving at the tiny port of Merat, the group of circuit riders gradually separated: some getting the short train ride to Jakarta, some moving on straight to Bali, and at least one person just hanging around

Merat. We chose taking the train to Jakarta. Monkey-boy had been fairly compliant during the ferry ride but was constantly hungry for bananas and peanuts; and would drink water whenever he could. Emptying his bowels also presented many situational problems!

We took the short train ride to Jakarta, keeping Monkey-boy close; found a cheap hotel in a poorer section of town, and settled in for a hoped-for quiet rest.

But rest would not come!

Our newly adopted son – Monkey-boy – was in perpetual motion moving about on his metal chain in our small nondescript hotel room. I tried sitting him on my lap for a while, which had been our custom on the train, but to no avail. Becoming frustrated with not being able to rest, we decided to abandon Monkey-boy in the room and go out for a much-needed dinner meal. Leaving him chained to a metal pole for safety and security, we needed to get away.

We found a clean-looking restaurant and had a relaxing time; feeling righteous knowing Monkey-boy would soon be in Bali. The meal was called satay and consisted of skewered meat (who knew what kind?), a large portion of diced potatoes, and with an especially good-tasting peanut sauce; and a small side-dish of hot-sauce; then topped off with fried bananas and coconut cakes for dessert. Cheap, too! Then we had a slow romantic walk back to the hotel; as traditional Indonesian music of drums, gongs, and flutes filled our heads from nearby public loudspeakers in the night sky.

We were feeling a light near-levitation walk toward the hotel.

Entering the hotel, and as we open the locked door, the romantic high feeling came crashing down to earth by the unanticipated destructive condition of the room. We were shocked! Monkey-boy had completely destroyed most of the contents of the room. He had pulled the pole down with his chain, freed himself from any constraints, and then used the room as his personal energetic playpen. The mosquito net over the bed was in shreds, the curtains were torn and on the floor, the nightstand was turned over, our backpacks were pulled off the hangers, there was feces on the floor, and a smell of urine pervaded.

We had a psychotic monkey!!!

Still determined to get to the monkey sanctuary in Bali, Monkey Boy continued to live with us. However, he would get extremely agitated if Buck was out of his sight, even accompanying him to take showers. Trying really hard to stay calm, I Arlene, held him on my lap thinking I can overcome my fears. After about 5 minutes of him sitting calmly, he abruptly turned to me and bit my arm. THAT WAS THE LAST STRAW. I told Buck, it's me or Monkey Boy!

Completely upset and on edge, I grabbed the chain and held it near his leather collar and rushed out of our room, breathing unevenly and hard. And, not sure what I was doing pushed through the main hotel entrance onto the pavement and held Monkey-boy on the chain with an outstretched arm; as some passerby citizens looked on in amazement. I bent my arm at the elbow several times nonverbally offering the chained monkey to any willing person passing by. Without hesitation, a passing young man in a <u>songkok</u> hat and a strong mustache accepted the somewhat sacrificial offer. With a smile, he continued walking away. We never again saw Monkey-boy. And with it ended the dream of returning <u>him</u> to the Bali sanctuary.

Chapter 16

BALI HIGH...AND LOWS

"In Bali life is a rhythmic, patterned unreality of pleasant,
significant movement, centered on one's own body to which
all emotions long ago withdrew."

–Margaret Mead, Balinese Character, 1942

We wanted to get away from the madness of the very large, loud, smoggy, overpopulated Jakarta, so we bought the cheapest tickets possible on Garuda Airlines ($25.00 each) to Denpasar, the capital of Bali. Once there, and from the airport, we bused it to Kuta Beach. We were there in what seemed like a flash, along with a handful of other circuit riders from different parts of the world.

We were led to Tegal Wangi, the main dirt street through Kuta, and all of us routinely secured one of the many well-weathered, white-washed cottages. The street was unevenly lined with these small quaint cottages – though not all so white or so quaint – and each had at least one, two or more circuit rider. There was not a tourist in sight!

We rested, then visited with many travelers up and down the roadway, having a toke or two, sharing storied experiences from travels all over the world. But we all agreed: Bali was one of the most unique and enthralling places we'd ever been. One of the more unique aspects of Bali was that it is predominantly an island of the Hindu faith and culture (83%) with some Islam and Buddhism, whereas the rest of the Republic of Indonesia consists of more than 17,000 islands of the Islam faith. Perhaps this may have stimulated such a great Balinese culture of art, dance, sculpture, painting, and music so prevalent there.

The Dutch ruled Bali since the 1840's (then called Netherlands

East Indies), and was occupied by the Japanese during WWII, and the whole nation achieved independence in 1949; led by Sukarno, and later by Suharto.

Great historians, scientist, authors, artists, and explorers have told of Bali since before the turn of the 20th Century and in their own discipline presented this mystic island into the world conscience until it has become a household name. Being none of the above, the telling of our experiences in Bali may appear somewhat kindergartenish, except to those who may have chanced to have been there, but these are our personal and collective impressions of thinking, feeling, which only traveling can bring to the fore.

We were visiting with a beautiful-looking Australian couple just a few cottages down, exchanging travel stories and philosophical thoughts, when we heard a commotion outside getting closer. There was music of an exotic nature. It appeared as if a small parade of Balinese, men, and women, dressed in ancient clothing; some with golden headgear, black eye makeup, and a variety of wooden masks. Close behind was a wave of musicians playing a large number of percussion instruments. There was even an ensemble of men covered in a long robe connected to a fierce looking and wildly painted dragon head. We were told it was an ancient ceremony heading toward a nearby temple. Some said the date for the ceremony was written on a calendar a thousand years ago.

The music, of course, was <u>gamelan</u> played with well-synchronized instruments of metallophones played with wooden mallets, small drums, xylophone-type instruments, bamboo flutes, and bowed instruments. Faintly, we could hear a female voice in the background. But the <u>sound</u> was totally immersive and inspirational at the same time; unlike anything we'd ever heard. Then there were young Balinese girls dressed in colorful traditional costumes, but barefooted, moving in such a smooth and erotic dance it almost reminded us of tai chi; except the speed would change from slow to fast without warning, then back again to slow, as they danced around the temple courtyard in total confidence. Without a script or any written materials, it was extemporaneous and yet so holistically synchronized.

114 |

Men began bouncing around, maybe 6 of them, as if in a trance-like state. Out came 2 covered figures: one representing a witch, one representing a dragon. Apparently, the witch represented death and the dragon representing life, and of course the whole show came to a climax with the dragon symbolically killing the witch invigorating the will-to-live. In the complexity of movements near the end some of us thought one of the tranced men may have pulled the head off a live chicken. We saw another ceremonial festival where, instead of a dragon the central figure was a lion; but the witch always dies. So, generally speaking, the Balinese represent a culture unafraid of death, despite the multiple external influences and environment experiences.

WOW!!!

Memory is a funny thing. A sound, a smell can trigger the rush.

A few days later a few of us took a taxi up to Lake Batur: a 50-mile drive, or so. It was a most beautiful integration of the beautiful landscape of Bali compared to the villages. On the way, the driver stopped to allow us to view the terraced paddy fields of rice and the especially impressive irrigation system developed by the local growers. It had been rumored that the US Peace Core went there to help improve the system but failed miserably. It seemed so perfect; with the layers of growing rice with the levels of water flow; all bending with natural curvature of the earth's high hills from the top to the bottom. And so very green; so fulfilling!

(We discovered later this system was developed in 9th century and was used as an ecologically sustainable irrigation system holding their agrarian society together. Under the authority of the priests at the nearby temples, they promoted the relationship between humans, the earth, and the gods. Rice was seen as a gift from the gods. This ecological system eventually became a UNESCO World Heritage Site.)

As we drove higher up the mountain road, we all became aware of the altitude and the cooler air. The taxi stopped and the driver said: "Here" in near-perfect English. It was at a small restaurant overlooking Lake Batur. Looking horizontally across to Mt. Batur, we were fascinated by its active volcano, 5,600 feet high. We had just gone from sea-level to a mile high.

It was a memorable time, and we shall always remember sitting at a small wooden table with 2 engaging circuit riders, eating delicious fresh fried fish netted from the lake 2,000 feet below, and having a slight giggle each time the Batur volcano would release a small puff of grayish smoke straight into the air; clocked every 20 minutes; actually, not quite _that_ precise. We believed the tiny explosions were synchronized enhancing our sense of togetherness, empowering the total experience.

Lake Batur

Sipping on the famous Balinese honey-ginger tea, watching slow moving puffs of clouds drifting toward us high above from the east, then passing over our heads, we could see small boats and smaller people on the lake below. The air was cool and fresh. Moments like these make all the hazards and hardships of travel worthwhile. In time the worries and hardships will be forgotten, but the sweetness and goodness of togetherness and awe-inspiring beauty remains, a forever value. Such a life!

The next day, toward the evening, we started watching a shadow puppet show, perhaps Bali's most enigmatic form of entertainment. And a small gamelan orchestra played in the background to add to the spellbinding atmosphere. The smell of hashish smoke drifted from the surrounding audience.

Created hundreds of years ago, they tell stories of heroes like Arjuna and Shiva from the Hindu tradition with observers on both sides of the theater screen. The "screen" is a large piece of thin cotton with lighting behind. The puppets are intricately carved out of pieces of stiffened water buffalo hide tied to a long thin piece of bamboo; usually several pieces of bamboo to facilitate moving arms or legs. The puppets are then brightly painted to reflect the image of their character as one person recites their story while interacting with a host of other characters telling an intricate story of gods, love lost or regained, and destiny: all with music, voice, shadows, with the ultimate conclusion of good over evil.

The shadow puppet stories are an integral part of the Balinese spiritual life. Unfortunately, for us, these ceremonies often last through the night. When our eyelids struggled to remain up, we retreated to our cabin for some easy sleep. Drifting off to sleep, I flashed on Plato's Allegory of the Cave; wandering…what was real? The prisoners in Plato's cave thought the shadows on the wall of the cave were real; for that was all they had ever known. But one prisoner breaks free and sees the sun but perceives it as unreal. Is this life just a shadow of a higher reality unable to be perceived?

Waking refreshed, we decided to go to the beach for some sun and surf. It was a short hike to Nusa Dua Beach, and, in a moment of wild fantasy, I wanted to try my body-surfing skills while Arlene sunbathed near a palm tree; having had some surfboard experience years ago in Southern California. Swimming out past the breakers, I had no idea what I was getting myself into and soon realized I was way over my skill-level. The waves were huge and breaking left! Guessing maybe 20 feet, or more (the older I get, the bigger I envision the size of the waves). Realizing my serious mistake, I wanted to get back to the safety shore, and Arlene, ASAP. Hoping to catch the next wave in, I swam onto the crest; and it was a nightmare from then on.

It was a total wipeout after wipeout! Not able to sustain the crest, I immediately was swept under the powerful thrust of the wave and my body was violently tossed and turned, tossed and turned inside the crashing curl, like a rag doll! Just when I thought I could no longer hold my breath my head popped to the surface; but I could see I was still a long way from shore as I tried to stroke toward the trees. But the strong undertow forced me out, away from the short, returning for the next wave. Within uncountable moments, the next wave came crushing down on me with the same result; being twisted and flipped about like a feather in a fierce wind.

This same wave-crashing happened 3 or 4 more times before I was able to swim free of the numbing violence, breathing in quick full breaths. Fortunately, I was in reasonably good swimmer. Returning to Arlene lying on a sarong, still sunning herself, I felt too embarrassed to tell what had happened; plus, I didn't want to disturb that sweet look of serenity in and through her eyes.

Actually, when Buck was fighting the gigantic surf some of the locals came up to me (Arlene) anxiously sharing that the Balinese do not swim in the ocean because it was so treacherous. The Balinese people were wisely afraid of the surf. I may have looked serene but was far from it until Buck was out of the water.

On our way to the Nusa Dua beach, we passed a hand-painted sign with an arrow reading: "Bali Marina". On a lark we strolled around the marina before trekking back to Kuta.

It turned out to be a life-changing decision.

Being Westerners, it was easy entering the marine clubhouse. Our slight hope was, perhaps, of getting a sailboat trip across the Pacific to Hawaii or even California; hence completing a circumnavigation of the world.

Life, however, was full of serendipitously surprised beginnings!

Walking around the inside of the club we noticed a sketched note on a raggedy note-board: "Crew needed for sailing, Binasu II". Still in a whimsical mood, we boldly walked out to the mooring slips until we found Binasu II with the stern tied on the floating walkway, among a dozen or so moored sailboats of various sizes and styles. Then we yelled to see if anyone was aboard. Our ardent hopes remained to catch that sailboat trip across the Pacific and back to the States; a mere 13,000 miles.

The cabin hatch slide back and out popped a redheaded woman followed by a tall slightly hefty man, speaking English. We introduced ourselves, they on the boat and us standing on the wooden slip. We shared that we had read the notice for needing crew members for sailing; and wanted to know where they were headed. "_We're sailing to the Seychelle Islands, leaving in 3 days, and need 2 more crew._"

We couldn't believe what we were hearing! **_The Seychelles_**???

(Up to this point we'd been thinking about how to cross the Pacific Ocean and returning to California.)

After giving a quick salubrious answer, the man, obviously the captain and owner asked some very pointed questions relating to any sail experience. Arlene had only a tiny bit of sail experience since we owned a sailboat while living in Venice Beach, next to the Marina Del Rey in California; a 30-foot gaff rigged boat; sailing occasionally to Catalina Island and beyond. On the other hand, I shared my extensive experience; boatbuilding and sailing in the China Sea off Okinawa, and the 2 transatlantic crossing; the North Atlantic and the South Atlantic. Raising his eyebrows, the captain tried hard not to show his elation and asked a few nautical questions to ascertain my earnest knowledge and honesty.

We had up-to-date passports and pretended we had plenty of money; again, thanks to the Indian scam.

He said OKAY, yes, he would take us on as crew but without pay. Also, he wanted us to take 24 hours to first think about it. It will be a long journey, he added.

Back in our cottage at Kuta Beach, we looked at each other and agreed it was a supreme and impactful decision to make; Arlene did not know how to swim, and I had long ago given up dreams of small boat sailing. At this stage in personal development, we knew it was important to go into private and separate meditation/contemplation sessions to seek an answer; at opposite ends of the cottage.

Which we did, all the while asking ourselves: "Am I meant to be doing this trip NOW?"

We spent hours of sincerely, honestly, openly seeking an answer. And we each received our answer. I, become physically ill with fever and flu symptoms while my anxiety increased about the possibility of dying on such a voyage. Since I was four years old when my grandfather died, I would have panic attacks with the mere thought of death. And I couldn't swim! All of a sudden, I heard a clear calming, reassuring voice say: "**IF YOU'RE AFRAID, DO IT!**" At that moment my *fever broke, and I jumped out of bed with the certainty of the decision of sailing to the Seychelles.*

My answer was: "**_A MAN MUST DO EVERYTHING!_**" Strange, but I heard this voice inside my head (or outside?) so clearly, authoritatively, and succinctly at the height of my meditation. It startled me at first; and tried to be sure that no persons were nearby because it seemed like a male voice. What did it mean – do everything? Was it my subconscious talking to my aware consciousness, or my superconscious talking to my lower consciousness? It was the first (and only) time in my life I ever heard an inner voice speak. The emphasis, though, was firmly on **_doing_** – something - and obviously the meditation was about just that.

The meditative thought was not a negative; *not* doing something; but about what to do. So…I had my answer! If a man must do everything, then I must take this sailboat journey to the Seychelles as an inclusion of my doing everything. After all, it was a long-cherished dream to travel to the Seychelles, anyway.

(**_Always_** will I remember the experience of hearing that voice, and it remains clear as ever to this day! Now, whenever confronted about whether to experience something, invariably I choose to *do* it. For me, doing something it better than doing nothing; mistakes are inevitable.)

We conferred, and after sharing our meditative directions, headed straight to the Marina and the Binasu II to tell the captain and his wife – Don and Carolyn - of our unequivocal decision to join the crew on the sail to the Seychelles if they would have us. They smiled and simultaneously said "Good" and told us two other American crew members – a guy and a girl – had already agreed to go. They were waiting in anticipation of 2 more in order to have a full crew of 6, 3 women and 3 men. We were asked to bring our personal belongings on board as soon as convenient.

One last night at Kuta Beach sharing with strongly admiring friends and travel comrades was a wonderful sendoff; buying two batik sarongs as we departed.

Passports, money, and destination, and out the door we went.

Chapter 17

AN ISOLATED PLANET OF OUR OWN MAKING

"Twenty years from now, you will be more disappointed by the things you didn't do than those you did. So throw off the bowlines. Sail away from safe harbor. Catch the wind in your sails. Explore. Dream. Discover."

–Mark Twain

Once on the Binasu II we were introduced to the 2 other members of the crew – Sarah, 23 and Paul 31 years old, both circuit riders. Sarah had a slight body build, with short blonde hair (unusual for that era), and with a quick reserved smile. Paul had a rugged lean body type, with long, nearly bald, stringy blonde hair, with a square jaw and an easy-going quick smile. They were *not* an intimate couple, having only recently met on Bali as backpackers.

Captain Don encouraged us to bring our backpacks and personal belongings onboard and showed us our berth (sleeping quarters of 2 each); ours to the starboard aft, and Sarah and Paul to the port aft. Each had a small cabinet for storage. Carolyn took the women aside and talked about cooking, cleaning, and general maintenance of the cabin; especially the "head", or toilet.

The cabin was beautifully and newly finished with Filipino cherry wood, a propane stove, 2 tables and a couch. Don took Paul & I on deck and instructed us on the workings of the steering, location of the cleats, the jib and main sheets, and the storage of the sails in the forward hatch. Don asked pertinent questions about our knot tying skills – square, double half-hitch, and bowline – and especially if Paul

.. knew how to use a navigation sextant.

Paul was a little awkward with knot tying skills, and neither of us could use a sextant. In all my sailing experience, and much to my chagrin, I had learned the sextant for triangulating positions at sea only minimally; certainly not enough to help. Don, on the other hand, was a retired airline pilot, and well-trained and skilled with the navigating and the sextant. I was a good knot tyer and could back splice rope ends.

Don and Carolyn brought us all together below deck at the opened table for a brief outline of our trip: the guys would be holding watches at the helm (3 on and 6 off) and each responsible for presenting themselves for their watch. Tomorrow would be used to complete taking on and stowing supplies, engine fuel, water, fresh fruits and vegetables, and dried food like rice, beans, flour, and pasta, etc. We would leave on the first wind in 2 days.

Leaving Bali on Binasu II with Sara

It was mid-July 1971, around noon, when the captain told Paul and I to raise the jib, and without fanfare, or use of the motor, we eased the Binasu II out of the mooring, past the breakwater, and into the open sea. Then the mainsail went up; tightly. We were all on deck to capture the excitement of the departure into the Indian Ocean; easily overcoming any lingering anxiety. We constantly looked back at the dwindling island landmasses and looked forward to the horizon and the perpetual movement of the water. In a 40-foot sailboat, 6 of us were about to sail approximately 4,000 miles; calculated in a straight-line distance.

Sailboats, because the necessary tacking to get from point A to point B, could sail twice the distance of a straight line. But we didn't care how far away or how long it took us, we were on our way; with a sublime confidence of arriving there. For those glorious few moments, without thoughts of what adventures or dangers might lay ahead, we were caught up in that moment that seemed to last forever. We were headed westward on the circuits of the equator.

As a 40' yawl, the Binasu II was a beautifully built sailboat; all white, with a thin blue streak near the waterline; new and built for comfort. It was a little unclear about the origins, but we understood Don and Carolyn had it built in Hong Kong and towed to Singapore to be outfitted with Dacron sails, then sailed it to Bali; whereupon it became obvious for the need of additional crew for the long trip to the Seychelles.

Although somewhat unclear, the owners explained the name "Binasu" meant, something like, "beauty" or "Venus" in Japanese, giving less understanding of the "II" in the name.

It had a beautiful teak deck, a wide beam, and a 5'8" draft with a ballast (iron) keel of 7,700 lbs., which later proved to be critical. The cockpit was spacious with padded seats in "U" shape around the wheel-helm and leading down into the cabin. And, being a yawl rig, the mizzen mast (shorter, and toward the aft, past the location of the rudder) was behind the cockpit and easy to manipulate. However, its newness became the weakness.

Amazingly, nobody became seasick! Sarah complained a little, Paul toughed it out, and Arlene was stable after the first 24 hours. The sailing was easy the first week; each getting accustomed to their job without noticeable personal tension. The 3-hour shifts on the helm took some adjusting, and during the late nights and early mornings each man was solo; without companionship; the ladies slept through the night. Most of the sailing was with the main sail on a "beam reach"; off to the starboard side about 10 or 15 degrees, the jib the same on the port side and the mizzen for stabilization; and we sailed into the sunset each evening. We had a few rain showers one evening, but of no severity or concern; and only 4 to 6-foot waves.

Then things amongst us got a little strange!

Paul lit a joint one evening while on watch. Captain Don, smelling it, came rumbling on deck and said: "That stuff is illegal, and I don't like it, and don't want you smoking that stuff while on this boat and especially when at the helm!" He stormed off down into his cabin. It all seemed rational except...by this time we knew both Don and Carolyn were drunk by 5:00 P.M. dinner time every night. The 4 of us later hysterically exaggerated: **they had more vodka on board than drinking water.** The situation was pregnant with hypocrisy.

After the next 2 weeks of sailing, with only essential conversation between the owners and the crew, we spotted land. It was on August 8, 1971, that we pulled into Flying Fish Cove on Christmas Island, and Australian territory. Our main purpose was to restore perishable food, especially fresh vegetables and fruit. But it was refreshing to get off the Binasu II and interact with others; mostly Australian merchants of Chinese-Malaysian descent speaking English. Also, it was early in the season, but we saw thousands of red crabs crawling all over the place.

We also met a few other yachtsmen going west across the Indian Ocean. The most interesting was a young Australian. He was sailing a "double-ender" sailboat; where the stern was shaped "pointed" like the front, or stem; similar to a canoe.

What was especially interesting about the captain/owner "Charlie" of the double-ender was the fact of his solo sailing; alone, without crew. He apparently set-up an elaborate auto-pilot system for steering using the tiller and a mixed configuration of ropes. This allowed him to sleep and eat without the necessity of being constantly holding the helm. He was young, muscular, had a very positive can-do attitude, and was just "heading west" to where he was uncertain and didn't seem to care; maybe South Africa; maybe around the world.

He was one of us – a circuit rider in a sailboat.

About a week after waving goodbye to the Christmas Islanders we hit our first real storm. It came from the southeast, and soon caused twenty to thirty-foot troughs and near-gale winds close to 50 MPH. The light of day was beginning to fade with threatening black skies and raggedy grey clouds. Captain Don seemed a little tipsy but took the helm and started barking out orders to Paul and me. First, we lowered the main sail and lashed it down, then lowered the mizzen sail with only about 2 feet of sailing surface, and then we tightened the jib. Raindrops struck our bared skin like shooting hail stones. Frenetically the women jolted around the cabin lashing or locking down everything flying loose, which was a lot!

The captain quickly rejected my suggestion to lower all sails and use the stabilizing sea anchor because it would stop forward progress. Everyone eventually wore safety straps to move from spot to spot as the skies darkened into night, closing all hatches, and tightening any slacked turnbuckles. Near the midnight watch, the captain relinquished the helm, turning it over to me; notifying all that the light in the compass had broken during the chaos; despite its luminescent numbers. He jury-rigged a battery powered light and tied it onto the compass post for temporary light through the night. Becoming more and more verbally authoritarian, he strongly reiterated that our compass course must follow 285 degrees as westerly as possible. The storm was pushing us southward; farther south of the equator than hoped for.

Waves came over the deck and drained through the toe rails throughout the night, and, luckily, the cockpit had a good self-drainage system as the rest of the crew tried to sleep. By daylight, the wind died down, but the waves remained with high whitecap sea foam breaking high over each wave as far as we could see in every direction. By mid-day we were back to full sails again and moved along briskly about 10 or 12 knots.

Thereafter, it became clear to everyone the Binasu II was slowly showing signs of deterioration. Several cleats required regular tightening with a screwdriver, and, worst of all, the bilge had to be hand pumped. At first, we thought it was drainage leftover from the water taken on from the passing storm, but soon recognized the incoming water was from an unknown leak, and the captain ran the mechanical pump at irregular intervals.

Relations between Don and Carolyn and the 4 of us, became even less cordial; almost secretive. Don relieved me at the helm each watch change, and we would briefly discuss the sail settings and the general handling of the boat. He showed a forced smile with his now bearding facial skin, as if being gratuitous, but always returned to his point-of-sailing skills. Paul often complained because Don always came on watch with a cup of hot-chocolate or some warming drink which none of us had access to, confirmed by Arlene and Sarah. Don would sometimes smoke a cigarette while on watch and the unsavory smoke would drift into our sleeping quarters.

After losing sight of Bali, we had been at sea for about 6 weeks (3 weeks from Christmas Island) when we again spotted land! This time it was the Cocos Islands (sometimes called Keeling), another Australian territory. With only about a third of the population compared to Christmas Island (1800 to 600), they were more welcoming probably because of the rarity of visitors. Most were of Malay Islam (Sunni) descent and very unselfishly helped us load the Binasu II with fresh supplies of water, fish, fruits, and vegetables, and except for the water, of less quantity than Christmas Island.

The scuttlebutt among the few other boaters in the harbor was that Charlie and his double-ender sailboat was still on Cocos. We thought we had seen him in one of the harbor shops but didn't recognize him, and he chose avoidance, and we were not able to spot the double-ender. Unable to escape the embarrassment, he told the story of his solo sail from Christmas Island when, about halfway, his propane cooker blew up, causing the scraggly look on his face. And several teeth were knocked out! Astoundingly, he was able to craft himself a 3-tooth set of falsies out of a mix of epoxy and corn meal (I believe) allowing him to chew food. Amazing! He was trying to get some better and more permanent dental work done on Cocos, and some of the interior cabin wood was being refinished from the blast. What a guy!

We never saw or heard of Charlie again. And the Cocos Islands were the last of any humanity we would see for a long time.

Relentlessly, the Binasu II continued westward, the sun warming our shoulders early on and brightening our faces in the evenings; sometimes there were large schools of dolphins following/chasing –

sometimes leading. Somehow the dolphins always appeared on our starboard side; playfully breaching the water and returning just as quickly; often getting very close to our bow as we'd reach out trying to touch them. Always, we sailed into the sunset.

After 2 weeks of steady sailing in nearly stunted silence, we all became aware of the food shortage. Captain Don produced a large fishing hook 4 or 5 inches long and some good strong string stating: "See if you can catch some fish." Paul and I rigged it altogether, scrambled around for some dried organic food resembling bait to tie onto the hook, and tossed it in, trailing behind about 30 or 40 yards.

Of course, we had no way of knowing if/when something might "bite" and be hooked; and after taking turns holding the line, we decided to tie the end to the mizzen mast and wrapped it around one of the cushions. Then sure enough, after about an hour the string went taunt and we could feel something pulling. Paul and I took turns pulling in the line, at the end of which was a very large fish. Getting it onboard, we realized it was a <u>dorado</u> <u>dolphin</u> – commonly called Mahi-mahi in restaurants.

It had a long blue dorsal fin down its back and a blunted flat head, with dazzling side colors of green, gold, and an iridescent blue; and was about 3 feet long. I took out my trusty knife (always with me since my old sailing days), gutted it, and carried it into the kitchen below for the gals to cook; beautiful to look at and delicious to eat.

After that, we had plenty of raw guts for bait and caught more dorado dolphins; as well as an occasional small shark, and other odd-ball types of fish. And we learned another neat fish-catching trick. After allowing the hook and line to fully extend with the end securely tied to the aft shroud, we'd pull the line in 12 or 15 inches and tie that also to the shroud; but with a much lighter and thinner line. That way, when the thinner line snapped with a *twang*, when broken, a fish was hooked; the helmsman didn't have to be distracted from the compass and sails by having to watch the line too frequently.

Another fish story: Despite, or perhaps in accordance with, ***flying fish are*** ***real***!

Because the luminous compass light was broken and unfixable since the last storm, the captain rigged a propane-powered lantern with the light just above the compass. It had a metal cylinder and plastic window, making it safer and durable. The additional benefit – or liability - was it emanated a strong bright light. Over the nighttime watches, the captain, Paul, and I began seeing small fish landing on the Binasu II deck and into the cockpit: literally flying fish. They had large pectoral fins that act as "wings"; being aerodynamic and translucent allowing them to glide above the surface of the water for fairly long distances away from predators; probably the dorado dolphins. But flying toward the lights on our boat seemed to contradict that notion.

Realizing our good fortune for easily accessing food, we decided on a wholesale approach: bringing several lights on deck for several hours during the middle of the night, we suddenly found the Binasu II deck filled with flying fish. Flying fish are sweet and delicious tasting but with each containing a zillion bones.

Confident in our abilities to adapt to the rigors of life at sea, we continued westward; and as always, just below the equator.

Chapter 18

THE REAL YOU COMES OUT

*"The fishermen know that the sea is dangerous and the
storm terrible, but they have never found these dangers
sufficient reason for remaining ashore."*

–Vincent Van Gogh

The monotonous sailing was broken one day when we entered a
non-weather cell of complete calm: no wind whatsoever in any
direction. The clear blue ocean water had no white caps; nearly lake-
like, except for the slow rolling waves. So, like all good sailors, we all
went skinny dipping; just the four of us. Fun as it was, it seemed to
somewhat exacerbate the continued tension between Sarah and Paul,
mostly because of Paul's continued pursuit of Sarah for sex. Of that,
and his claim to fame, as frequently mentioned, was a sexual
relationship with Allen Ginsberg. Paul retraced some of Ginsberg's
travels through India and spoke saintly thoughts about him and his
wellknown poetry expressions of angst. But no sex with Sarah.

It was a beautiful cloudless day. Except for the drifting motion
of the natural ocean currents, we swam over, around, and even under
the Binasu II; checking the rudder, propeller, barnacle attachments,
and any debris inhibiting the smooth glide of the hull's forward
motion. Generally, all was good. There was some barnacle growth; but
I'd seen worse. We could see no points of leakage, even though the
bilge now required more daily pumping, and guessed the seeping water
entered where the rudder entered the hull.

The respite was invigorating.

It's a tribute to the human condition how, given enough time, personalities adjust, even in the harshest conditions. Living on the tiny planet of the Binasu II in the middle of a grand ocean, constantly in motion, for days, weeks, and now months, allowed for penetrating new thoughts and the ruminating and restructuring older ones. Emotions would ebb and flow as if in perpetuity. Adjust or adjust.

The mind circuits were opening.

It'd been more than a month since Cocos Islands – and this was our now reality. We were six individuals, collectively sailing the endless wind and eternal water: the sky above adding yet another dimension. Sometimes after midnight, barely needing to focus on keeping the sails full, I'd turn off the compass light and stare into the stars; steering only by the heavenly North Star compass; as did the intrepid days-of-yore sailors seeking unknown lands, and an unknown destiny.

The ocean's enormity, the power of its presence, moved only by the moon, and we're only a drop on it. To know the ocean, to **really** know her, requires all your ability to focus, all of your attention. And then…and then… she knows you better than you will ever know her. Who could know something so infinite? Yet the infinite knows you.

Ahh, the North Star. So steady, so consistent, so comforting; always bright. High off the starboard of the main mast, it was easy to know its position; about an arm's length when looking up. The vastness when peering upward opens the mind, and the mind's eye. It is as if you unwittingly get to feel it's part of you.

The starry nights were so astoundingly bright because the Milky Way stretched elongated across the sky, inviting and beckoning wonder. Millions and millions and millions of stars varied in hues, brightness, and size poured instigating thoughts of time within. It was as if we were there in it. With each hesitant thought a shooting star flashed downward as a reminder that, somehow it was alive, a **living** cosmos.

The sound of the bow slicing through time and plowing through space kept a pulsation within the body. The faintest sound of a tiny drop of water splashing the deck from the misty sails keeps the true believer on task. The energy waves synchronized with the rhythm of blood with each beat of my heart, allowed a feeling of one with it all. Can we be up there looking down and be down here looking up at the same? There must be billons of beings scattered throughout that vastness. But why? There must be some sense of <u>unity</u> to it all.

The **solitude** of the helmsman on a sailboat in the ocean hundreds of miles from anywhere during the starkness of night was...the ultimate solitude! The universe provided the stars. The planet provides the ocean; we make the boat. Nature gives us wind; we adjust the sails. Who makes us and provides the guidance? Solitude was not loneliness. The surrounding of hundreds of people can cause loneliness. Self-examination while knowing any small error at the helm at any time could cause disaster; and yet feeling on autopilot gliding through life, the ocean, and even the universe.

There was one moment in time that seemed to last forever standing alone on the deck steering into a new dawn. The Binasu II had been following the mesmerizing brightness of the moon the entire time, diluted only by the many starry systems. The copious sails, the movement of each new wave, the outward bow sprays, and every visible fixture of the boat were indelibly etched into a surrounding view waiting to be painted. It was the <u>Alpha and the Omega</u>. The sun was rising, and the moon was setting – in perfect synchrony – at that moment; both peering over the oceans edge in opposite ends. Yet it all seemed so...

Could it be that my mind, at age 31, was like a blank sheet waiting for the universe to write its script; like the mind of a 5-year-old?

Transcending, I was beginning to sense a new belonging, not only to the world, but somehow part of the larger whole...of creation. Why not? Surely, in all the starry grandeur there must be other inhabitants with thinking, motivated to go and to grow, explore, and sail their oceans. Are thoughts from an original thought, persons from an original person? Origins. How did it all begin? There had to be something in the beginning to create a Big Bang. The Alpha and Omega ensure no end.

Will I someday be absorbed into that grandeur of the vastness of the oneness? Are our travels just beginning and showing the way?

Questions of mystery while allowing me to follow a sequence of thought, watching Orion's Belt sink into the horizon.

Oh, the Oneness of it all.

The circuits had carried us so far from Israel, Afghanistan, India, Nepal, Bali…

"LAND HO!!! LAND HO!!!" Those ancient and deep resounding words echoed by Captain Don, woke me near the end of my allowed sleep period; remain a clear memory. We all rushed topside to view the stationary object. It was visibly a small and low volcanic atoll and our first encounter with the Chagos Archipelago. It seemed surreal to see seagulls gracefully hovering overhead and to concentrate on something stationary, something that wasn't in motion; didn't move!

We sailed into the horseshoe-shaped bay seeing lots of coconut trees and ferns at the south bend. To our great surprise and happiness, there was another boat anchored near the western end; a white 45' ketch; a little larger than the Binasu II. Two middle aged men came on deck to wave at us as we slowly slid by; both sides shouting "Hello!" and smiling. We anchored nearby.

Not remembering their actual names, we'll call them Ian and Lucas, they invited us all onto their boat for some snacks and cola drinks. Ian and Lucas were from Cape Town, South Africa and were heading in the opposite direction, to Bali, wanting to escape the political turmoil surround the ruinous apartheid, while never revealing if they were for or against that great human struggle for freedom.

The next day was a day of rest. Ian, Lucas, Paul, and I decided to do some snorkeling in the clear water of the lagoon. They provided masks for Paul and me, but no fins and, we used their wooden dingy to row about 100 yards from our boats; anchoring in about 20' of water on a reef. The underwater view was spectacular, and brilliant! So many varieties of coral, seashells, and fish, it seemed unreal. A giant clam, at least 45" long and fully open caught my view; the largest bivalve mollusk of its kind. But no pearl within (ha, ha).

Within seconds my good humor was interrupted by a violent sting!

Gliding underwater a few feet below the surface, my right arm suddenly felt as if it had been pierced by an arrow! Looking, I saw a small florescent blue sea creature with a long clear tentacle wrapped around the pain spot. Surfacing, the intense pain radiated up my arm and into my chest, as I pulled this predator off my skin. I thought I was having a heart attack!

My "AAHHH" and "HELP, HELP" screams were of terrifying life-threatening intensity and loud enough to quickly alert the others. Sensing an emergency, and my plight, they quickly pulled me to the dingy and lifted me onto it. But the severity of the pain continued throughout my body causing deep groans. I could barely breathe as my mind raced through dozens of life scenarios; most about death.

The Binasu II was closest; all the crew and the 2 South Africans lifted me onto the deck and down the hatch and laid me on our mattress. Captain Don quickly opened the emergency first aid kit, and, not sure of the problem, poured lots of alcohol on the swollen red spot. After a while, he rubbed some topical cream around it, and gave me an aspirin.

Calming down and describing my recollection of what happened, Ian and Lucas surmised it was most likely an Australian Bluebottle jellyfish that stung me. With long tentacles, their sting can kill fish, and occasionally humans; so, I was lucky to be alive; and thankful for all the hovering assistance. The South Africans chuckled, in a hesitant way, acknowledging that they may be going to Australia after Bali.

The next day, I felt better and the 6 of us rowed the wooden dingy to land at the curved end of the horseshoe shaped atoll lagoon; to explore; Don and Carolyn remained on the Binasu II. After dropping off some extra gear and agreeing on a central gathering spot, Ian and Lucas stayed on the dingy to go spear fishing. Arlene and Sarah walked through the palm trees, Paul and I walked across the narrow band of land to the seashore to observe the Oceanside surf. We were both amazed at the thousands of dead seashells crushed by the waves and washed up on the beach. Mostly of the cowry variety, the dead and cracked seashells made it virtually impossible to walk from the sand to the ocean's water. And this site stretched all the way up and down the curved beach. Totally unreal to see!

Meanwhile, Sarah and I had a <u>chicken</u> encounter. We were walking through a coconut grove, and gradually began hearing the clucking of chickens walking around and nibbling off the ground. Not wanting to disturb them but fascinated and wondering how and why they were there, we continued toward the lively bunch. Then, out of nowhere a <u>man</u> appeared. We introduced ourselves and he said he was a local islander. He lived in a nearby shack and said his job was to care for the chickens and help the flock grow in numbers. Between the French and English languages (I recalled some French I studied in college), we found out that an occasional islander would stop by for some chickens and available fresh eggs. He was extremely introverted preferring to live alone. (The islanders spoke a type of French Creole; being mostly African, with Indian and Malay ancestry; many carried there by French boats.) The reality was he was hiding from the British and Americans because he wanted to remain on <u>his</u> island.

We had a wonderful evening together, each sharing our own stories of the day's adventures by the campfire and eating the fish Ian and Lucas had speared; and adding some personal history. In such a short time, we felt a group cohesiveness and consciousness, a feeling we hoped would never end.

But with silent happiness, our crews and boats went in different directions shortly after sunrise the next day. It was a clear day for sailing.

Refreshed we now welcomed the accustomed chores of 24-hour sailing the Binasu II through the Chagos Archipelago. Our next stop, and a 2-overnight trip, was the island of Diego Garcia, the largest of the archipelago (76 square miles); and proved to be an indelible stop on our journey.

The US government had somehow finagled a way to secure a contract with the British Indian Ocean Territory (BIOT) and take control of Diego Garcia. It had become a British colony after the Napoleonic Wars as part of the Treaty of Paris in 1814. In 1966 the British government gave the United States a 50-year lease agreement, with a 20-year extension, to use Diego Garcia for purposes of defense. Shortly thereafter, the US began the process of "<u>decreasing the island population</u>" of over 1,000 inhabitants.

To implement this, the British & US first disallowed any natives leaving Diego Garcia from returning, whether for vacation or medical reason. Next, those still on the island had restricted food and medical supplies with the hope that those remaining would leave "willingly". The tactics of killing the islander's pets was used to motivate the locals to leave. (We now were beginning to understand the pleas of the chicken-man from the previous island.).

By March 1971, when the first US Seabees arrived (about 6 months before us), and except for a few helpers, all of the remaining Islanders had been forcibly displaced and taken westward to Mauritius, the Seychelles, Reunion, or other islands in the Western Indian Ocean.

(What an abomination! What a travesty! Such arrogance! The talking heads of the military-industrial complex would justify this shameful behavior, but it will never satisfy my benign sense of power, justice, and sovereignty toward others. Dastardly behavior! When will we ever learn?)

We sailed into the rather large lagoon and promptly anchored in the crystal-clear water. After radio communications with the command center, Captain Don was rowed ashore for the purpose of scrounging food – any kind. But it was expressly stated that <u>none</u> of the crew, and especially <u>women</u> were allowed on the island; guessing the all-male military crew were dangerously horny. We were dismayed because the captain stayed overnight on shore; and Carolyn never came out of their forward cabin.

The guy rowing Don to shore was a native, and on the return trip, he hesitantly looked me in the eyes for what seemed a long time. Words cannot express the length, depth, and breadth of his expressions. I hope you can imagine.

During the moonlit night, Arlene and I composed a short song:

♫ Diego, Diego Garcia
Isle of a thousand dreams
Won't you please come to me♫
♫ Diego, Diego Garcia
Isle of a thousand eyes

Won't you let us return
To our home by the sea♫♫
♫Let the darkened and demons go away
And the light and life shine in
Through the breeze and coconut trees
And the grains of sand offer peace…♫♫♫

They rowed back to the Binasu II the next morning and…surprise!!! Along with their sizeable catch of non-perishable foods procured, we were each handed a 6- ounce container of vanilla ice cream; cold and mushy but memorably delicious and refreshing. We all gobbled it down practically without breathing. The time used for slobbering down the melting ice cream allowed for some of the resentment to abate; although we remained suspicious that some of the returning boxes contained alcohol.

It was the same native Chagossian who had rowed the captain the day before. And, he had pretty much the same facial expressions, with an obligatory thin smile. I secretly wanted to take him with us, but knew it was impossible.

Of course, the US went on to build a huge naval and air force base there for US missions in Afghanistan, Iran, Iraq, and throughout that region. It was intimated, on the dark side, that Diego Garcia was also used by the CIA as an interrogation/torture camp for captured terrorists. But…such is life on such a war-torn planet.

Chapter 19

SAVED: BY THE KEEL

*"Facing it, always facing it, that's the way to
get through. Face it."*

–Joseph Conrad

With Diego Garcia and the Chagos Archipelago to our backs, we again charted a course westerly with a full set of sails and a good 1,000 miles to go. The first week of sailing was fairly smooth, with consistently favorable winds from the East. Captain Don set the sails using the "wing and wing" method; the jib was opened to catch the wind on the port side, while the main sail was pushed to open on the starboard side. The main sail boom, when at nearly a 90% angle with the length of the boat, requires a "boom vang", basically a strong set of adjustable rope pulleys lashing the boom to the deck; preventing the wind from causing the sail from accidentally flying back to the cockpit; possibly lopping off someone's head or knocking them overboard during the backward swing!

Memory is a funny thing. Fact or fiction?

Even I, (Arlene) know this detailed information about sails and "boom vang" has relevance to our story. So, get ready for the rest of the story.

We had become habitually accustomed to our chores. Paul and I fished during daylight hours and the captain would require us to make sail adjustments on his watch; if necessary. Arlene and Sarah were very consistent with preparing hot food for most of the watches. Carolyn seldom spent time with the crew in the cockpit.

One day, during Paul's watch, he excitedly called for all of us to come on deck! We soon became equally excited at the site of a very large **blue whale** following our course through the water; no more than 10 to 20 yards to our port side; even closer sometimes. It was a magnificent animal, **and** longer/larger than the 40' Binasu II by 10' or more. Soon Captain Don became alarmed and asked us all to be quiet and for Paul to attempt to steer away; slightly to starboard. We could smell alcohol on his breath and later gave a possible reasoning for the closeness to the whale. He thought the whale might side-swipe the hull of Binasu II consequently cracking it open. Because Don thought, the whale might assume the boat was another whale and sideswipe it in the process of mating.

(Later, we thought, whales would be smarter than what the captain believed. But when talking with other sailor-folk, they said whales do sometimes crash into sailboats, but for uncertain and murky reasons.)

Another incident between the captain and me happened when I wanted to follow an old sailor's tradition. I had an old glass bottle and somewhere found a tight-fitting cork and was about to write a paper note with personal pertinent and sailing information and put it adrift, hopefully to be discovered on some strange and wonderful shore on a faraway beach. The lucky finder would, perhaps, eventually contact me with the time and place it was found.

Something I always wanted to do.

Instead of just throwing the bottle overboard, I first told the captain what I was about to do, thinking he would get a chuckle out of it. His reaction was just the opposite. Loudly and aggressively, he told me NOT to do that because it was polluting the ocean, and the bottle belonged to him and Carolyn anyway. He pulled the bottle out of my hand, and I never saw it again; nor did I have another opportunity to do another bottle again. I held resentment over that childish incident for a long time.

Then began a sequence of events that ultimately became the identifying marker, and the most deeply embedded memory of the entire sailboat circuit ride.

Sarah, Paul, and Arlene were sitting around the cockpit as I was on the helm. It was early evening, as the sun was setting, and the sky was mesmerizingly beautiful. The longer we set there, the more beautiful was the sky! Eventually the air became saturated with tiny droplets of moisture and, glowing through the rays of the sun, casting a most brilliant and colorful reddish-violet hue. It was all around us and into the horizon as far as we could see. We sat speechless and motionless, in oneness, not wanting the tantalizing event to end.

But there was a foreboding! The problem was: to our backs, and coming upon us from behind, was a very large, black set of clouds dominating the sky. A storm was brewing, the wind began increasing in intensity, and was the actual cause of the moisture droplets we so admired. But still, a beautiful sight to behold. It was obvious to us we were in for a windy and salty time; and all agreed something had to be done with the sails! And, as stated previously, the Binasu was running wing-and-wing for a maximum of sail efficiency and speed with the direction of the wind.

Yelling down to the Captain, Paul alerted him of the approaching weather and for, in our opinion, the need for the sails to be trimmed. Captain Don came strolling up the companionway stairs and stuck his head above deck and looked around, mostly to the stem, port, and starboard. He looked sleepy and hung-over, and said "NO, we're okay. Don't change anything." And he returned to his cabin.

Even, I (Arlene) by these times, a somewhat experienced sailor, saw the imminent danger and knew the wisdom of trimming the sails.

The sun set and the black clouds engulfed us into a great darkness. The wind was of high-pressure speed and began to swirl, and the Binasu II started bouncing between the waves and became nearly impossible to control with the wheel and direction of the boat. The winds soon reached gale force (34-40 mph). The girls jumped into the cabin below, Sarah, whimpering near fear, while Paul tried to tighten the sheets as best he could in the now darkness. Raindrops pelted our skin like blasts from a paint gun.

Then it happened!

The swirling wind got <u>behind</u> the main sail (to the fore) which remained held immovably in place by the boom vang. The determined fierce wind began pushing and tilting the boat over to port until the main mast was close to the water. The jib was partially filled with water, holding the tilting boat on its side.

Sarah and I (Arlene) were trying to stabilize flying objects in the galley. Sarah had always affirmed that she was unafraid of death. I on the other hand, as you may recall, was quite aware of my fears of dying from age 4 on. At the moment the boat went on its side, Sarah was petrified and tightly holding on to me was crying with fear. To my complete amazement, I felt a calm acceptance of the certainty of my death at that moment in time. My thoughts were: "I guess this is my time God!" My only regret was that my mother would grieve never knowing what happened to her one and only daughter. My parent's first child, a girl died at 3 years of polio within a week of getting sick. When we returned home, my father told me that my mother experienced seeing me in darkness and was hysterical believing I was going to die.

Now I knew the reason for the voice I heard in Bali while struggling with the decision to take this trip; "If you're afraid do it." I have little doubt that this voice was that of my spirit helper. I faced death and was not afraid. The lifetime panic about dying has never returned since this experience. The thought of death now brings me peace with a sense of curiosity and adventure about the next stage in my life.

The captain slipped and slid his way to the cockpit and began shouting for us to loosen all the sheets and/or cut all the lines that were taut.

Having my personal knife always on my hip, I desperately tried to maintain uprightness while easing my way forward to the boom vang; and began cutting any line where there was tension. Captain and Paul did the same, cutting stiffened lines; perhaps more. Cutting was much quicker than trying to undue the lines tied to the cleats. But at least 2 cleats still tied to their lines flew around in the air like unseeing bats. Paul eventually cut the lines holding the main sail tension.

There was a lot of shouting and foul words used in this chaotic confusion! The boom of the main sail, now freed from the boom vang, wildly flopped back and forth like a giant wand swatting insects. The mizzen mast lost a shroud, becoming weak and unable to hold a sail and nearly fell over. The sheet holding the tension on the jib was cut by the captain afore the winch. We were once again standing parallel to the deck; trying to get a footing onto something in the strenuous disorientation! And, except for one dim light in the cabin, it was in total darkness. The entire port side was at water's edge, and partially opened porthole, allowed an opening for the saltwater to rush into the cabin.

(Ah, a Darien Jungle near-death post-traumatic-syndrome moment!)

Then, just when we thought we were dead, a miracle happened!

The Binasu II righted itself. With no sail tension, and not too much water in the hull, the iron ballast keel (of 7,700 lbs.) and nearly angled out of the water, fell into the water forcing the hull to right itself and was again level with the sea; albeit the waves were running at 30' high; so, being <u>level</u> couldn't be the best word to use. The deck was a mess, and we all took turns pumping out the bilge; even as the storm continued. The captain agreed (finally) to put out the sea anchor to stabilize the boat until the storms passed, giving us more stability and time to restore the condition of the boat to maintain sailable living.

We batten down the mainsail boom, tied-up the jib, and stabilized the mizzen mast, and tied-together the cut lines with the easy-to-break bowline knot. We went below to rest or sleep until daylight; knowing there was nothing else to do, and the boat was stabilized by the steady sea anchor.

At first daybreak, the storm had mostly passed, the seas were calming, and we all went on deck to help get the Binasu II again sail worthy. It didn't take long. The captain had plenty of extra new rope available for replacing the cut lines, put new turnbuckles on the shrouds to stabilize the mizzen mast, and tightened the screws on the 2 loose cleats. Then there were several hours of taking turns pumping the bilge. The gals reorganized the various components of the galley and made some hot tea; grateful the stove remained operational.

Slowly we hoisted the main sail, testing the new sheets for strength, and then up went a very wet jib; after a few hand-sewn stitches. Finally, the Captain felt confident enough to the get mizzen sail up. He took the first watch, and we were once again on our way; each tired but serenely happy to still be afloat.

Reminiscing about that near fatal event, we were thankful for the skills and strengths each person used to keep the boat afloat, and for the quick response to such an adrenalin laden situation. Initially, as crew, this made us feel closer and unified. Then slowly the old consciousness of separation began to again creep in between us; the old versus the young, the alkies versus the dopers, the establishment versus anti-establishment, the power versus resistance.

As the days passed, a new unspoken wedge appeared in the team's crack. Somehow, "they" took the stance that "we" were responsible for the near disaster of nearly sinking; more especially, me, because I was on the helm at the time. It was an issue without resolution, even if there had been a real and serious discussion relating to the sequence of events.

To the Captain's credit, he functioned well in the emergency, and was a great navigator. He would regularly get on deck about midway and pull out and open his trusty sextant; typically, at noon to catch the overhead sun; or occasionally at night to catch the moon or the North Star. I never learned much about it, but…the practice was to use the sextant to get "sights" of a celestial body with the horizon, and measure this angle using the sextant, and ocean charts can show your approximate position; sometimes called triangulation. It assumed your position within a mile of accuracy, which is very good at sea (compared to today's GPS of being within one foot of your actual position). He got us dead-on to Christmas Island, the Cocos, and Diego Garcia. But, because he was an airline pilot, his feel for ocean motion and ocean winds was somewhat…less than his navigational skills.

There were times of flexing muscles, straining the brain, and believing without seeing; coupled periods of doubt, confusion, and utter blindness. But always we'd be enwrapped by a strong sense of sublime uncertainty; not knowing where we were going or if we'd get there, but that translated into a solid travel feeling. Though not forgotten, the conflicts were sublimated, and cooperation dominated. For unknown reasons, the times at the wheel, the cooking, fishing, and sail changing seemed easier, pumping the bilge, bordering on fun. After all, it was all we had to do, so why not do it well!

There were many days of cloudless and near cloudless skies, with favorable winds pushing us along a straight course; hardly changing the sail settings. We had been to sea just over 3 months.

The unforgettable memory of that _**first speck**_ of land, a barely visible stationary stone, sticking out of the water was seen several miles to the fore of Binasu II. And as that speck of stone grew larger with our forward movement, it was then we knew, for certain, it was the Seychelles Islands; dead ahead! It was an unforgettable moment; stunned by a rapturous feeling racing through our reawakened human circuitry of body, mind, and spirit!

Two brilliant white seagulls circled above the mast.

We had made it!!!

Chapter 20

OUR MOMENTS IN THE SUN

*"I was rich, if not in money, in sunny hours
and summer days..."*

–Henry David Thoreau

Being late in the evening, the captain decided to slow down our forward progress to allow for an early morning arrival in Victoria, the capital on the main island of Mahe. Pulling into the dock seemed a little surreal, to think we'd sailed from Bali to Mahe and lived to talk about it.

We docked between an old iron freighter and a ferry boat and could see large colorful fish flitting about in the clear water nearby. A few dark-skinned islanders moved about the nearby wooden buildings quietly chatting, as the sun was rising just above our mast. The air was fresh and clean with seagulls searching above for food, as we stared at the lush greenery of the nearby hills. (Perhaps best denominated as mountains because the highest peaks of the Seychelles were Morne Seychellois at 2,969', with Mont Dauban at 2,427'. and was that **first speck** of land we sighted when approaching from miles away.)

The captain was casually escorted by 2 men in wrinkled beige-colored uniforms, unarmed, of course, returning about 30 minutes later saying he and Carolyn had been cleared through customs and immigration and were free to debark. It was then we learned of their motive for sailing to the Seychelles – they had planned to **retire** there!

At first the 4 of us didn't realize the significance of this, but soon learned of the nautical rules when clearing customs and immigrations. Turns out, crew members of any type of boat entering a foreign country can legally stay in the country **so long as their arriving boat remains there!** So…we could stay in the Seychelles as long as we wanted because the Binasu II owners were retiring there, i.e., staying for the rest of their lives.

We were ecstatic, of course. Forever in paradise! What a deal! Suddenly all the working hardships, near sinking, conflicts and jellyfish stings were pushed into the recesses of our minds. It was a complete feeling of freedom after the previous 3 months of confinement!

There was a short but interesting time processing through the legal system. Not knowing for certain, but suspecting, the captain and his wife may have alerted the officials of our dope smoking habit because they seemed to make an extra-special effort while going through our personal belonging. But by then, we had been out of any type of THC for a long time; probably just before Diego Garcia. Eventually they cleared us, and we were free to enter.

Except for one accidental meeting, and without interaction, we saw Captain Don and Carolyn at the marketplace in Victoria a few days later. After that, we never saw them again.

We stuck close to Sarah, Paul, while on Mahe; finding a place to live close to each other and learning the ropes of how to live amongst the Seychellois, i.e., monetary system, local food, and ways of getting around Mahe and between the islands. We soon parted ways, enjoying the comforts of our own unique rhythms as a couple.

During this political era, the Seychelles remained a British Colony (again, the Napoleonic Wars) but growing toward independence, and a population of 54,000; descendants mostly of African, French Europeans, and Asians creating a Creole culture. Their language is a Seychellois Creole based mostly on French, with a smattering of English. We found it easy communicating with all levels of their society.

Like all the Indian Ocean islands, there was no indigenous population to the Seychelles Islands until the 16th Century as the French and British competed for control. (Some local scuttlebutt has it that French pirates carried freed African slaves there to live together; but this version was difficult to find in any "official" island history.)

Officially it was named after <u>Jean Moreau de Séchelles</u>, King Louis XV's Minister of Finance in 1756.

Our first bed was, shall we say, a bit difficult; not very kingly. As a matter of fact, it was a single bed we squeezed into every night, Arlene against the wall.

I remember times being on the outside with leg hanging over the bed. My choice since I frequently needed middle of the night bathroom visitations. But the rest of the ground floor house was spacious, composed of 2 rooms with a bath and a ceiling fan: a luxury in those places. The owners were locals and baked us a chocolate coconut cake and gave us plates of bake breadfruit. Paradise on $5.00 per week! Lightheartedly we walked around Victoria getting "the lay of the land".

Talking with fishermen, businessmen, and any rare travelers, we soon discovered the best place-to-be was on one of the two other inhabited islands – Praslin and/or La Digue (there are 155 total islands in this group, with 42 of them being of the granite type, and only 3 of them populated by humans: Mahe, Praslin, La Digue). It was an easy choice for us, taking the next available 27-mile inter-island ferry ride to Praslin.

When we told Sarah and Paul of our plans, their response was that they might possibly join us there someday soon; or possibly on La Digue. We never did meet up with them again in the Seychelles. However, we somehow kept in contact with Sarah for many years, exchanging Christmas letters and occasional telephone calls. Our bond was strong!

It wasn't long before we were on Praslin and had a house rented. The friendly neighbors acquainted themselves by guiding us on short walks to the beach bay, just across the dirt road from our house. It was maybe 30 or 40 yards from our open doorway, through a small grove of trees, and onto the soft glistening sand of the beach with picture postcard overhanging coconut trees. The feeling of warm sand on bare feet and opened toes…became transformative.

The $35.00 a month rent included a housekeeper who came daily to clean and cook for us. She taught me how to gather and break open a coconut, and after drinking the hydrating coconut water, grate the flesh and add it to any and every dish we prepared.

AND I was able to buy a good set of snorkeling mask and flippers for practically nothing; each in near-new shape. VHAT A DEAL!!!

The yearly temperature range averages from 75 to 85 degrees, and, unlike the more mountainous Mahe, the smaller islands get under a hundred inches of rain per year with only moderate humidity; and the islands are outside the cyclone belt. The sea temperature was ideal for swimming year around – 79 to 86 degrees. Perfect for skinny dipping, free diving, and snorkeling.

Once under the surface, it was like a new world, a world of its own! How to describe? The water was as crystal clear as a cloudless sky, with the underwater vision ranging as far away as…exaggeration…50 yards or more. The islands are ringed by coral reefs containing such a myriad of underwater life as to make it difficult to document, producing an expanding collage of vivid colors causing me to often be agog, motionless, for long periods of time; not sure if I wanted to or could move while restfully breathing through the snorkel's air valve. Like on another planet, another universe!

And it wasn't very deep; usually 10 to 30 feet; an easy depth to reach. Large and small schools of fish would swim by; some casually drifting nearby checking me out. Swimming farther out the reef dropped off into an abyss with large, graceful stingrays; again, some of them coming close checking me out, usually as I was making my way back to the secure confines of the glowingly vibrant reefs. So full of life!

It was conveniently easy to observe and learn the habitat of the colonies of lobsters. After bartering for a 3' long aluminum spear from a local, it was easy, daily, to have lobsters for dinner; sometimes sharing extras with neighbors who taught us how to clean steam and prepare the lobsters.

(The trick for cleaning freshly caught lobster, we learned from them, was to first break off one of the antennae, and the soft tip end, to then force the sturdy antennae up the inside of the lobster tail, twist and turn it several times, then pull it out; with it comes the intestines and with the internal waste; ready for cooking.)

Fresh lobster with sliced and ripened mangos was…memorably

delicious; especially with chocolate coconut cake afterward; yummy. Anyone?

Praslin was an interesting and exotic island for us, in many regards. Besides the enchanting beaches and enticing crystalline water, the people, and the weather, there was the Vallée de Mai. It was an easy walk there from our small Anse Volbert Village; the entire island being only 7.5 miles long and barely 3 miles wide. But the island has a height of 1,204' allowing for a jungle-like drop into this valley, only a mile and a half from our house. Walking down into this valley on a narrow earthen path, we became completely engrossed by the non-threatening multitude of green leaves and floral. We were nearly speechless, and the native guide remained quiet!

The sounds of low synchronized volume of birds and insects enhanced the view. The largest overhanging fern leaves we'd ever seen minimized our stature as we brushed against some. Skinks and geckos scurried across our path, and several wildly colored frogs blended with the trees. Some trees grew to the heights of 80 to 100 feet, and these were the world-famous coco-de-mer (coconut of the sea) found only here, grouped in bunches near the top. A bi-lobed species of a rare coconut palm tree, some laying half-rotten on the jungle floor, others in various stages of losing their husks; the largest and heaviest seed in the world; some weighing as much as 50 pounds when fully ripened.

These are from the female trees. The male trees produce a yard-long phallic-looking growth called a catkin, helping to produce their mystery of pollination. So, it was easy to understand the islands legendary beliefs, with the coco-de-mer having a shape like firm human buttocks and the long and thin catkins, of them going down to the sea to embrace for pollination, hence the name, coconut of the sea.

The mushy content of the coco-de-mer was considered an aphrodisiac by the islanders, although the taste didn't go well with our palates. Eons ago, after shedding their outer husks and the inner contents dried-out, the coco-de-mer would sometimes float on the ocean currents to faraway lands. Arriving in places like Africa, India, and SE Asia these were considered great treasures by kings and queens, and often on display with trophies of gold and gems. But their origin continues to remain a mystery even to world botanists.

The sun was setting but we didn't want to leave <u>Vallée de Mai</u>. Many sizes and colors of orchids were enchanting to us, as a vision of the Garden of Eden. The very rare black parrots flew nearby in pairs; unafraid. And for us? It seemed a timeless place, or at the beginning of time. We had traveled so far to get there! But every short, long, and intermediate step of the way was more than worth it!

I felt like Alice in Wonderland!

We loved to hike around Praslin on the dirt roads; there were a few trucks on the island, but not many. One evening toward sunset, we saw this incredible spider web stretching across the road near the beach. It stretched between two palm trees many feet above us. The sun was shining directly through the thickness of the web as it shone a glistening golden thread. It wasn't a perfect spider web as seen in books or pictures, but a hodgepodge of many webs, adding to the brilliance. Moments like this were captured in our minds as a secured forever memory. So, we can now write about them.

One thing we learned the hard way, very early on, was that <u>every</u> coconut tree anywhere on the island was owned by <u>someone</u>! I remember finding a large coconut in the sand near the beach and started to walk away with it. Midstride I was politely accosted by a young native asking for payment, saying he was the owner of the tree from which the coconut had fallen.

Relaxing and Sailing the Islands

If you wanted a fresh coconut for cooking and eating, it was a process of learning who owned that particular tree, finding them (or they would find you), and bargaining for a price; rarely costing more than a half, or no more than, one Seychelles rupee; equivalent to18 cents US. The copra was their primary source of income (then), with tourism and the service industry rapidly taking over. (Copra was the white meat inside a coconut shell from which food and oils are extracted.)

Our months on Praslin were wonderful, mystifying, and enriching, and the mythical "island fever" never streamed into our emotions or consciousness. We had grown accustomed to their rhythm of daily life following nature's beat conjoined with each individual and collective personality. We had no idea what the population was at that time, guessing to be around 3,000. The total population of the Seychelles at that time was slightly above 53.000. Everyone recognized us and we connected with many, and they with us; and they would look us in the eyes and smile as we passed by; as if we were brothers and sisters; but always a slight suggestion of admiration both ways. A few were there to help us with our sparse belongings getting onto the old slightly unstable ferry boat as we left the island.

We had a calling to move on. And La Digue was next! La Digue was the smallest of the 3 inhabited Seychelles Islands; most remote and least traveled to, so it fit our needs perfectly. The inner desire was always to explore places as of yet unexplored by the seasoned travelers. We were excited! A bit of an ego thing, I suppose; but soul-satisfying and fun.

La Digue had a land mass of only 3 miles long and 2 miles wide, and an elevation of 1,000 feet. It was only a quick one-hour ferry ride across the 7 miles of sparkling water bubbling up; seen as the noisy one-lung engine churned the propeller. And although it rained often, the downpours lasted usually less than an hour. The Seychelles in general are out of the tropical storm area, and tsunamis never reached there, so the year-round weather was glorious. (The Seychelles are only 900 miles below the equator and less than a thousand miles from the East coast of Africa.)

It was so easy moving into the island milieu. Someone directed us to a very large wooden house for rent; above ground with seven steps going up to the main door, a spacious and airy living room, dining room, and great kitchen. But the best was a most inviting bedroom, with a king size bed and a mosquito net hanging above. The owners, living 2 houses down the dirt road, thought we would balk at the $35 per month price, were surprised at the quick acceptance. We couldn't believe our luck! The owners gave us some dried fish and fresh mangoes and bananas to help us get settled in.

Chapter 21

ENDLESS ARRAY OF VISITORS

♫ *"By the sea, by the sea, by the beautiful sea,*
You and me you and me, oh! How happy we'll be..." ♫

**–By the Beautiful Sea, 1914 song, by Harold Atteridge and
Harry Carroll**

My continued preoccupation with the sea became...snorkeling; and <u>seashell</u> <u>collecting</u>; greatly raised to a passion. There was such a numerous variety of shells and in copious amounts as to cause a stuttering of awkward swimming motions. The sheer beauty of living seashells when in absolutely clear water created in me an eternal attraction to all things beauteous. Surely, it must reflect the source of original Beauty.

<u>Cowry</u> seashells were the most plenteous, and so shinny with their hard porcelain shell. The Tiger, Gold-ring, Arabian, Hundred-Eyed, Serpent's Head, Depressed, Map, and Money Cowry, to name a few, were quickly added to my collection.

Once, while diving near the edge of a reef where it drops into deeper water, I saw a large school (blanket-like) of Money Cowry covering a 20 X 30-foot area: hundreds, probably thousands. The reef area shone in a bright gold color; reminding me of the old adage of "streets of gold". What a sight! I went back 3 or 4 days later, and they were all gone; somehow, somewhere disappeared.

My next favorite seashell was the cone shell; the Textile cone, Geography cone, Striatus cone, Tessulatus cone, Aulicus (or Princely, a favorite) and the Hebrew cone. Arlene, ironically, found a Hebrew cone shell one day while snorkeling together. The Glory of the Seas was the most sought-after textile cone seashell, of any kind, because of its rarity and beauty; though not in the vicinity of the Seychelles.

It was important to remember that the cone shells, especially the Textile type, could be extremely venomous and even deadly. So, caution was needed when handling them. With their elongated shape, they have a hypodermic needle-like spear coming out the smaller end. When the toxins from the harpoon get into the fish it paralyzes them; making them ready to eat. With humans, the venom contains a wide variety of peptide toxins that sting and sometimes kills humans. Handling them by width, not length, was safe.

(Some of the scuttlebutt going around the islands was of the American CIA willing to pay top dollar for just one, intact, Textile cone shell. For what, we can only speculate.)

I met a Seychellois with Asian relatives who wanted to work together to retrieve Indian Ocean <u>sea slugs</u> and export them, a sought-after delicacy in some countries. His name was Gérard, but I called him Jerry. We dove together several times as he pointed out the slugs; easy enough to get because they just lie there unmoving. He wanted Arlene and me to finance the venture thinking we were rich Americans. Of course, we refused.

Jerry also liked to dive for octopus, because the locals would buy them and often preferred them to fish; but mostly because they were tasty, but difficult to catch. Difficult because they'd quickly change colors to match the surrounding reef and would spray a milky substance when in danger, and most importantly, their 8 tentacles could be as long as 30 or more inches each.

Late one afternoon, when diving more than a hundred yards but offshore in an area of the reef we were both familiar with, Jerry pulled an octopus out of its lodging hole and hauled it to the surface next to me. Gleefully showing off his catch before bagging it. Within an instant the wily octopus began wrapping its agile tentacles around Jerry's lower left forearm. Instinctually moving his right hand over attempting to pull the many sucking cups off his skin, Jerry watched helplessly as <u>both</u> of his forearm's quickly became encircled by the remaining flailing tentacles, holding him in an absorbing and captive grip!

With panic in his eyes and dire urgency in his voice, he screamed: "COME ON! Come on! Get my knife!" For an eternity of moments, we stared at each other. Somewhat shocked, Jerry was getting out of breath and tired from treading water without arms, and I…seemed to be…frozen in time and space; unable to move.

Natural reflexes then kicked in. Jerry tilted over on his side showing the sheathed knife belted around his waist. I pulled it out and feverously began cutting the tentacles in a line between Jerry's forearms, with the head the octopus underwater, emitting a dark substance. Its flesh was so rubbery; making it very difficult to cut; plus, Jerry's knife was less than sharply honed. My rough hacking on the tentacles was hampered by my fear of cutting into Jerry's arm, because the distance between forearms was so close due to the tenacity of the tentacles holding them together. The length of each tentacle was able to be wrapped around his forearms several times; so, it required more than just cutting one of the 8 single tentacles.

After cutting through about half of the wrapped-around octopus's flesh, Jerry was soon able to pull his arms apart as the octopus released its hold and tried vainly to swim away but was quickly captured and placed in Jerry's holding bag.

Neither of us had ever seen or experienced anything like that before.

Swimming to shore, we could easily see the discoloration on Jerry's arms from the suck-marks of the tentacles; happy to have survived the ordeal. Gratefully, the idea of a sea slug export business never resurfaced again.

Another imbedded memory was of our neighbors who lived a short hike back into the hills from us, away from the beach. They were a very old couple! They were Mr. & Mrs. Gibbs, Allan, and Jeannie, living in a dilapidated thatched-roofed building with an uneven foundation. Embittered ex-patriot tobacco farmers from Rhodesia, Africa their main source of sadness was having been forced off their private land. Their political justifications were so convoluted as to be difficult to follow; something about race, majority, minority, independence, and British rule.

154 |

Allan was, naturally, a heavy tobacco smoker and was diligently trying to grow tobacco on his La Digue land; about 10 acres, only half of which was even partially able to be cultivated due to the wild jungle-like conditions. But they tried. Jeannie was a passive type with sparkling eyes and a willingness to help any person any time. It was obvious to us that they loved each other and were loyal to their newly adaptive way of life.

Allan was very thin; especially his skinny legs, and always wore boots, khaki shorts, a faded white t-shirt, and a pith helmet. He talked a lot and usually diverted the conversation back to his war-time experiences as a British officer in the North Africa campaign in World War II. Jeannie never changed her bra-like top, and flowery wraparound skirt. We'd talk with them for hours over tea at infrequent sittings inside their hut; Allan being the center of attention. They seemed mildly interested in the hippie culture, and especially of our travels; primarily of how we could afford such travels. They were obviously rich in life's experiences, but monetarily poor.

They taught us the importance of cutting down banana trees; after the bananas are fully grown but <u>before</u> turning yellow. First, by cutting down the tree, soon thereafter a new stem begins to grow and a new tree forms, and second because bananas taste better and are more nutritious if ripened <u>off</u> the vine giving time to arrive at the marketplace. To support the Gibbs, we would sometimes buy their bananas and vegetables, and listen to their farming woes.

One day, after a brief exchange with them, we decided to explore the path further back into the jungle: mostly walking uphill to an open area. Getting close to the top, we were astounded at what we saw!

Just before us, no more than 5 yards away, was this giant <u>turtle</u>; blotchy tan in color and seemingly oblivious to our nearness. It had to be over 3 feet high. We weren't even certain it was alive, and then it stuck out its neck and started eating plants on the ground. We just sat nearby in wondrous observation, at this unusual product of nature, until the sun got big and heavy and dropped low.

(As we discovered, it was an <u>Aldabra giant tortoise</u>, found mostly on several of the Seychelles Islands. They live to be well over 200 years old and can weigh over 500 pounds in a 4-foot-long body. These relics of the past are herbivorous, eating grass, herbs, and other plant stems close to the ground with their very long neck; even sometimes reaching up for food from hanging trees.)

Passing through the Gibbs compound on the way home, Allan was intensely interested about the turtle wanting an exact description of what and precisely where it was seen. We never understood this interest, nor cared.

As weeks turned into months and our house became a well-known community fixture, we were accepted participants in the La Digue society. One of the benefits of this community-known image was the regular influx of foreign travelers (mostly circuit riders) visiting La Digue; and for obvious reasons were directed to our place because of their appearance! We offered them a clean place to "crash", water for bathing, some books to read, conversation and storytelling. The only thing we asked in return was to help with purchasing and cooking food, which they graciously accepted.

This also gave us an opportunity to catch up on world news and events: the Pentagon Papers were released, proving, that the Pentagon had been lying about Vietnam, Jim Morrison had died as did one of the Allman Brothers, India and Pakistan were still battling it out, another American had walked on the moon, Idi Amin took over Uganda, etc., etc., etc. Hearing it all, we were supremely satisfied to be away and disengaged.

There were too many people passing through for us to remember them all, but a few stood out.

Memory is a funny thing. It gives voice to the soul.

There was this young couple – yes, younger than us. Jack and Beth were Americans coming up from South Africa on their way to Kenya for a flight back to the States. The unusual take on this couple was their constant talk of continued world travels, even though, to us, Beth looked very much into 3 months of pregnancy. But she/they were in total denial about it; she more than him. We quizzed them several times about it, always with the same response of denial. Jack and Beth stayed with us for about a week, and then moved on, as wannabe circuit riders

I remember sitting on the stairs to our house asking Beth about the signs of pregnancy. She in fact had not menstruated for 4 months and had tender swollen breasts. Even though she agreed those could be signs of pregnancy she continued to be in denial acknowledging she and Jack were not ready to have a baby and wanted to travel. Ahh the power of the need to escape reality.

Then there was the middle-aged kind of scraggly looking guy; maybe a burn-out from too many acid trips. But he was fun, and always kept a positive approach to things; even when he once bought some fruit that turned out to be too wormy and rotten. He so appreciated us for letting him stay with us, he promised, when he got to his next destination in Uganda Africa, he would send us some <u>bhang</u>, which he claimed was the best shit in the world. We said yes, that would be great; but we immediately blew him off thinking it was just another innocent gesture of projected gratitude; ultimately to be unfulfilled. Nonetheless, he was a true circuit rider!

But sure enough, about 3 weeks after he left La Digue, we received a small package delivered by the local postman; post dated with stamps from Uganda, Africa. Cautiously, we unwrapped it. The initial appearance was as an ordinary paperback book; with an unremembered title, maybe 4 X 6 inches, but thick. Drawing back the cover, we gleefully discovered the pages were carved-out and the cavity was filled with marijuana! And he was right! It was some absolutely good stuff.

Our next visitor was the lovely Theón, and her boyfriend John. John didn't loom large in our memory, but Theón remains. It began almost immediately as she extended herself in friendship to us in loving help around the house, shopping, and having great spiritual conversations without judgment. We clicked! She was from San Francisco having traveled up and down the coast often; remembering her stays in Venice Beach. As a journalist, she wrote musical reviews for the rock industry; her most recent writing on the Beach Boys. We almost laughed, thinking the Beach Boys were pretty light and old stuff in the music world, but she ably convinced us their latest album "Pet Sounds" with songs: "Sloop John B" and especially "God Only

Knows" were becoming true classics and was having a great impact on the rock music world and a renaissance for the Beach Boys.

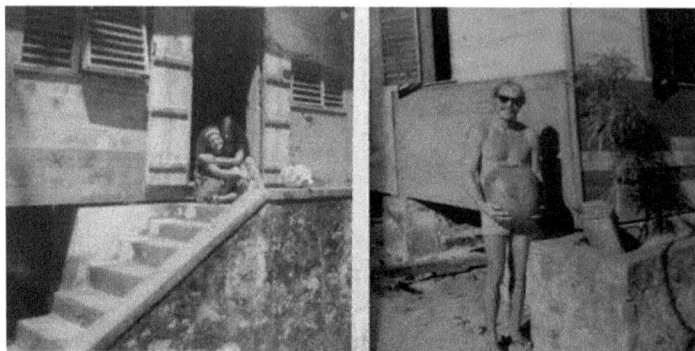

On La Digue, Arlene & Theon – a Coco-de-Mer

Theón also liked to snorkel and was delighted to have me show her around the nearby reefs. It was just she and me, because John didn't enjoy the water much, although he dove with us once. She showed great enthusiasm when finding live seashells of different types. We were stoutly disciplined to not take away more than 2 of any type, mostly cowries; even though, with some, there were hundreds for the picking. In our house, we had a long 6-inchwide slightly warped board, maybe 6 feet long, resting on some bricks several inches off the floor, displaying the varieties of collected shells; after learning how to boil them in water to extract the organism inside. Each was in pristine shape, untouched by the direct rays of the sun. It became an attraction to guests, neighbors, and other locals.

One of my great fantasies while there was to make a night-dive by the full moon. Which I did! On this particular night, I waited until the moon had risen high in the sky then waded slowly into the water; no flashlight needed because of the brightness of the moon, and an intimate familiarity with the beach, surf, and reef in that area. Pushing off by the edge of the water, I first saw only the sand; which by itself was incredibly bright white; glistening off the reflection of the moon light. Of course, it was a violation of the cardinal sin of diving alone.

Approaching the deeper area of the actual coral reef, my eyes beheld a new horizon! It was an entirely different specter; initially frightening me because the view was so different and lacked familiarity. The schools of fish were gone! No seashells visible! And lobsters must have been well-hidden. And especially the colors were different, everywhere I looked. Like viewing a channel on the TV, there were sea urchins, coral shrimp, and several octopuses freely roaming about looking for prey. Most impressive was the coral itself. Not all, but much of the coral during the day tended to be somewhat flat in color and shape. Whereas at night, on this night, they were fluffy looking with their polyps outstretched and moving with the flow of the currents. And to top it off, some of the coral polyps were bioluminescence color; some psychedelic green, others not-as-bright purple or blue; even though the water was brightened by streaks of moonlight. Who needed LSD?

I saw a small sand (tiger) shark at a near distance off to the left. Again, unusual because I'd seen many during day dives because they typically lie on the sandy bottoms during the day; but these sharks apparently feed at night. That, combined with a light-flashing weird looking jellyfish, helped me to determine it was time to get to the safety of the shore, and reality, seeing lots more coral shrimp along the way. But the entire experience remains.

Chapter 22

ARLENE'S GOOD DEED

"No one has ever become poor by giving."

–Anne Frank

Our reputation amongst the Seychellois, especially within the close knit La Digue community, had steadily grown upward over the months; mostly because we had stayed on their island longer than previous "tourists" and interacted with them in a loving, respectful manner as equals. We relished it, but there was a downside as well; for us. Arlene had easily established a reputation as a peacemaker with relationships and with a calming influence when talking with others, even with groups of other locals. It was not known if they knew she had a degree in psychology, but...

One day around noon, 2 women rushed up the stairs loudly knocking on our open door and in high-pitched voices asking for Arlene to go with them, which she did. The ladies hurriedly led Arlene down the road about 2 blocks away to a two-story commercial building with a small crowd of people looking up in the same direction. Standing on the corner of the roof, was a man threatening to jump off; threatening to harm himself. It was doubtful if the building was tall enough for the man to actually kill himself had he jumped, but certainly the fall would have caused severe bodily damage.

Arlene being Arlene quieted down the crowd and spoke directly with the distraught man; in between his expressions of anger and crying in despair. In what seemed like a long time, but in reality, was only a few minutes, Arlene skillfully had the man agree to allow his friends to raise the handcrafted wooden ladder to the roof, allowing him to climb down. And as agreed, she privately spoke with the man assuring him of additional talks, as needed. It was an obvious huge success for everyone; always to be remembered.

I (Arlene) was surprised by the man's willingness to be saved, realizing he just needed to be heard. Of course, lots of credit needs to be given to the community of people gathered who truly wanted him in their lives. At that moment I began to realize it was time to leave the Seychelles and make our way back home. I began to have more confidence and faith in myself as a counselor, believing I could be most helpful to people of my own culture.

For me, there was a very different kind of diving-by-the-sea experience.

Over time, more and more foreign travelers/tourists were coming to the Seychelles and to La Digue. And, of course, the main attraction was the beautiful remote beaches and the beyond-description snorkeling on the reefs. Soon I was called upon to lead the newcomers to the beaches, Anise Beach especially, and toward the best spots on the surrounding reefs. In effect, I was becoming a tour guide! It was fun at first, but gradually began gnawing at my degraded sense of tourism.

One day, 6 or 7 of the newbies practically begged me, even offered money, to lead them on a reef snorkeling dive. With a mixture of guys and gals, we went pretty far offshore about a hundred yards or so, when 2 of the divers began to express being out-of-breath with extreme tiredness. We had barely begun to survey the reef; but perhaps I was judging them too harshly. After months of daily diving, my physical habits had become robust. Nonetheless, I felt responsible for them, so we began to slowly swim toward the beach.

About halfway back, we swam over a large bowl-like sandy area. Looking down at about a 30-foot depth, I could see a large seashell, and, calling all divers attention to it, suggested each to dive for it. But none accepted the offer, after expressing doubt and uncertainty about the depth and their skill level. So, I did. And much to my surprise and amazement, I scooped up a large Pacific Triton Trumpet; at least 14" long! WOW!!! It was the one shell I'd been searching for and hoping to find since arriving in the Seychelles. And it was still alive; meaning the leather-like "foot" when closed was still intact – like its own fingerprint.

(Also known as Triton's Trumpet; as the son of the Greek God of the sea – Poseidon and has been used for centuries by many cultures by blowing into a notched end and making signaling, trumpeting, or ceremonial sounds. They typically feed on starfish.)

Several of the accompanying divers offered to buy it. Arlene boiled it and the inside meaty body was easily removed and the beautiful specimen was placed in the seashell collection for all to gaze in wonder at its shiny beauty.

Our moment in the sun was nearing a close. We had lived in the Seychelle Islands for slightly longer than 8 months; and loved it, of course, having been fortunate enough to participate in this great culture with its gracious people. But it was time to head back home, wherever that was. Arlene's parents were in Brooklyn and my mother in Columbia, Pa. But we really had no place to call home. The world had become our home, maybe even the cosmos. We spent long hours in the evening and nights discussing "home", where it was and what it meant to us. We knew we had to choose somewhere to go and call home; having been to so many places and experienced so much. We could literally choose from hundreds of places.

But, also, we were running out of money! Time to be out the front door and onto the circuits again.

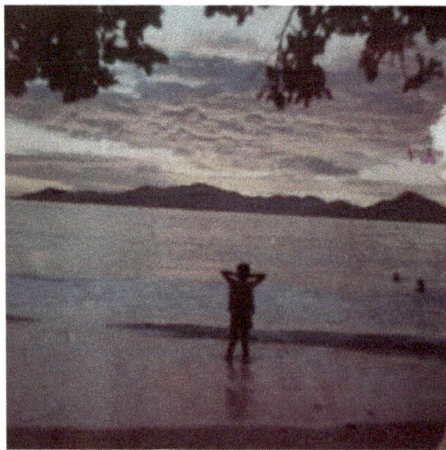

Saying Goodbye to the People and the Islands

Chapter 23

NEVER ENDINGS, ALWAYS BEGINNINGS

"The moments we share are the moments we keep forever."

–Author Unknown

Passports, money, and destination, and out the door we went. In a deep sensuous state of preoccupation between grieving reluctance and anticipatory excitement, we began to plan the return circuitry. We had to first get back to the main island, Mahe. We'd heard from some of our guests about freighters going to Karachi, Pakistan sometimes taking on passengers; having used that simple and cheap method several times in the past. From there, we reckoned we could trek our way back to Europe and to the States. (Simple enough, huh? Ha, ha.)

With a continued aggregation of unresolved mixed feelings, we said goodbye to those we had become close to on La Digue, uprooted ourselves, and took the ferry boat to Victory; seashells, coco-de-mer, tons of memories in haul. And, within a seemingly short time, we were the only Western passengers, much less circuit riders, on a Pakistan freighter plowing northward through the Indian Ocean to Karachi; 2,280 nautical miles to be exact.

It was a deeply reflective journey, reviewing our traveling experiences thus far. Travel-hardened, we knew we could easily sustain the circuitry home; again, the word "home". The "how, when, and where" of the return ride did not concern us; like a vehicle going downhill. We knew we would get there! But the uncertainty of "home" pervaded our unconsciousness.

The captain gave permission for us to dine with him and the officers at the captain's table. It was intriguing to watch the crew member break for prayer time with their prayer rugs and have one of the officers pointing out to them the direction of Mecca. Their dedication was sincere and admirable; even as the seas of the Indian Ocean rolled around.

Karachi hit like a bomb shell of overloaded stimulation! All the layers of serenity absorbed during the months on the islands was suddenly dissipated by the hustle and bustle of 3 million people rushing around: seemingly going nowhere, and everywhere. The real world? What had we done!? Left Paradise for what? For this? Smog, horns blaring, tall buildings, loudspeakers pounding out unknown sounds, and people; people everywhere.

We knew we had to get out of there, and <u>fast</u>!

But fast was a rather relative reality for us, when considering each new culture, city, monetary system, food, language adjustments, and eliminating digestive wastes. All of which took time; time for adjusting. ("<u>Adjust or adjust</u>" was a euphemism often heard.)

We hopped on a series of cheap buses to Hyderabad, then on to Kaipur, and finally to Quetta; in anticipation of crossing the border to Afghanistan. The trips were long and arduous; again, in the old uncomfortable buses, crossing mostly barren lands and some mountains, sprinkled with small villages with flat roofs and few people. Somehow the uncomfortableness of the buses seemed less uncomfortable than on the original rides last year from Turkey to India.

The running of the slow buses covered nearly 500 miles, and most of the food was very spicy hot; eating lamb kabob, rice, flat chapatti bread, and yogurt, if lucky. For drinks, it was hot weak tea and bottled water; when available. We met none of our like-minded circuit riders on this route. So, we were beginning to feel a little isolated.

The boarder crossover trip from Quetta, Pakistan to Kandahar, Afghanistan was short (150 miles) and without incident. The Pakistani officials had no concern for us leaving Pakistan heading into

Afghanistan because we would be leaving Pakistan, not entering with hashish. Whereas the Afghanistan border guards were smiling and happy to stamp our passports and the customs officials did not check our bags.

Once in Kandahar, the atmosphere of moving around the city was without concerns and we were directed to a good hotel by travelers encountered at the bus station, who had a hard time separating from us because of their desire to know about our time in Bali and especially the Seychelles Islands.

The hotel had cold running water, a mid-sized bed, and a balcony for us to look over the city from the 3rd floor and watch the sunset; a habit we loved and had grown accustomed to. Dope was everywhere and easy to get, but we were a little shocked to know it now actually cost money; ever how little. Kandahar was close enough to Pakistan that we could sense the trade indulging influence between the countries.

Because of our desire to head westward toward Europe and America, it was an easy decision to bypass Kabul and bus-it the 350 miles directly to Herat; one of our favorite cities, anyway.

The bus ride to Herat was surprisingly easy. The terrain had few hills and no mountains, and the macadamized road was unusually smooth, despite the ancient slow-moving bus with irregular seats and nonadjustable windows. It was a typical Afghan bus. A ton of assorted boxes and hand-wrapped packages were tied or strapped to the outside top. The sides were painted in wild bright colors with large Islam symbols drawn in black; and of course, every seat was occupied. In addition to Arlene, there were 2 others, well covered, females: and an agitated goat. It was told to us by an Afghan, speaking broken English, that the road was built by the Soviets in the early 60's; but he didn't seem so happy about it.

It was a good road, but the bus was very slow, forcing an overnight journey. Arriving early in the morning, it was somewhat like returning home, buying some hot Naan bread directly out of the kindled ovens from a familiar corner shop and picking up a couple of lamb kabobs from a street vendor on the way to the same hotel.

Checking in, the owner said he remembered us from a year ago (questionable, whether he did actually remember us), then added 2 cold Coca Colas to our room tab.

Afterward, we went strolling down by the market streets, nodding our heads at the many circuit riders there. Probably because of our travel-tested personas many were attracted to us wanting to hear our tales of travel; as we had done with worn travelers on our way through the year before. Surprisingly, we met an American <u>family</u> of circuit riders. They were walking near a row of Afghan rug sellers because they were very intent on buying; at least a small one. They invited us back to their hotel, to sit in the lobby, smoke, and share experiences.

Theirs was of a higher quality hotel, and obviously more expensive; and it had a large lobby with a round table and soft chairs and couches surrounding it. The father's name was Howard, the mother/ wife Gloria, and, they had a 14-year-old son with them, Jeremy. They were completely self-disclosing about their story: Howard, now gaunt looking, had worked for a large corporation in California, Gloria had been involved in a non-profit company and was painfully thin, and Jeremy, energetic, was a high schooler, and hated it. They had liquidated all personal belongings and gave up their high-powered lifestyles because Gloria had uterine cancer.

So, to satisfy Gloria's wants, needs, and desires, and to get the most of her remaining life and their family time together, they decided to "travel the world". (Reminding us of a mid-1960's TV series called: "<u>Run for Your Life</u>" starring Ben Gazzara as a man with a terminal illness seeking adventure; until the end.) Theirs was a gentle family without remorse, fear, or anger, and definitely living in the moment; the now, more than ever. As circuit riders, they flew from California to London, traveled across Europe, Turkey, and now in Afghanistan; then were heading to India. After telling them of our time in Bali, the three quietly stared at each other for several minutes and nodded their heads. They were so easy going and so open and attractively loveable.

We shared many nights sitting in the hotel lobby together and were soon joined by a young Australian couple, the red-bearded Lucas, and the blonde Evie. They met while attending school in England and decided to travel overland as their way of returning to Australia.

Lucas had an obsession: he always wanted to be a cowboy as portrayed in the early American Western movies. Somehow, somewhere along our travels, I had acquired a pair of brown leather cowboy boots; and I showed them to Lucas. And he completely exploded with unbridled enthusiasm and said he would give me anything for this pair of well-worn boots. Even after trying them on, they appeared very tight and small for his foot size, he persisted in his desire to have them.

After verbalizing several different offers in quick succession, he said he would give me <u>anything</u> for the boots. In his emotional state, he held out his 2 hands, pleading. On his right hand was a gold ring, actually his high school graduating class ring. He saw me looking and said it was valuable because it was mostly gold. I had a secret motive for wanting gold, so I relented and made the deal: the boots for the ring. Lucas could not have been happier. Evie didn't seem so happy about it, but…

The motive for wanting the gold, especially while in Afghanistan, was to have a hand-crafted gold earring made. Lucas was okay with me having the gold melted down and stretched into a rounded sailor-type earring. All good.

But the problem was - none of my ear lobes had ever been pierced!

Enter Arlene! She remembered an old sail needle in the trusty doctor's bag used during the Indian Ocean crossing on the Binasu II. After that horrific storm it was to sew the seams in the jib blown open by the gale winds. It was a large needle with a few rusty spots.

I, (Arlene) cautiously agreed! Alcohol was impossible to acquire, but miraculously, we were able to connive the hotel owner into giving us a few small cubes if ice; an absolute necessity for this operation.

Thoroughly, washing the needle with soap and cold water and wiping it dry with a clean towel, I placed a cube of ice on the back side of Buck's left ear lobe and gently began to push the needle into the tough skin. The toughness of the earlobe caused me to stop and reflect on my ability, strength, and guts to accomplish this task. I knew Buck really wanted his ear pierced, so I girded myself and began to push the needle more aggressively through his earlobe, pushing, pushing, and pushing as Buck responded with a shriek with each push. Eventually, my persistence paid off and the needle broke through the lobe to the other side and into the ice. It was barely bleeding.

In an expert manner of someone familiar with the process, Arlene slightly separated the gold ring and forced it through the recently opened hole and closed the separation. It was done! And knowing the gold would not cause infection, I slept soundly that night. Miracles of miracles, it never got infected.

As our money was dwindling, we gave notice to the hotel owner that we would be leaving in a few days. He seemed truly dumbfounded! "Why" he argued? He countered our short-funded position by stating: "Not a problem, you can stay here for free!" It was our turn to be dumbfounded. Then, after a few minutes in his office, he came back to the counter, opened a 10" leather bag displaying an array of dazzling semi-precious stones. Including: several colors of quarts, small pieces of aquamarine, some turquoise, amethyst and 2 chunks of their beautiful lapis lazuli, and others we couldn't identify; all were unfinished and in natural form.

He could easily see we were attracted to the lapis lazuli, so he pushed 2 rough golf-ball size pieces of lapis to us; followed by pieces of beautiful amethyst quartz, and a red garnet.

"There," he gestured "for you." Adamantly refusing any money for the unfinished jewels, he returned to his office shaking his head in continued disbelief of why anyone would want to leave Afghanistan.

(The Hindu Kush Mountains are fabled for the variety of precious and semiprecious deposits. But their mines are also known for the gold, iron ore, coal, lithium, marble, petroleum and natural gas, rare-earth elements, as well as uranium; and more.)

The next discussion we had with the owner, gave us some insight into his motivation. He confirmed our feelings of a subtle but pervasive change over the Afghan culture from the time of our first visit, i.e., a slightly less happy-go-lucky tenor. He was distraught because many people from the Soviet Union were moving into Afghanistan, and not as tourists, but businessmen, contractors, and

168

other high-level professionals. And he didn't like them very much, preferring the non-threatening and peaceful hippie circuit riders.

(Of course, we consequently learned of the Soviet invasion that started in December 1979 and lasted until February 1989, in defeat at the hands of the mujahedeen supported by the USA, until February 1989. Again, my indignations are aroused by the thoughts of war. Then the USA invaded Afghanistan in 2001 under the guise of driving out the Taliban, morphed from the mujahedeen, preventing a base to the al-Qaeda. The USA military is still there, as of 2020, and has become America's longest war; but also doomed to be lost. More dastardly behavior by the warmongers of the world. But the will of the Afghan people, and the world, shall ultimately prevail.)

It was time for our last hurrah and to get out the front door.

We gathered the Howard, Gloria, and Jeremy family together, then Lucas and Evie before their departure, and had a marvelous full day together. Howard and Gloria loved our newly obtained jewels, and we liked their new Afghan clothing, and Lucas admired my earring while continuing to showoff his cowboy boots; as Evie seemed to have come around to accepting our bargain of boots for the ring. Then we shared a great lunch in the back-yard garden of Howard's hotel, sharing travel stories and histories of our pasts.

Someone said: "Let's take a picture!"

With great group cohesiveness, we went straight into the downtown marketplace and did what true friends would do. The one place in town with the word "PHOTO" hanging from the wall, was a man welcoming us into his world. For the picture, we were backed into a tiny, wood-framed spot against the wall with only a well-worn blanket loosely hanging in the background.

Actually, he was a "street photographer" and his shop was only a small, framed backdrop. His camera was of a large box-type mounted on an unsteady tripod requiring him to do some quick adjustments that we didn't pay much attention to. But he opened a small door in the back of the larger box, made more adjustments, and told us to be very still. Evie was agitated as Lucas tried unsuccessfully to display his boots in the picture. We all did the best we could to inter-communicate as one. He showed us the negative and we told him we wanted 3 copies; and he took a picture of the negative. (This process of photography is called <u>karma-e-faoree</u>, or Afghan Box.) The camera was reminiscent of the late 1800 in the U.S.A.

This picture continues to hang on the wall in our bedroom to this day; after 48 years. When I look at it, a flood of warm loving feelings and comforting memories fill my mind and soul. We remember those friendships, of those beautiful, idealized days of travel, and of an eternity of traveling circuits. No accidents when people meet, and the moments shared are of lasting value and an end in itself.

Classic Pic

That evening over dinner, we laughed at each other's look in the picture. The picture somehow captured our essence, the 7 of us, even though it looked like one of those "old tyme" western style pictures made in modern USA for nostalgia; also made in Australia. We smoked and lifted glasses of tea saluting each other, and vowed friendship forever; and to keep in touch. We exchanged mailing addresses; but sadly, we never saw or heard from them again. They were true circuit riders, and we loved them.

A lifetime of human experiences. All good experiences are balanced with the grungy ones. We knew we had to get moving again. Time was not on our side. On a rough bus ride to the border with Iran we fully felt the drawing need to return home, although it was with much reluctance on leaving Afghanistan. We crossed the border at Qaderabad; essentially retracing our steps from more than a year ago.

The outstanding memory when crossing the border was going through the customs check, no problem with immigrations. Our appearance gave us away for what we actually were; shoddily dressed traveling hippies. The leading customs officer literally called the two of us into his tiny ill-lighted office and asked many unmemorable questions. But the memory that remains was watching him sift through our backpacks, especially when he pulled out my shaving kit of toilet articles, zipped it open, and very slowly pulled the kit up to his face and directly under his nose. He gave a full lung inhale, hoping, we suspected, for a whiff of hash, or any illegal drugs.

(We can still see his oily skin, narrow mustache and squinting eyes holding the kit up to his face as he hopefully smelled; and was probably trained to do so. Luckily, we had no hash within our backpacks or doctors' bag. However…we did have a few grams of hash stored on our body. And again, fortunately, the customs officer had no reason for a strip-search, so he released us to continue our travels. If they would have found the hashish, we would have been locked in an Iranian jail never to be found and wouldn't be writing this story. Our angels were working overtime.)

The remainder of our time busing through Iran – Mashhad, Tehran, and onto Tabriz, near the Turkish border - was with few significant memories but highlighted by a few short often intense conversations at bus transfer stations with European circuit riders heading toward Afghanistan and India, some hoping for Nepal; albeit, sometimes responding with occasionally glazed eyes with the mention of Bali.

Our lack of recall for this period of circuit riding may have been because we were hardened travelers and were less in awe of everything. And, we had been there before. Or, it may be just the opposite, we were so aware of our total surroundings that we had little time for conscious invasion of specific details of people and places; instead allowing everything to automatically flow into our subconscious or super-conscious memory.

Chapter 24

EAST MEETS WEST AND
ANOTHER GOOD DEED

"The most important principle of divine philosophy is the oneness of the world of humanity, the unity of mankind, the bond conjoining East and West, the tie of love which blends human hearts." '

–Abdu'l-Bahá

The bus ride from Tabriz to the Turkish border, again, was slow, dusty, and uneventful. And passing through customs and immigrations was a breeze when compared to the crossing from Afghanistan into Iran; although the Turkish immigrations guy did have enlarged pupils while spending a little extra time viewing our passport pages - full of the many stamps from everywhere we'd been (but, of course, NO Israeli stamp).

Once inside the country of Turkey, it was an easy ticket purchase to good old-Erzurum because of the felt familiarity with its inhabitants and environment; having been there before and generally liking the cultural and academic surroundings, with a general look of old Russia. After an efficient overnight hotel rest, we boarded a bus going through Ankara and on to Istanbul. We were also feeling uplifted because the bus was a more-modern type with soft seats and air conditioning; and with windows that were actually easy to push up and pull down. It was our first modern bus trip since leaving the States and was to be about a 1,100-mile journey to Istanbul.

It was a long ride, and we don't remember exactly where it started, with this major incident; but sometime after we'd changed buses in Ankara. We were seated about 4 rows back from the driver and awakened by the sobbing eruptions of an Islam woman dressed in a traditional black burka with no face covering pleading with the driver for help – we assumed - because everyone spoke in Arabic. The bus driver was irritated and tended to ignore her while a man, dressed in a wrinkled Western suit, began pulling and screaming at her, again our assumptions, attempting to force her back to their seats. But she refused, clinging to the upright chrome poles by the driver; and now crying with her head bowled even lower.

Sensing a female in crisis, Arlene jumped to her feet and moved toward the young woman in an assertive motion. The driver, a heavy-set man in a short sleeved company shirt, tried to explain to Arlene, as best he could with limited English, what was happening. His agitation increased because, while trying to be empathetic with the woman and talk to Arlene, he was responsible for keeping a bus full of people on the road; all in the darkness of night. The disgruntled husband returned to his seats in the back of the bus; probably not wanting to appear as the bad guy. Both appeared as if they were in their late twenties, early thirties; so, from an age perspective, we could identify with them.

As best as I could ascertain, this was the problem: the husband was an unfaithful partner with several mistresses, so he was wanting to "get rid of" his wife by declaring her insane and the bus trip was designed to take her to an insane asylum near Istanbul and return to his wandering ways. In their culture, the men have all the rights and the feminine has little or no rights. This lady consented to the trip, but as they neared Istanbul she was hoping to be "rescued" before arriving at the mental institution because Turkish people were generally considered more liberal; perhaps more Western, than some of the more conservative countries. If for no other reason than the geographic nearness to Europe may seem influential.

I understood her feelings of desperation and helplessness and sitting next to her, held her hand and she began to calm down. She began to admire the various types of jewelry I was wearing, and I expressed liking her burka as we continued to hold hands, which showed no wedding band. The woman was emotionally exhausted and probably sleep deprived because she fell asleep soon thereafter and remained quiet through the remainder of the night.

Pulling into the Otogar Bus Station in Istanbul, the woman's husband grabbed her by the arm and ushered the somewhat dazed woman off the bus and into the crowd. I felt sad and helpless not being able to save her from her fate and of course never saw or heard from them again. I can still see her face clearly and feel the warmth of our connection, grateful that for a while she had some relief from her anxiety.

Istanbul was fabulous! We loved it! Strolling around the outside a mosque we experienced its unique structure and the pilgrims on their spiritual path; called the Blue Mosque because of the hand-painted blue tiles on the interior. After only a few minutes of walking around and paying the cost of admission, we then went inside. The Hagia Sophia Museum provided such eye-opening beauty. Built around 537 AD, and as the Eastern Orthodox Christian cathedral, it was the seat of Patriarch of Constantinople (the former name of Istanbul); then fell to the Ottoman Empire and converted into a mosque in 1453. But it remains an impressive structure with its giant dome, tall minarets, and combination of Christian and Muslin symbols.

And also, within walking distance, and actually paying again, we entered the Topkapi Palace; and were happy we did pay to get in. (What? Were we being hypocritical and playing tourists?). Once inside and encased was the single most beautiful <u>object</u> we'd ever seen, to this date. It was the **Topkapi dagger**. What a breathtaking stunner; and to say it was gem-encrusted would be like understating a cat has fur. The handle and sheath had a gold foundation, and the blade handle had 3 of the largest and most beautiful (Colombian) emeralds ever; sprinkled with sparkling diamonds. Thirty-one diamonds at the base of the sheath with another 21 diamonds higher up; and a diamond studded gold chain attached. Beyond words! It was created in the mid-18th century during the Ottoman Empire.

Such are memories.

Coming out of the Topkapi Palace, a young Turkish guy intercepted us and said: "Come with me." We followed him for about a 10 or 15-minute walk, during which he said nothing. He led us to – the now famous – Lale Restaurant; aka "Pudding Shop". We could see the Blue Mosque and Hagia Sophia from there. We'd heard stories about this place from a couple of circuit riders along paths of our travel from Afghanistan and Eastward. It was like any ordinary restaurant with plain off-white and somewhat stained walls, a few pictures and paintings, some big couches to lounge on, and an ordering bar.

Except for the staff, every customer was a circuit rider, or facsimile thereof; many of them staring at the large bulletin board near the door. On it were myriad of hand-written notes; mostly asking for rides or cheap hotels eastward, to Afghanistan, India, or Nepal. Some were just love notes and others were anti-war statements. We ordered some baklava and a dish of their famous pudding (pounded chicken breast, rice flour, milk, sugar, and topped with cinnamon), and soon were in travel conversations. By this time, most of the conversations were simple or naïve; almost irritating.

Unimpressed, we moved on.

A memory that remains vivid was our walk along the waters of the Bosporus Straight. As usual, and as was true most of the time, we were needing to *eat*. And to our delight, we were about to experience one of the great treats of Istanbul; or anywhere. Casually walking, we encountered many colorful boats tied to the quays selling fish sandwiches, a simple yet delicious nutritious meal.

Called _balik ekmek_ by the Turks, it consisted of grilled white fish from the Bosporus, raw onions, and some greens on a half loaf of elongated warmed bread. Vat a deal! And, so incredibly good and cheap, I ate two! Arlene had one.

Memory is a funny thing. A veritable storehouse of wealth.

And, of course, what trip to Istanbul would be complete without a visit to a Turkish bath? We went to the closest one, walked inside, and were soon separated, to the feminine side, and to the male side. We didn't see each other until the experience ended.

After undressing and having a thorough bath with buckets of hot water splashed over me, I was given a white towel and permitted to enter the main chamber. It seemed rather dark at first, giving my eyes time to adjust, and the interior was of graying stoned archways on tall pillars. The large pools of water gave off copious amounts of steam; refreshing my travel withered body and thirsty soul. I leaned and rested against the marbled edge of the largest of the steaming pools looking up.

High above this main pool was a large concaved domed ceiling with intricately inlaid squared pieces of thick glass circling around the dome, getting obviously smaller nearer the top. The apex was fitted with a cluster of the same glass, but without an apparent pattern. Then, as my inner self quieted down, I began to see and hear the somewhat heavy droplets of moisture falling from the many pieces of glass from the dome resulting from the rising steamed water. And I swear (not done often), the sequencing of the droplets into the water began to have a melodic sound as if coordinated with the height and separate distances of the glass inlays.

At one time, the direct rays of the sun shone through the ceiling glass squares creating a series of dynamic light rays brightening one side of the bath, causing me to wonder how old this bath was and how many people have had the joyous opportunity of using it: probably hundreds of years old, and thousands of visitors from many places around the world. It was a hallmark memory.

My experience was less appreciative of the surroundings, feeling somewhat awkward surrounded by nude strangers. I do remember admiring the enormity and antiquity of the baths. I so appreciated the warmth of the water and for the first time since Katmandu felt clean.

Totally refreshed, we knew it was time to plot our continued movement Westward toward Europe. We had no idea of exactly where we were going or how to get there. Our habitual modus operandi was the cheapest way possible without much regard for challenging hardships or possible dangers. We had faith in the circuits.

Passports, money, and destination, and out the front door we go.

Chapter 25

THE LONG AND WINDING ROAD – TO THE US OF A

"…We're on our way home/We're going home… you and I have memories/longer than the road that stretches out ahead"

–Two of Us, The Beatles

We departed from Turkey at Edirne riding on another comfortable bus for the (approx.) 400-mile overnight trip to Belgrade, Yugoslavia.

(Yes, it was still called Yugoslavia. Yugoslavia as a country ended in 1980 after the death of Dictator Josip Tito, and consequently broke up into Bosnia & Herzegovina, Croatia, Macedonia, Montenegro, Serbia, and Slovenia. Kosovo was also a part of that dividing up of land. National countries may do better to be uniting and seek strength in their ethnicities, instead of using that as a reason for division. Paramount to world peace is the necessity of world's leadership (religious and political) to grow in the understanding of the 2 principles of <u>sovereignty</u> = the part and the whole!)

Interesting enough, our main memory of Belgrade was the small hotel room we rented from an older, plump, gray-haired lady, with a continuous slight smile. It was a medium sized room, but full of beautiful wooden furniture; making it seem small. There was a very tall and darkly stained closet and a long dresser with tight drawers. But most impressive, and memorable to us, was the headboard to the bed. It was obviously hand-carved with several types of unusually shaped animals surrounded by an elaborate array of leaves and flowers. The overall headboard was outlined in a darker stained wood carved in indistinguishable but in a beautifully consistent pattern.

Funny, the things remembered.

Getting a cheap bus trip ticket from Belgrade to Milan, Italy, sounded good, so we booked it. Being in Italy gave us a definite feeling of being in the Western world and closer to home. And, although Milan was considered a fashion capital, few people seemed to care about our out-of-place dress which was an eclectic combination of many cultures and places we had been. But naturally, Italy had a hippie population, too.

The food was outrageously plentiful, good, and cheap with the benefit of being able to eat anything without worry of "the crud". We wanted to see Leonardo da Vinci's painting of "The Last Supper" but getting in the Santa Maria delle Grazie proved to be difficult, and expensive; still regrettable. So, we hung-out at the Simpione Park warming in the afternoon sun; resting and fantasizing our next move to get us closer to the States.

Sitting on an isolated bench staring at the peaceful surroundings of green trees and beautiful array of flowers in the park, we began chatting with a young Italian hippie (are the words young and hippie redundant?) who was alone and casually passing by. Let's call him Lorenzo. Lorenzo seemed like a pretty cool guy with long black stringy hair and a very thin face. He was short with a slim body but talked and projected a strong, almost baritone voice. His English enunciations were good, although his grammar needed an occasional correction; corrections he encouraged. Our Italian was limited to the usual few words learned from our American culture.

I knew more Italian than Buck since my best next-door neighbor and best friend growing up was Italian. I spent many hours in her home listening to her grandmother speak Italian and enjoying the scrumptious food!

We spoke mostly superficial hippie-talk about the continuing Vietnam War, excessive materialism, and repressive governments around the world; and, of course, how drugs should be legalized. He expressed amazement at our time in Kathmandu, Nepal. The conversation took a more serious turn when Lorenzo said he may be driving to Amsterdam within a few days and asked us if we wanted to travel there with him. He had a car, and only expected us to help with paying for the petrol fuel; about a 650 or 700-mile journey. He talked in rapid short sentences.

Without much discussion or realizing our serendipitous luck, we said "yes" nearly simultaneously. He requested we be at this same bench in the Simpione Park the next day and would then confirm the details of the trip to Amsterdam. Again, we gave a strong affirmative. Without asking at which <u>pension</u> we were lodging, Lorenzo changed his mind and asked us to return to this bench site ready to go with belongings by early noon the next day. We thought the whole episode was a bit odd; but much of our circuit riding was odd and faith-filled by this time.

Sure enough, Lorenzo arrived at the park bench site greeting us just before noon. He asked us, in a low ominous tone, if we were carrying any dope, and we said "yes", having a small piece of hash tucked in Arlene's underwear. He smiled, said "Good" and waved to stuff our backpacks in the opened front <u>lid/boot</u> of the aging Volkswagen; the engine being in the rear. He had surprisingly little personal belongings on board; from what we could ascertain.

And away we went, driving North toward the gradually empowering Alps, with the anticipation and enthusiasm of an early morning hiker. We sat together in the back seat.

Viewing the snow-capped Alps in Italy kept us at peace and nearly speechless. And even as we effortlessly crossed the border into Switzerland, our mesmerizing gaze continued skyward. We passed by what seemed like a very long and beautiful lake and were soon in Ticino. Stopping only for soda and sandwiches, Lorenzo insisted on continuing, disappointing us with the little time for absorbing the magnificent beauty.

It was nighttime when we reach the border town of Basel near Germany, and we were expecting to look for a cheap place to spend the night and relax. But again, Lorenzo pressed for continuing. After all, it was <u>his</u> trip. We sensed him becoming more hyper and anxious with each border crossing; not the happy-go-lucky guy at our first meeting. We were shivering cold since this Volkswagen had a very poor mechanical heating system.

Crossing the border into Germany at late night didn't instill confidence; but there we were. They closely checked Lorenzo's vehicle papers first, then looking under the body of the Volkswagen with mirrors they asked a few questions in Italian and stamped his passport and papers. The guard, unarmed, shined the flashlight on us and our passports, and asked us to get out of the vehicle; with our backpacks and doctor's bag and asked if this was our total belongings; in near perfect English.

On a table inside a large near-empty and uninspired and undecorated room, 2 guards went through our belongings; as the proverbial saying goes: as if <u>with a fine-tooth comb</u>! Again, our appearance betrayed our counterculture habits. After finding no contraband or drugs, they carefully watched as we replaced everything, stamped our passports, smiled, and said we were free to leave which was music to our ears! We'd only been on the road for around 12 hours. It seemed like forever.

Lorenzo appeared much lighter and with a brighter confidence driving into Lörrach, Germany where we stopped for a few hours of sleep in the VW. Awakening at daybreak, he drove through Germany persistently, but within the speed limits, almost as if robotically possessed. Arlene and I nodded off frequently. He appeared to have a strategy of bypassing all the major cities, which was fine with us.

We just remembered the "Cologne" city signs, the "Düsseldorf" lights as dreamlike. Crossing the border into Netherlands from Germany was a breeze, since the border guards just checked our passports. Lorenzo's entire demeanor changed, to calm, smiling, and laughter. And in less than an hour we were in Amsterdam. It seemed like only yesterday we were in Herat, Istanbul, Milan, and now Amsterdam.

Ah, the wonders of traveling; circuit riding! Adjusting to the many wonderful cultures, languages, and lifestyles and feeling the rhythm of the buses, planes, trains, boats, and automobiles had morphed our bodies and minds into a human jazzy type of improvisation.

Lorenzo dropped us off at a youth hostel in the Jordaan area and, after thanking him profusely, he drove off and we never saw him again.

(We didn't know for certain, but we later suspected he was most likely transporting drugs from Italy to Amsterdam and using us as a type of decoy; diverting the attention of border authorities.)

The Amsterdam hostel was fabulously accommodating! The English-speaking desk clerks, one male and one female, were most helpful in making us comfortable with having a space to sleep, showing the clean bathrooms, explaining our location in the city, understanding the pot laws, and directing us to their large living room which was well populated with a horde of variegated circuit riders: and fresh hot tea. The smell of pot, while not prevalent, was detectable. We felt rewarded with a great sense of inclusion, reminiscent of the feelings of belonging in Afghanistan yet in a more modern version.

The canal bridges, mostly open-air cafes, the multi-colored tall-bricked buildings, and good food made it all seem so refreshing! We could drink out of any water fountain or spigot we saw; and most people could speak in relatable English. But…one overlaying problem remained: we were running out of money; the Bitches Brew (Miles David)!

The universe economy happens by intake and output; and not to be escaped. We knew this, or at least learned it over time.

We held many and long discussions with our travel comrades, most of whom were travel-wise; especially about getting from North America to Europe. The consistent message for cheapest transport to the US was by air from London to New York; and, if we were lucky, we could catch a chartered flight; the absolute cheapest from Amsterdam to London was by bus.

Passport, money, and destination, and out the front door we went.

Leaving two days later, and with a tingling of reluctance, we were sleeping on the bus heading to London as it ferried across the English Channel.

After an efficient bus ride from Aldgate Bus Station to Heathrow Airport we made a flurry of inquiries on charter flights to New York. Surprisingly there were quite a few. We learned of a US charter flight arranged by <u>birdwatchers</u>, of all things, which had come to England. Unexpectedly, permission to travel with this group on their chartered flight had to be granted by the civilian organizer of the event; an always smiling mild fellow. He looked us up-and-down and correctly assessed we would be unable to afford to pay much for a seat on the plane. Jumping at the offer of $100 each, the organizer said he would clear it with the airline manifest. We were to be ready to leave the following morning with passports and shot records in hand.

We slept uncomfortably on the Heathrow carpeted floor that night.

Arriving early, we received tickets and cleared customs and immigration, and were guided to two seats on the left side just over the wing. We were still feeling a little like being in "The Twilight Zone" because of the circumstances and speed with how it all happened that we were so quickly guided to a plane flying back to the US; and to New York, no less.

It was just about 2 years after the wedding and our departure.

The cabin seats were completely filled. They were all Americans with clean well-scrubbed faces, brightly colored clothes, and well-trimmed hair. Some couples, but mostly men, with lots of cameras and binoculars in cases appearing upper-middle class. Everyone seemed cheerful, happy to be going home, too. <u>Our</u> dusty crusty appearance, multicultural well-worn clothes, and long hair were obvious and starkly marked us for separation. Our minimal interaction was opposite of the experience at the youth hostel in Amsterdam. Most assuredly it was not the first time nor the last time we experienced that division. We just did not "fit in". Or was it, by now, <u>they</u> did not fit in"?

About mid-flight across the Atlantic, the captain announced that, due to weather conditions, it would be impossible to land in New York City and that Philadelphia was the alternate airport landing destination. The airlines were arranging for buses to transport the passengers to NY from Philadelphia. Most of the passengers began expressing discontent after the captain informed everyone that the bus trip to NY's Grand Central Station was not free and would have to be paid for by each passenger, because of the charted flight status. It especially shocked us because, after paying the plane trip, we were left with only the cost of the bus and pocket change to our name.

It felt good to be back in my birth state of Pennsylvania and in Philadelphia; only a short distance to Lancaster County where the images of gooey shoofly pie, warm salted soft pretzels, and hot cheese steak sandwiches made my mouth watery. Just thinking about it, imagining the taste of it all, punctuated the memories of those early years of misbehavior.

But no time for that! Upon arrival, we were shepherded onto a bus, as were all passengers, and promptly motoring on our 100-mile journey to New York and Grand Central Station. Sitting on soft cushioned seats with a slightly cool air-conditioning breezing past our faces produced a certain satisfaction and a feeling of equality with the passengers.

We had been in many "grand" and many "central" stations during the past 2 years throughout the world, but none compared to New York's Grand Central station. The station's Celestial Ceiling with the 12 zodiac constellations, the big golden clock facing in 4 directions, the mesmerizing stained-glass windows; on and on. It truly was grand!!!

*I was now in my familiar environment and quickly found our way to the system of subways, changing once, leading us to the 86th St. and 20th Ave. station in Bensonhurst, Brooklyn. We had barely enough coins in our pockets to get through the gates; but still had the (scam & unusable) set of American Express Travelers Checks. I called my parents from Grand Central station to let them know we were on the way home with **10 cents** to spare. I vowed never again to worry about having more than enough money to do everything God wanted me to do. No perfection on that one!*

Chapter 26

STILL ANOTHER CIRCUIT TO RIDE

"What we've got here is failure to communicate".

– **"Cool Hand Luke", 1967 movie**

(It would have been easy and pedestrian to end our travel-adventure stories of circuit riding here; at the time we had made it back to Brooklyn. Much of the familiar culture had changed a lot during the missing 2 years, while much had remained the same causing much bantering and some serious deliberations. Finally, we agreed on the importance of additional chapters for you, our beloved reader, to peruse. Hopefully, this would give a fuller in depth understanding of us; and the circumstances of why and how we ended up in Pueblo, CO as our nesting place.)

The arrival reception received from Lilly and Louie (the parents) was widely mixed; reminiscent of The Fiddle on the Roof song: **Sunrise, Sunset**... *"...laden with happiness and tears♪"*. Like all caring parents, they were supremely happy to see us home safe and sound after a 2-year absence; most of which was incognito. We had our first hot-water shower in a long time, followed by one of Lilly's scrumptious meals, and they put us up in their front room by 21st Ave. on a foldout couch bed. Great for us!

My parents had bought this, the first home they owned when I was 9 years old, and the room was originally a porch which was now closed in with big bay windows. It was the family T.V. room also used for large family gatherings. Comforting, memories flooded my mind, as I thought of the Passover Seder celebrations. My parents were verbally and visibly concerned about our future and expressed the stress they experienced while we were traveling and out of touch for months at a time. Privately, my dad shared with me a story about my mom when, one night about a year before, she awoke in a near-panic state; saying she saw me in pitch darkness and feared for my life. Crying, she was nearly inconsolable. Perhaps a dream, but the feelings lasted with her for a long time. It was a sharp and clear reminder of the near-death experience I had while sailing the Binasu II during a severe gale while crossing the Indian Ocean. There was a symbiotic connection between us, my intense thoughts about my mother during those moments of dire stress, and her waking up in a type of nightmarish trance, at probably the same time. Coincidence? Probably not! Just an example of the significance of human interconnectedness, despite distance or circumstances, it remains an incident that will surely remain a part of our relationship forever.

Over the next few days, we had long discussions with them about our adventures, illuminations, elations, and the sheer drawing power of travel fulfilling our deepest needs. They tried to understand, but it soon became obvious they were not grasping the significance of our journey; especially when compared to their travels as teenagers fleeing from the Pogroms in Poland/Russia. They talked much about themselves, Arlene's 2 brothers, and the relatives.

Lilly was especially elated that we returned with the leather jackets she bought us at the beginning of the journey. A quick realization creased a smile across her face when noticing the many scraps and scratches on the jackets that could have been on our bodies. Louie's seltzer water business was continuing to go strong; although he admitted "Carrying the boxes of bottles is getting heavy".

We knew the honeymoon was over when Lilly asked: "Buck, did you ever want to be a girl?" in a baffled reaction to the round gold earring in the pierced left ear lobe; at the hands of Arlene in Afghanistan. Responding generically, I said it was a common practice of sailors. With the long hair and beard, this was a not-so-subtle reaction to an unknown culture, and with some anxiety.

It was time to get started, again, looking toward the next circuit.

Good fortune was about to smile on us again. And why? Who knows? Are these things foreordained and predestined, by strings being pulled from above or from within our minds? Or was it just blind luck and pure chance, happenstance? There are so many things that

186

happen in our life it's difficult to pinpoint the cause or causes, and sequence of events leading to an experience or experiences. But, invariably choosing to gain the most out of that or those experiences coming our way, according to the cumulative result of the wild combination of heredity and environment.

It was the next chapter.

Memory is a funny thing! My one plus your one can equal a thousand.

I began telephoning every colleague and contact I could remember, asking for information on available jobs with my degree, skills, and background; anywhere! I can't remember who, but someone responded and said a teaching position was available at Florida Tech University in Orlando, FL. I called the head of the Psych Department, and, as if out of desperation, they did a telephone query and hired me without a face-to-face interview. It was a one-year position as an associate professor filling in for a professor on sabbatical. PLUS, the school was willing to pay for our flight down from NY and help find a place to live.

And out the front door we went, one more time, and with money, passports, and destination.

We were in Florida about 10 days before the start of the school year, moved into a one-story house with several orange, lemon and grapefruit trees; and, most incredibly, there was a large papaya tree in the backyard. One of the staff in the Psychology Department had a decent old Chevy he sold us for cheap; so we were ready to rock n' roll!

But cultural problems befell us! There was this saying: "You don't get any further South than Florida." It was another struggle of "us against them" or the conformist vs. the nonconformist or hippies vs. the … Well, you got the idea.

(Also, Disney World had just opened in October 1971, and NASA was launching Saturn rockets from the Kennedy Space Center only 75 miles away - so the feeling in administration at Florida Tech and the city officials was to present Orlando as "squeaky clean".)

Arlene's tenure in the Psychology Department and at FTU was rough, to say the least. Her attire was reflective of our lifestyle: long skirts and loose blouses, usually with bright colors and tie dyed, and lots of jewelry. And I continued with my beard, long hair, and earring. Consequently, selected types of faculty and students were attracted to Arlene; others were turned off. Many of the foreign students fully accepted her; especially those from Costa Rica.

I began to have a series of "encounter groups"; sometimes called T-groups or sensitivity groups in one of my psychology classes. It was about small group process, and through the interaction with each other, problem solving, and role playing, participants could gain insights into themselves, their relationships and cooperative group process. Psychologist Dr. Fritz Perls initiated the encounter groups in 1964 and practiced at the Esalen Institute in Big Sur California and continues today.

All was well and good until one of my students, a man in his early 30's, participating in the encounter groups began filing for divorce. The angry wife went directly to the Dean and complained that I (and the encounter groups) was the cause of their divorce proceedings. Without debate or reasonable discussion, the encounter groups were promptly and unceremoniously ordered ended. Such was life in those days.

Another memorable experience centered on a 70-year-old female student. I had agreed to drive her home after classes since she did not drive. Consistently, I would come home and complain of feeling tired which was unlike me, since I typically felt energetic and positive. Eventually, I told the woman that I would no longer be able to drive her home after classes because of this tiredness. The woman quickly responded in a clear and sincere voice: "You're right! Every time I get around you, I take in your positive energy. You're always so positive!" Well, that ended that!

The next event was a radio talk show. Having established a reputation for bringing fresh ideas as a teacher, and being new in town, I was invited to be interviewed on a local progressive radio talk show with a young and friendly DJ. After the usual pleasantries opening the hour-long interview, followed by my history, education, and current activities, the DJ began asking a series of controversial questions. He asked about my views on marijuana, which I responded to by reporting the pros and cons. And of course, I presented myself as an anti-Vietnam war advocate. But the clincher came when asked if I believed people were born into sin! With passion and some righteous indignation, I gave a strong response that was neither Christian nor Jewish but represented modern thinking – that children are born naturally positive and that emotions as guilt and shame are learned.

Well…there was a heavy backlash from that and from the whole talk-show in general. Granted, the DJ was purposefully instigating controversy and succeeded with my interview. Again, feedback from talk show listeners, faculty, and students at school, and even some worrisome telephone callers had a negative effect. But I had supporters also; some students, young acquaintances, and the lady I had been driving home. The fallout from this interview resulted in me being asked to leave my position as soon as possible with pay, since my contract was good until the end of June. I graciously declined, feeling loyal to my students, and continued to teach until the end of the school year.

And that was just the ending of the first semester!

We consciously decided to divert all the unwanted negative energy into works of creativity. Since moving to Orlando, we became vegetarian. We occasionally ate a little fish, but Arlene became an expert at cooking soybean dishes, and we cultured our own yogurt. And we easily picked oranges, lemons, and grapefruit from our backyard trees, with an occasional papaya.

The creative part came when we made a vegetarian cookbook called: "Cosmic Cookbook – A Natural High" (which we still have, and recently shared with our sons and their wives.)

It was 26 pages long of Arlene's recipes and most pages with my drawings. The introduction said: "Remember, we love you, so have a nice trip" and concluded with:

"INTUITIVE TRUTH:

✞ Life is pursuing knowledge relating to the oneness of the universe and the cosmos. You can make it joyful – love is. Truth lies within; all else is illusion of rational ego. Discover all of yourself, and you know all there is to know. It's free and happening NOW; you live what you believe. The path begins at home with a body in tune with nature and a mind soothed by meditation.

✞ Eliminate all refined foods, especially sugar – it's valueless. Replace sugar with honey; white flour with whole grains; brown rice, etc. Gradually phase out of or eat lean meat. Alcohol, coffee, tobacco, uppers, and downers are no-noes.

✞ Breathing exercises, lots of sleep, proper eating, and regular workouts are necessary habits. Books and people only guide; you become aware of your own vibration level by knowing yourself through life's experiences.

✝ These recipes offer alternate eating habits without refined foods and meat. It'll blow your mind.

And in conclusion: "Dedicated to the Universal Unity in God"

In retrospect, the cookbook was a good collaborative effort, albeit very amateurish, but still amazes us when reviewing. The symbol used above equating the Egyptian's hieroglyphic representation for love and eternal life. Also, in our haphazard and shortsighted philosophical/theological conclusions we naively <u>missed</u> one very important aspect (learned consequently, as timed passed), of the significance of unselfish service to our brothers and sisters. But eventually, we got it!

For the next creative project, I bought an old dining room coffee table and used the top as a canvas on which to paint. It was about 40" X 20" and 4" thick. Then, in very strong and bright colors of red, white, and blue, I painted an American flag on the surface of the table; followed by an intricate painting of the 50 stars. Next came the finish: a quart of spar urethane for boats which I gently brushed over the entire table; legs included. After allowing it to dry, steel wool was used for smoothing the raised tiny spots; followed by another coat of spar urethane. Five times this process was completed until the finished product looked like a shiny precious stone. (Keeping in mind, those were the days when flag desecration – burning or otherwise – was considered a huge sign of national disrespect.)

Many house guests commented on the flag-table because it seemed like a glowing gem and several inquired if it was for sale; and was eventually sold prior to our departure.

Another great experience was watching the <u>night</u> launch of a Saturn V rocket carrying 3 astronauts in December 1972. There were an estimated 50,000 mesmerized observers near the Kennedy Launch Center watching: a truly indelible sight.

Shortly after the beginning of the second semester, I brought home a book and plopped it on the flag-table and said: "Here, take a look at this and see what you think." I was teaching a course on personality, and one of my students, a Vietnam

Vet with PTSD (Post Traumatic Stress Disorder), gave me this book. I remember him saying: "If you want to learn something about personality not found in any psychology book, read this!" He admitted to never having read the entire book, but said he somehow felt it was the truth!

It was a large hardbound book with a white and blue cover of 2,097 pages (referred to as **The Book**). *I, on the other hand, had absorbed volumes of books acquiring my Ph.D. and didn't want to read another big book. I also was satisfied with my new-found faith and a personal relationship with an all-loving God who gives us free will. However, after about 2 months of observing Buck reading* **The Book**, *he became more sensitive and responsive to my needs and in general more loving. I then became intrigued and was motivated to read at least part four of the book about the life and teachings of Jesus. I enjoyed reading biographies about people who were inspirational, and it helped me in my own growth about living the good life.*

I had been currently absorbing D.T. Suzuki's: "Zen Buddhism"; plus, our travels in the major religious cultures allowed for open-mindedness and new sources of thought. But perusing the table of contents of this book let me know I was in for an incredibly big ride on the mental/spiritual circuits. (In time, it would be *the* transformative experience of our lives thus far.)

By midway through the 2nd semester, we had gathered with a selected group of students and friends for evening discussions; about anything and everything. A few of the foreign students were from Costa Rica. We had recently acquired one of the great all-time counterculture books *"The Last Whole Earth Catalogue – Access to Tools"* put together by Steward Brand. It was a mind blower; to say the least!

On the front cover was a spectacular picture; the first American photograph of the "whole earth" taken November 9, 1967, the from Apollo 4 spacecraft at a distance of 9,850 miles. The opening statement began with: "We are as gods and might as well get good at it." It was a very large 450-page paperback covering an endless array of everything from Buckminster Fuller, Synergetic, General Systems Theory (first I'd heard of it), and even Maslow's Hierarchy of Needs, and drawings with instructions for building chicken coops. And each topic provided instructions for mail ordering (hard mail; hee, hee). We found ourselves reading about subjects we didn't understand but loved it because it was riding mentally expanding new circuits.

Of course, a favorite part of "The Last Whole Earth Catalogue" was a fictional story threaded through the entire book with several paragraphs on nearly every page, entitled: "Divine Right's Trip" by Gurney Norman. It was a story about a guy, and usually with a gal, driving across the US in a mini VW van during the late 60's, who was stoned most of the time; or on something. The many storied adventures and people encountered by DR (Divine Right) during the journey were fun and fascinating.

My favorite was the story of The Lone Outdoorsman. DR and his woman, Estella met The Lone Outdoorsman at a campground site. The Lone Outdoorsman was polar opposite of DR because usually he carried an automatic rifle, a pistol, and wore a military-style helmet. He invited DR and Estella for a steak BBQ by his tent, and DR asked him why it was he always armed himself. His reply was classic: "Well," he said, "…**you never know**…" DR continued to press him, and The Lone Outdoorsman again replied: "Well…**you never know**…you know…**trouble**!"

Chapter 27

THE GRAND EXPERIMENT

"I have nothing new to teach the world. Truth and Non-violence are as old as the hills. All I have done is to try experiments in both on as vast a scale as I could."

–Mahatma Gandhi

As often happens while brainstorming when collectively high, we, probably 15 to 17 in the group, made up mostly by Arlene's students and their friends, somehow came up with the wild notion of creating our own community; of living on a spiritual commune! The ultimate "turn on, tune in, drop out" scenario as advocated by the then very-popular Timothy Leary. After several <u>sober</u> gatherings discussing the real possibility of an actual <u>commune</u>, we began to look at any and all possibilities; the where, when, and how's of it.

Enrique, the obvious and natural leader of the Cost Ricans in the group, boldly stated his family owned lots of mountain land in Costa Rica and was certain they would grant permission for us to "live off the land". Gary, one of the non-student friends, proudly said he knew of some old school buses, and as a mechanic, he could pick out a good one for us to fix into a camper and drive from Orlando to Costa Rica. It was a mere 3,400 miles of engine time; give or take. Eric and Rosalie, a young handsome couple, had recently consummated a fairly large dope deal and had plenty of cash to help get the project started with little or no financial strain. Doreen and Henry were fully behind it. Doreen was heavy-set with a sweet smile and Henry was thin with a mustache; and constantly in-and-out of a relationship of intimacy.

Each was amazed at the other's acts of selflessness and cooperation while inputting enormous amounts of positive energy into a project so unfamiliar; and get it off the ground. But such was the group energy displayed in eagerness for travel, adventure, and desire to seek a new way of living.

For me and Arlene, anticipating the non-renewal of the teaching contract at FTU, it was an easy decision to make when the regular school year ended.

Selling the car and what little furniture we'd accumulated would be a piece-of-cake, especially the waterbed. The various tools and kitchen utensils we'd gathered would be saved for the commune, along with several selected books. By this time, **_The Book_** had me enthralled and hooked, absorbing hefty portions of it into my consciousness daily. Much of it was beyond my comprehension as the student admitted when giving it to Arlene. On practically every page something would jar my consciousness into a higher level, seemingly propelling my spirit into the cosmos.

An inner echo said it was truth.

Led by Gary, he and I traveled north from Orlando looking at some old school buses. We returned with a well-scarred yellow 1955 Ford school bus with 80,000 miles already on it: but road worthy. We bought it because of the roof rack and rear ladder, most of the seats had been removed, and almost all the windows were in one piece and easily slid up and down. Gary said the engine was reliable because it was a Ford and would be easy for him to overhaul and find spare parts for it along the way. Structurally it was sound. We paid $300 for it and considered ourselves lucky.

With increased teamwork, we completely removed all remaining seats, overhead bins, and linoleum flooring, then painted it; inside and out. Two windows needed replacing, and 2 new tires were put on. On the outside we touched up all the rust spots with whatever color of paint available. Then came the <u>final touch</u>. With complete consensus we painted, in 12" bright red letters, **GOD IS LOVE** across the outsides; figuring it would protect us from the police, _bandidos_, demons, and other miscreants.

We'd been listening to a lot of the Moody Blues and Santana music; both playing loudly when working on the bus. All our community-making and survival equipment ordered from <u>The Catalogue</u> had trickled in, tents stoves, etc., as we all began; excitedly exhorting the feeling of "This is <u>really</u> gonna happen!"

The personal love between Arlene & I strengthened during this time. It was difficult to describe how or why because love was like that, and at a time when we felt the bond could get no stronger. But it was a period of transformations, acts of selflessness, a union of souls, and actualizing potentials. Traveling throughout the world with someone inculcates that myriad of experiences, mutual decision-making, and multi-growth levels as to render a relationship inexpressibly united. No differences of thought, feeling, or action could or would separate that. We simply wanted each other to be the best we could be and supported each other in doing that.

Our team was slowly but solidly coming together as we got closer to the departure date. Interesting because of the initial hang-out group there were many volunteers willing to make the trip to Costa Rica and build a spiritual commune. But when push came to shove, and when it came time for applying for passports, only the loyalists remained. Nine of us, out the front door we went and into our **Yellow Rider**; Gary, the mechanic; Enrique & Mauricio, two native Costa Ricans; Henry & Doreen, the couple that wasn't; Eric & Rosalie, the wanna-be Circuit Riders; and us as Ma & Pa.

***

It was an interesting shakedown cruise from Orlando to New Orleans; and uncertain why we went to New Orleans, except it seemed to be what everyone wanted. Gary made an adjustment to the carburetor, Enrique & Mauricio were mostly quiet, Henry & Doreen constantly jabbered at each other, Eric & Rosalie were wide-eyed, and Arlene & I kept everything on track. The guys took turns driving, and the girls kept the food end of it together. We decided not to push through the nights, so it took us 3 days to get there.

Though not Mardi Gras time (usually in February), it was still fun being there, on Bourbon Street, with brassy music in the air, the smell of seafood filtering through our nostrils, and laughter and giggles from dark and unseen places. We stayed an extra night there because it was fun and cheap since we slept in our home on wheels.

(Groups are extraordinary entities. Each one is different; every moment, day, or gathering is different. Each person, couple, unit struggles to go their own way, or stick with the group. To lead or to follow. And yet, they are the same; longing for identity, unity; belonging.)

From there, and over to Texas, we crossed the border into Mexico at the southeastern corner of Texas at Brownsville. The strategy was to follow the Atlantic coastline down Eastern Mexico, which we did. Always, we'd search for the shortest distance between two destinations.

Crossing the border into Mexico was…unusual, though not unexpected. Of course, they went through the **Yellow Rider** with a fine-tooth comb looking for any signs of marijuana or drugs; especially on all the equipment and baggage loaded on the top. They snickered after finishing, leaving everything a mess for us to again repackage and lash down. And, since we had all agreed to NOT take any drugs or contraband when leaving Orlando, we were unflinching to the customs officers; and they knew it!

Immigration was not an issue for us, Americans, but the officials started giving Enrique and Mauricio some flack, and their Spanish became quite heated. However, Arlene and I had already secured a visa for Costa Rica in our passports while in Orlando, which helped convince the immigration officials that we were all together going to Costa Rica. They allowed us entry into Mexico.

We were on the road again and were cheerful and full of anticipatory hope; as a fisherman in the early hours. It was a looong, hot, and dusty ride the 600 miles to Vera Cruz. Consistently, we had to deal with food, water, urination, and defecation along the way. And, of course, gasoline became a huge problem; or at least, finding a gas station. PEMEX (Petroleos Mexicanos) was the Mexican State-owned petroleum monopoly; and though relatively cheap, the stations were few and far between. Always, after filling the gas tank, we would fill the extra 5-gallon can strapped to the front near the doors; often used.

Gary kept the **Yellow Rider** in good running condition and the tires inflated.

The night lights of Vera Cruz came into our welcoming sight. Collectively, we agreed to stop there for a while, check into a motel and chill-out. There was a pool at the hotel providing us with time to have some fun in the sun and relax, have a few cervezas and reminisce. Gary got a little drunk; and talked a lot about home.

This was my second time in Vera Cruz. The first time was around Christmas of 1964; and now it was the summer of 1973 – do the math. Riding my trusty Honda Cruiser, and by way of Mexico City, I'd crossed over the nearby Mt. Orizava during a treacherous snowstorm to arrive in sunny Vera Cruz. Again, to relax and have a few *cervezas*. Of course, it was while on my way to Panama partaking in the infamous trip through the Darien Jungle and into Colombia.

Memory is a funny thing. Stunting or stimulating growth.

We continued driving south; pretty much following the same routes used during my motorcycle trip. And, by this time, I was doing most of the driving as we crossed over southern Mexico heading toward the border of Guatemala, landing at last on the Pan American Highway; also called the Kings Highway, or El Camino Real. We knew then it was a straight shot through Guatemala, El Salvador, Honduras, Nicaragua, into COSTA RICA (yeah).

Crossing over the border into Guatemala was easy; almost fun because the customs and immigrations guys were chuckling as they processed us; mostly because of our "God is Love" message on the bus, while Enrique repeatedly quipped **PASAJERO AMARILLO** in loud and clear Spanish. It was June 19, 1973.

Enrique and Mauricio adamantly suggested we take a side trip to the fabled mountain village of **Chichicastenango** before continuing to Guatemala City. It was only about a 30 to 40-mile veering-to-the-left trip up the mountainous road. None of us realized how bad the road was and how difficult it was going to be to get the long **YELLOW RIDER** around some of the hairpin turns.

At one turn (we were actually going slightly downhill at this point) it required backing the bus up and repetitively turning the front wheels at least 10 times to navigate the bus around the turn. And everybody except the driver was watching from <u>outside </u>the bus for fear it might roll down the mountainside.

At one point the front right wheel hung off the cliff and I started screaming in panic mode. Eric the driver was skillful in getting the bus back on the road. However, soon after that the bus stopped in the middle of the road and died. Gary and Buck walked to the nearest village a few miles up the road and found a mechanic who agreed to drive back to the bus and diagnose the engine problem. He removed the engine, driving us and the engine to the town of Chichicastenango. It took him 2 days to get the engine fixed and placed back in the **YELLOW RIDER** *at a reasonable price.*

At an altitude of 6,447 ft., it was a center of Mayan culture and population, Enrique and Mauricio somehow knew this was a memorable place to visit. We were fortunate to have been there on a full market day, with an amazing display of handicrafts, pottery, candles, incense, and even machetes. Their textiles were particularly brilliant in color. Each of us bought something; Arlene getting a hand-woven bag with a long shoulder strap of bright blues, pinks, and brown colors, and I bought a machete; thinking it would be helpful in the Costa Rican mountains; which it was. We also peeked inside the 400-year-old church and were enraptured by some of the nearby ancient carvings.

Somehow the return trip from Chichicastenango to the Pan American Highway was a lot easier, and it wasn't long before we were refueling in Guatemala City, continuing southward.

Passing through and out of the small country of El Salvador was a breeze; so much so, we barely remember much about it. By the time we entered Honduras, Gary had become fully agitated and forcefully expressed his desire to return home, to Orlando. He knew if he had dialogued with us along the way, we would most likely have persuaded him to "stay the course"; at least until we got to San Jose in Costa Rica.

But there was no dissuading him as he strongly and repetitively stated he missed his ex-wife and daughter. We knew not that he had a daughter and there was no refuting the sincerity of these feelings. Enrique and Mauricio obtained information about the Honduras

Toncontin International airport, a dangerous airport in a mountainous region, but Gary was assured of a flight to Miami. With a mixture of sadness and hope, Gary unloaded all his gear; leaving a few tools with the bus before adjusting the carburetor one more time. And he told me to keep an eye on the tire on the passenger side; it would need an occasional filling.

Gary was a true genius of auto-mechanics! He took an old, dilapidated school bus that could barely run, fixed it up, and governed it the nearly 3,000 miles to Honduras; and that took some great length, depth, and breadth of mind and character. For that we were all so grateful, hugged, kissed, and bid him bon voyage home.

But we still had about 450 miles until San Jose, and the bus was slowly showing its wear and tear.

Of all the countries, when passing through the usual customs check with the **YELLOW RIDER**, Nicaragua was the most difficult, although the reasons were a mystery to us. But it seemed, sadly, as if Nicaragua was always at war with itself!

Politically, the era of the Somoza family dictatorship still governed.

But...the FSLN (Sandinista National Liberation Front) had already begun a guerrilla movement against the regime; likely fashioned after the tactics of Fidel Castro and Che Guevara in Cuba against the Batista government; and probably for similar reasons.

The border guards exhibited some resentment and paranoia toward our peaceful and freedom loving lifestyle; as their eyes projected anticipation of finding drugs, arms, or other contraband on the bus. But regardless of which side of Nicaraguan politics was favored, most of the people held old resentments toward Americans resulting from the "Banana Wars" (1900-1934). The United States dominated the economics and politics in Latin America as the way to gain easy access to tropical fruits, which continued for most of the Twentieth Century. It was a form of neocolonialism, specifically by the United Fruit Company; later transformed into Chiquita Brands International.

(And, as unpopular as it seemed, the Catholic Church was often a defender of the brutal political ruling class during much of this time, as **their** primary source of funds. Ahh, then came the Latin Liberation Theology in the 1960's)

In the end, Enrique and Mauricio let us know, the officials wanted a cash bribe, but we were united and steadfastly refused. After a long and frustrating interaction with the chief honcho, permission was granted for us to pass through into Costa Rica.

Transiting from Nicaragua into Costa Rica was, to Arlene and me, slightly reminiscent of traveling from Pakistan into India; the difference was so stark. Admittedly, it may have been a placebo effect in our heads. But the plants and vegetation seemed greener, lusher, and more plentiful. The locals we saw at stops or along the way were better dressed and smiled when reading the "God is Love" message on the bus. It was a friendlier atmosphere to all of us; something we all had become collectively sensitive to since leaving Orlando.

We spent only a few hours in San Jose, the capital. After a quiet short telephone call, Enrique directed us straightaway to the town of **Heredia**, about 8 miles northeast of the capital and about 3,700 ft altitude with a population, at that time, of approximately 22,700. Heredia was also the full market-center for the region, nicknamed, and for good reason, the "City of Flowers".

We drove a few short kilometers up a dirt road toward the mountains, to where Enrique told us to pullover and stop, pointing and loudly exclaiming: **"Up there! Arriba, Arriba"**!

Following examples of Enrique and Mauricio, we began caravanning light loads of personal and camping paraphernalia up the trail. It was about a 400yard trip. The hilly path went through open fields with cows, a few rocky and stony patches, and then into areas moderately populated with trees; 6 to 8 inches thick. What appeared to be midway up the mountain, Enrique stopped and, waving his arm and body around, proudly stated **"Aqui - Here!"**!

It was about a quarter of a mile up from where the bus was parked and took about an hour of strenuous chugging.

Chapter 28

ON THE MOUNTAIN TOP

"Toto, I've a feeling we're not in Kansas anymore."

–Wizard of Oz, 1939 movie

A small creek ran downstream to the right of the area chosen to pitch personal tents and get settled in; each at least 25 yards apart. Our tent was a large square with canvas flooring and poled corners. Arlene could stand up in it, but I had to crouch a little.

We had a double sleeping bag with a 5 x 5 foot 2" thick foam pad underneath for my, the city girl's comfort.

Plenty of tools were purchased from the Last Whole Earth Catalogue; hammers, saws, measuring tapes, machete, etc. And **The Book**!

Starting from scratch, we were basically living a pioneer-type life on a new land and in a new world! But we were committed, determined, and…in a bit of a fantasyland. We were young and dumb, but stalwart!

Our first collective task was to build a central gathering place for food, and a centering place for collective minds to grow. Several bodies had schlepped the heavy-duty tarp, previously used to cover our gear on top of the **YELLOW RIDER**, up the hill. We tied one corner to a tree and used whacked-off tree branches for the remaining corner, then used rope and pegs for stabilization. The kerosene stove was pumped and started; and boiling water would become our primary source of drinking water.

I along with Doreen, and Rosalie cooked our first meal of pinto beans, brown rice, and some legumes on the gas camping stove. We were satisfied campers that night, falling asleep exhausted.

Each tented couple dug their own long, deep, and narrow trenches for human waste, and found our own spots at the very cold stream for bathing.

Every morning at daybreak, I would drink some hot tea, eliminate in the hole in the ground while breathing in the beauty of the lush, green growth with gratitude. I would then gather our previous days soiled clothes and head down to the stream where I scrubbed the clothing on a huge rock and hung them to air dry on rocks. I learned that the morning sunshine would turn into afternoon showers and would take our dry clothes into our tent before the downpour. Most days others in our commune would come to me for dry socks. My pattern of being caretaking "Ma" was ingrained. I remember spending hours embroidering an apron for my mother. I had come a long way from the Jewish princess big city girl. My confidence grew in my abilities to adjust. An outward-bound experience?

Arlene Washing Clothes in the Creek
(Our only picture of Costa Rica)

For inspiration, there were many and varied species of birds, including: psychedelic blue and green hummingbirds, parrots that always seem to fly in pairs, and an occasional trogon (birds with continuous and unmelodious sounds) with their extremely long tails. We were regularly flabbergasted by the unusual variety and species of **frogs**; separately seeing a batch of red ones, then a batch of what looked like albino frogs!

Then there was the incredible array of flowers, many of which were **orchids**, personal favorites. We didn't have to travel far into the woods or up the mountain paths to find them, squatting on tree branches, and other unexpected places. Some tiny, and some as big as your fist, but there was always one in our tent, and several at our headquarters around the heaters which was used for tea-making.

It was decided that our first major project was to build a pyramid-style building large enough to live in; out of wood! Of course, none of us had any real experience with structural framing or building; let alone with the exactness and complexity of a pyramid. Henry had worked in construction, and Eric's father owned a construction company; but only built large office buildings. Nevertheless, we went full steam ahead; believing pyramids had some mystical quality. Enrique and Mauricio, through their families, provided much wood, nails, and saws, as well as shingles for roof covering.

Without a foundation, we marked off a 30' square and pounded large studs into the ground at each corner. After much sweat, tears, and no little knuckle bleeding, it was completed - as best as we could, under the circumstances being that we were high most of the time, lacked knowledge, and were without precision measuring equipment.

The main flooring was a few inches off the ground, and the room was divided into 2 sections; the second floor was divided into two parts and barely large enough to stand in upright; the 3rd floor was just a tiny space for squatting. But we were happy with it and felt much joy upon completion.

A genius built the pyramids in Egypt. We were just a couple of wide-eyed hippies building something that was neither structurally sound nor geometrically accurate. But it was ours from beginning to end. And we took great pride in it.

Enrique and Mauricio graciously, again, provided the commune with a milking cow, and a week later came with a large black horse (stallion?). Sometime later, they carried up several dozen small cherry tree planters. We were starting to feel like a viable community.

Magically, during the many return trips from Heredia for lumber, food, and other necessities (and our favorite Costa Rican drink *papaya con leche*, basically sliced papaya, milk, and ice smoothie), we discovered fresh <u>mushrooms</u> (psilocybin) growing out of the many piles of cow dung on the hillside leading up to the commune. The fleshy toadstools were everywhere and easily spotted with each having a dark brown ring near the top of the stem.

So, we had a constant supply of psilocybin; and for free! We would eat them raw, cook with them, but mostly they were boiled into tea, producing a warm energy drink. It provided a light visual hallucination accompanied by warm feelings of love and a deep sense of a broad social connection between us and the universe.

I never did try them being concerned about the possible side effects to my intestines, mental state, and fear of feeling out of control.

With this came many collective discussions on expanding our time/space perception and gaining feelings of release from hereditary and environmental constrains. A fantasy, of course.

There were no shortages of volunteers for the necessary runs to Heredia because of the attractions of the satisfying *papaya con leche* drinks and the consequent ingestion of mushrooms. (VHAT A DEAL!!!)

All-in-all, the resulting sense of "settling in" allowed time to focus more on personal spiritual growth and a collective consciousness – the primary motive for embarking on this communal journey in the first place. One collective technique was to embark on a "no talk" day, when we would go about our daily habits and chores without speaking to anyone: even to our spouses and partners.

One day Enrique mysteriously arranged transportation to take us to a private house in San Jose and introduced *"Pepee"*. Pepee had a local and national reputation as a mentor of spiritual wisdom, a meditation guide, and somewhat of a guru.

Unlike some gurus he did not appear to be seeking devotees, living a very simple life. He never once asked for donations. Meditating with him brought me into the greatest stillness and sense of peace I had ever experienced.

Strongly steeped in Buddhism, he was short, squatty, and of few words, and even fewer words of English. Probably in his mid-sixties, we were attracted to him immediately! He cast an aroma of love, with an inviting smile that constantly exuded friendliness to all. Interrupting Enrique in mid-sentence, he invited us to enter into meditation. That was his aura and style; and it was attractive.

Focusing on the light of a candle with incense burning and Zen Garden meditation music filled my soul. I continue to this day to meditate to this same flute music which triggers a great sense of peaceful joy and gratitude.

After our second visit to his home, he stated with adventurous eyes, that he would be coming to the commune to spend the night. After dropping off his sleeping gear and food, he joined us for tea, of the non- psilocybin type, of course. Finishing the evening meal, and as the evening darkness settled in, Pepee found a small grassy knoll nearby, sat cross-legged, and invited us into meditation. Without an awareness of time, we were collectively and individually in and out of the meditative state trying to melt our thoughts into one; then to none.

The aroma and sounds of nature had invaded our senses, as a moist air enveloped the area. Pepee softly spouted a few unintelligible but pleasant-sounding words. Several of us started breathing in and chanting **Om** meditative sound of India that seemed to fuse our energies.

Without warning, Pepee stated in an authoritative voice: "el ángel" which we all knew was the word for **angel** in Spanish. Arlene and I, opening our eyes first saw the dim glowing lighting of San Jose 8 miles below, the nearby cloudy mist looking ahead, then saw flashing colors vibrating in movement through the levitating droplets. It could only have been angels; at least as we understood them.

My memory was that Pepee slept in our tent. I woke up in the middle of the night hearing him outside our tent. The next morning, I asked him if he had slept well. He said he looked into the valley near our tent and saw a host of angels saying that this was a sacred gathering spot for our unseen helpers.

For days afterward, we talked about that memorable experience; each expressing it differently and on different levels of awareness. We never saw Pepee again. Was it real, or just an optical illusion? Was it a collective hallucination, or mass hypnosis? Who knows? WE certainly didn't. But that memory lives with us today.

Someone, unknown to our memories, recommended we treat ourselves by going to San Jose for the (1972) movie: *"Brother Sun, Sister Moon"* – which we did. It was the story about St. Francis of Assisi and St. Claire and was the impactful message needed at that time in our spiritual journey; of which, many may be somewhat familiar. St. Francis, son of a wealthy merchant, just returned from war with the feeling of complete emptiness. After spending much time in nature, and to his father's ire, Francis denounced his wealth and gradually began helping the poor and downtrodden; some of whom were employees of his father.

He acquiesced to the inner desire to build, rebuilt, a church from the broken-down ruins of a previous structure destroyed by fire. The townspeople watched the young man selflessly carrying stone-by-stone for the restoration. He soon had a small following of like-minded men and women helping and willing to devote their energies in service to the poor.

He decided to walk and seek an audience with the Pope; a little over 100 miles. Francis was immediately appalled at the opulence and wealth of the Vatican and shared these feelings during his audience with Pope Innocent, who quickly rejected Francis as being "out of touch". However, after having second thoughts, the Pope recalled Francis and kissed his feet, declaring his example of innocence and as a true believer; later to be designated as a saint.

St. Claire was also born into a wealthy ancient Roman family, who owned a palace in Assisi. As a teen she heard St. Francis preach and asked him to help her live a life of joyous poverty, in selfless service following Jesus' life and teachings. Francis placed her in a convent of Benedictine nuns. She started the Order of Poor Ladies and had a following of woman who lived a life of poverty, austerity, seclusion from the world, and spent her days in labor and prayer. Clare sought to imitate Francis' virtues and way of life, considering him her spiritual father, and took care of him during his final illness.

After seeing this movie, I had a clear dream, seeing myself dressed in burlap sackcloth with my head cleanly shaven. I was shocked at this vision of myself since my curly hair was one of my most attractive physical features and wearing colorful cloth brought me joy. However, I felt a great sense of peace identifying with St. Claire and wanted to serve selflessly, giving up my ego attachments and vanity.

The impressions the story of St. Francis and St. Claire made cannot be overstated at that time and in our circumstances trying to forge our identity in the Costa Rican commune.

By this time, I had nearly finished reading the over 2,000 pages of **The Book**, and Arlene continued to observe a gradual change overcoming me, i.e., becoming move loving and helpful.

*This behavior so impressed me that I too wanted to start reading **The Book**. I decided to read the last part of the book about Jesus, since I learned from and enjoyed reading historical biographies about wise, great people who contributed to the betterment of mankind. I had to overcome my Jewish cultural heritage and upbringing which was **so** deeply imbedded. I simply reframed it by now seeing Jesus as a wise rabbi and no doubt one of the wisest, most loving men ever to have lived. In earnest, I immersed myself in the text as well.*

We sometimes lobbied in friendly competition for reading times. While Arlene was perusing, I would occasionally talk with Eric and Rosalie or Henry and Doreen about how impressed I was about the truth in **The Book**, but to no avail. I was not aware at that time of any translations, as an inroad to introducing the text to our Spanish brother.

I don't remember the date, but I remember the day, waking up in the morning looking outside the tent into the new morning feeling…a sense of joy, of liberty, of serenity and being overcome with a notion of oneness. A feeling of belongingness invaded my soul. Belonging to what, I wasn't sure; just to everything! My mind was unable to translate everything into words; ineffable if you will. I burst outside our tent and pranced up and down the grassy knoll hugging everyone and trees within my orbit. Then, I wanted to laugh and cry. A huge burden had been lifted. The demon had been vanquished!

Looking for my father
As a kid I never saw my father
So, I went looking for him
He was not inside a dank prison cell
Nor in the blast of an opening parachute
Even near death in a thickened green jungle
Or in the salty ocean air and gigantic waves
He could not be found in faraway countries
Though I kept looking never giving up
Not in the solace of a like-minded community
And especially with a mind full of chemicals
But knew to keep seeking I would find
And one day I woke up and discovered all
the while my father was inside me
It was a revelation!

I felt as if the old me had died, and literally a new me was born! Through the process of absorbing the revelations of **The Book**'s contents into my consciousness, and the totality of my life's experiences, I felt this freedom of accepting and knowing myself. And even greater, my self-reflective awareness permitted knowing God as my true and loving father, the source of love, of truth, beauty, and goodness.

I went around the campsite quietly shouting, "My father, my father, my father...I love you, I love you...and thank you soooo much...I love you." The others who heard and saw me thought I had probably drifted into a bit of delirium or some sort of madness. But Arlene knew as she always did.

Faith in my soul's reality gave me an acceptance of origins with true beginnings, while allowing a gateway to an eternity without end. I am a person, and God must also be an even greater person. Personality opened the door to a real person-to-person relationship with God my Father; and adding an indissolvable friendship made it even more stupendously remarkable.

The hole in my soul was filled! At last, that demon of not knowing and being without an earthly father's affection and direction was lifted, no longer having to constantly prove myself. The genetics of my biologic father, whom, as an adult, I had only met once for less than 10 minutes, had no resemblance to my real father. And now I had my eternal father; and, unknown to me, always did have. And I wanted to be just like Him!

This awakening was doubled when I then knew this same spiritual DNA belonged, inherently, to every other person in the world. We are all brothers and sisters in the family of God our Father. WOW! Finally, I belonged to a real family! A faith family with all conscious members trying to do the wishes of the parent(s) was so profound yet so simple – to love and serve. Finally, I got it; the real life and teachings of Jesus – as he loved God and served humanity. It was a transcendence of self. VHAT A DEAL!!!

My natural reaction was to return to our tent and grab Arlene in an unbreakable embrace. And she shared a similar experience. We wept together. No longer were there religious, cultural, educational, or ideological differences between us, we were together in spirit. We knew and accepted that it would last forever, throughout our eternal careers.

Sitting on a small grassy bluff looking down into the deep San Jose valley, as the sun broke through the clouds, we talked. It was one of those indelible memorable discussions.

We talked – much as we did during the first time we met in St. Thomas – but now very differently. Now we spoke of transcendences, of acceptance, of loyalty, of truth, beauty, and goodness welling up inside of us. And, for the first time, we sincerely spoke of settling down and having a family, having children! The model of Jesus as a parent gave us the confidence needed to overcome the previously felt limitations of our families of origin.

Up to this point I resisted having children and passing down my inherited Old Testament guilt and fears.

We wanted to live in a medium-size city - not too large (like Brooklyn, NY) and not too small (like Columbia, PA); realizing we could live anywhere in the world, for the world was our home. But we chose to return to our culture and homeland in the USA.

The model of Jesus as a counselor and selfless human being who spread good cheer as he passed by , gave me the needed confidence to realize my dream of becoming a therapist and use my education to be of service to other.

But all was not well in paradise.

Imperceptibly, the monsoon rains had gradually set in. The wooden pyramid showed its amateurish and shoddy construction with severe leakages on every level, offering little refuge from the constant downpour. Our tent's plastic ground covering began to rot, causing damage to some books, and most disheartening, to many of the remaining travel pictures. We had to raise perishables off the ground and onto tent poles.

The horse choked himself to death with the too-long halter lead rope, <u>our</u> serious mistake! All the men got shovels and began digging a burial hole. We were in shock, but knew the burial had to be done immediately to prevent decaying and the wild animals from feeding. It was rainy, wet, and hard digging because we had to dig near where the horse laid and go deep and wide because of the stiffened legs. It took a long time, and not an obvious joyful time. We all knew we did not give the animal the time and attention needed to maintain safety and good health. Enrique was especially perturbed because the black stallion was his family's property.

The next day we surveyed the planted cherry trees. They too were all dead; all 2 dozen of them! In shock again, we didn't know why they had died! But upon pulling a few of them from the soil we could see the roots had not much grown; had not thrived! (A quick non-scientific bit of research on soil pH levels showed Costa Rica to have typically high acidic levels and our cherry trees may have suffered from aluminum toxicity and moisture stress from the monsoons)

Another failed experiment!

By this time, Enrique and Mauricio were spending less and less time on the commune and had long-since stopped bringing their Costa Rican friends up to the pyramid to talk and share our activities. Less enthusiasm was displayed during much of the responsibilities for maintenance, organizing fun activities and group meditations. We knew that the best way to lead was to delegate, while leading by example.

Soon we found ourselves as the only ones going to Heredia for food essentials and schlepping the bags up the hill to the food storage bins. And when encouraging other members to assist (enticing them with a free papaya con leche), they usually made excuses. Whispers began circulating about "getting low on money". The realization that we had become the "Ma & Pa" of the commune had unscrupulously crept upon our reflective souls.

The guillotine fell on a Saturday when, after carrying a particularly heavy shopping load up the mountain trail but refreshed after another (our last papaya con leche?) we discovered the commune was completely deserted; devoid of humans but personal belongings remained. No written notes, nothing!

We made dinner and retired to our tent, read some of **The Book**, and went to sleep without hearing a sound; except the steady rain drops on the overhead canvas. In the morning, still nobody. But by midday they began trickling in, except Mauricio and Enrique. Their avoidance techniques worked until we decided to call an all-attendance meeting for some answers.

The answer was: they had all gone down to San Jose to attend a Santana concert! We couldn't believe what we were hearing! They tried to appease us by reliving the experience and saying how great the music was and wished we had been there. Though Arlene and I were great admirers of Santana and his music and have endlessly enjoyed "Black Magic Woman", (that had a spell on us too), but... Where was the collective consciousness, responsibilities, priorities, and loyalties to each other and the commune? When our resources were nearly drained and the physical conditions of the commune deteriorating... they went to a concert? I'm certain our age gaps were blatantly showing but exposed a real "failure to communicate".

"**The Book**" had brought us to a higher level of consciousness, awareness, and tolerance. It was time to manifest a new beginning; a new way of living; a real life. We easily forgave the other members for their irresponsible and immature behavior, but we had to "move on".

We envisioned a life of service, living in a mid-sized town, hopefully in the Rocky Mountains, having children, developing careers, and growing old together; all the while accepting all relationships as eternal.

It was with deep and conflicting emotions with constrained purposefulness that we began packing personal belongings in readiness to depart. Sad because we were leaving the commune we had conceived of, helped build and lived in for nearly 10 months. Grieving because we were separating from relationships groomed for almost 2 years and had grown to love. And, of course, we felt the loss of leaving the local environment of birds, frogs, endless variety of orchids, and mushrooms. We also would miss the Costa Rican people and the country-as-a-whole; easily the most advanced of the Central American countries.

The **YELLOW RIDER** had long since entered into a state of non-usability; so, it was not an issue.

It was the conclusion of a dream (with the understanding that there was no such thing as an end). But like all conclusion, and before the final act, there was present within us new adventures and opportunities to actualize and dig within for greater potentials. We were bursting with an inner ambition to begin a new life, a life with all humanity as sacred. Now with clarity of direction, we sensed this was the time; a new moment where we were united with all in the progressive evolution of planetary destiny as children of God.

Hugs and kisses, and we were on our way to the San Jose airport. Other than a very rare email, we never saw any of the commune participants again.

Chapter 29

BACK IN THE U.S.,
BACK IN THE U.S. OF A

Love is the desire to do good to others.

–Urantia Book, 56:10.21

When passing through the airport gift-shop we saw the impressionable Costa Rican t-shirt with printing either in black-on-white or white-on-black: "**NO ARMY SINCE 1948**".

Then we got it! We fully understood why Costa Rica was such a friendly, wonderful, and advanced culture when compared to other Central America countries. Instead of diverting huge amounts of their resources on wasted military arms, which are used to kill and discarded into the scrap heap of antiquity, the majority of their budget was returned to the people and the cultural needs. If only other countries were like the Costa Rican government and spent most of their revenues on resources necessary to help the people, like education, health care, transportation, etc. It's not a perfect country, of course. They do have a police force and rely on the US for military protection. Still…what if…every country in the world relied on one international military force while putting their resources into the people? But… perhaps I was dreaming again, or just espousing old hippie dogma.

Landing in NY, we took subways to Brooklyn to Lilly and Louie's home again. This time they were more welcoming, much friendlier. Perhaps they had become accustomed to our forays on the world travel circuits. Our first mission was to contact the Chicago headquarters of "**The Book**" inquiring about readers in Brooklyn or New York area and received the name and telephone number of a long-time reader. Within a few days we met our first "**Book**" reader. His name was John

Hales, one of the sweetest guys ever to meet! As a social worker in Brooklyn, he was observant without judgment, friendly without being patronizing, and inquisitive but not nosey.

Most astounding, John was a <u>second-generation</u> reader of "**The Book**"; his parents being some of the first readers during the time of its inception in the 30's and 40's in Chicago. So, he knew whereof he spoke! With a smile, John took one look at us, and pointing his arm in no particular direction, said: "Get yourselves to a study group!" He easily recognized our appearance looking as if we had just "come down out of the trees" and needed socializing with other readers which was so true.

Memory is a funny thing. The greatest of all memories are of the many loving relationships.

Shortly after our meeting with John in NY, we landed back in Venice Beach, CA.

We secured a beach apartment in a quadruplex, and soon started attending a study group at the home of Vince Ventola and his wife, Roxy, down by the canals in Venice. And John was so right! Sharing our thoughts, feelings, and experiences with the 6 or 8 others in the group proved so immensely satisfying, enriching: and humbling.

There were differences, of course, but we all unified in accepting the essence of "*The Book*" *believing we were all children of an unconditionally loving God and as such were all brothers and sisters. Our unique perspectives served to expand our minds and increase our compassion. Unity rather than Uniformity!!!*

Within a month, we heard about "**The Book**" society in the Los Angeles area, and they were soon having a conference. We couldn't believe our good fortune! After not knowing of another reader in the whole world while in Costa Rica, we were suddenly inundated with an amalgamation of stalwart believers, brothers, and sisters.

Attending, our most startling impression was of the diverse types of people attending. Besides the young, middle, and old agers, there were Asians, Blacks, and Latins; hippies, gays, bikers, conservatives, liberals; people from across the social and economic spectrum. That "**The Book**" appealed to such a grand cross-section of people was so very reassuring, making us desirous of wanting to remain; especially experiencing all the hugs, kisses, and exchanges of love. Collectively we intrinsically accepted our journeys as eternal. The topical presentations, games, and meals were all so joyful. This was our family, and we felt at ease and at home.

(There was a brutal reminder that not all was fun and games with "**The Book**" and it would not protect us from the vicissitudes of life after we learned one of our biker brothers was killed in a crash when on his way to one of these gatherings!)

We attended several of these conferences and gatherings while living in Venice. They were held near the home of Julia Fenderson, the grand dame of all the readers in Southern California. Her thick blonde hair was raised in pompadour style and her friendly face displayed an omnipresent broad smile highlighted with clear plastic rimmed glasses. But she loved everybody, and everybody loved her. While she didn't rule with an "iron fist", she did run a "tight ship", whether for a conference, a society officers' meeting, or a friendly social gathering.

One of her biggest concerns was that someone in the hippie segment of the society would get "busted" for smoking pot or other illegal drugs, and "**The Book**", **"The Urantia Book",** movement would fall under extensive legal scrutiny and doom the growth forever.

*She had gathered information on parenting, both from "**The Urantia Book**" and current literature as well as writing original children's songs. She passed all this work on to us, hoping that someday we would add to and edit these writings and use them as a guidebook for parenting. We taught our 3 sons her songs and used the writings to help us raise our children. Of course, we shared these pearls of wisdom, with friends, family and clients and did presentations both professionally and at conferences.*

Then there was this young energetic hippie wearing bib overalls and a red bandana around his blonde hair. Mo Segal said we should move to Colorado, where he was starting a tea company in Boulder. We heard Buffy Sainte Marie, the Cree Canadian American Indian folk singer and writer sing many songs. (Buffy won a 1983 academy award in music for co-writing the song "Up Where We Belong" along with Jack Nitzsche and Will Jennings for the popular movie "An Officer and a Gentleman".) Her song "Universal Solider" resulted in her being placed on the Nixon Administration's blacklist, making her an instant hit with most of us. "WOW"!!!

And, after attending one of his mind-blowing talks on the nature and structure of the Central and Grand Universe, we met Charles "Chick" Montgomery and developed a long, meaningful, and humor filled relationship. During our months in Venice, we often had small meditation and yoga classes at our apartment, and people would come and go because it was so close to the beach. Chick was a frequent visitor.

One night we heard a knock at our door, and it was Chick asking if he could stay in our apartment for a short while. He was separating from his wife and wanted a place to temporarily live; and without hesitation we said "yes". The humor started and revolved around his choice of where to sleep and keep a few pieces of personal belongings. And even though we had an extra bedroom, he insisted on living in our walk-in closet; easily fitted with a single-size mattress! So, he lived out of our walk-in closet for nearly 2 months. And for many years afterward, each time we meet, we always embraced with a remembrance laugh.

During our 9 months stay in Venice Beach, I taught several classes in the Psychology department at the University of Southern California. I networked with my old professors and looked at journals in search of a job that would fit my qualifications. Bursting through the kitchen door one day, I said: "I think I found it!" and went on to show Buck a listed "Chief Psychologist in Geriatrics needed" at the State Hospital in Pueblo, Colorado. PEERFECT, we agreed. I called the listed number and arranged for an interview. I applied for the position, and I went for an interview and immediately knew this was our future home. The position was a perfect fit which they immediately offered me, and Pueblo was a small city near the mountains, which we had envisioned while on the mountain top in Costa Rico.

Returning to Venice from the interview at the Geriatrics Division of the Colorado State Hospital in Pueblo, Arlene was itching with glee. The decision made, we were on our way with backpacks, suitcases, and doctors' bag in hand.

Chapter 30

THE CIRCUIT HOME

Be in the world
As if you are a traveler, a passer-by,
With your clothes and shoes full of dust.
Sometimes you sit
Under the shade of a tree,
Sometimes you walk in the desert.
Be always a passer-by,
For this is not home.

–Hadith, Islam

With what seemed like a million miles behind us, and a faith-instilled eternity before us, we felt rejuvenated, creative, and ready to plant some roots. And build a home life.

Ultimately, I guess, the home is where the love is, where peace prevails, where spirits are united, and children nurtured and learn moral decision-making, the crowning glory of our advancing lives.

The car ride from Denver's Stapleton Airport down Interstate 25 with George Baichek, the Director of the Geriatric Division at the State Hospital (who had hired Arlene) was spectacular. We were oohing and ahhing while gazing out the windows off to the right toward the mesmerizing snowcapped mountains, the brilliant blue sky, and beautiful tree-covered hills, when George interrupted to ask: "Do you like those pine trees?" Answering in the affirmative, he then added: "Take advantage of them now, because you won't see many in Pueblo!"

It was December of 1974, and we spent the first 6 weeks in Pueblo living inside the Colorado State Hospital Nursing Quarters. It was a bit of a dreary and gray Holiday season; the steam radiators clanging, unworkable window curtains, and little human laughter. But we had each other, and knew we were on the cusp of another and different glorious adventure.

George, being the only person we knew, introduced us to a cheerful real estate agent – Bud Brown. One snow covered day we looked at the outside of 3 or 4 houses. That night I had a dream of the house, 419 W. 22nd St. and knew without looking inside that this was to be our home. Walking through the rooms validated my premonition. The kitchen and bathrooms were remodeled since the double brick corner house was built before the turn of the 20th century. It was owned and lived in by Bud; and chosen mostly by me because I wanted a "corner" brick house like the one in which I grew up. His wife Marylin and 2 children had just moved to another residence. The bad news was we didn't have money for a down-payment. The good news was the community was desperately trying to attract professionals of any type to Pueblo because of the recent downturn of their largest blue-collar employer; the CF& I Steel Mill.

Because I had a contractual professional job, borrowing money was reasonably easy. Bud took us around to 3 banks/lending institutions saying that we wanted to borrow funds for furniture; a partial truth, since it was mostly used for our $5,000 down payment and for some furniture, and we formally closed on the house of my dreams in February 1975.

Our first son, Jonathan, was born August 25, 1976, when I was 33 years old with a long hard labor and fast easy delivery. After working at the State Hospital for 3 years I decided to get my license as a Clinical Psychologist in private practice in order to work part time at home while raising our family. Buck got a BA degree at the University of Southern California and worked at Parkview Hospital until retirement. Our second son, Matthew, was born July 12, 1979, and I was ready to birth our son in the car as we rode to Penrose Hospital in Colorado Springs for a very quick delivery. We wanted him to be born in a birthing room and never dreamt the labor would take only 45 minutes. After the initial shock of an unplanned pregnancy, we were given a wonderful gift of our third child, Adam on May 31, 1981, at Parkview Hospital in Pueblo after a relatively easy 3-hour labor and somewhat more difficult delivery weighing more than our first two sons.

The boys are riding their own physical, mental, and spiritual circuits now, and we've remained in our home on 22nd Street. And the rest, as they say, is recorded in our spiritual records on the Mansion Worlds to be reviewed upon our arrival; especially those which memory has failed to retain.

The great benefactors of this manuscript are our children and 5-year-old granddaughter, Zoe. From the 2 of us, there are 8 in our biological family now representing our greatest achievement. Truly, the love that we have for our children is the closest we will ever come to understanding the Love that God has for us.

Matthew, Jonathan, & Adam
Memory is a funny thing.

THE POST-SCRIPT

Reviewing these travel experiences, and to say we personally grew a lot on many levels, would be a trivialization of the entirety of such a life. But were we part of, or serving, a higher purpose, something greater than ourselves? We would hope for a hearty decisive YES!!! Travelers, regardless of the circuits or distances, serve to promote and increase the brotherhood of humanity, our planets' inevitable destiny. We are beings of experience, and experience is the only truth we know with any degree of certainty; morally and ethically.

Perhaps an <u>ending question</u> could be: Why isn't every responsible citizen of the world free to travel wherever, whenever, and however they please? All arguments against traveling are based on fear, and that fear is based on future uncertainties. Of the 2 kinds of fear, reasonable and unreasonable; most are unreasonable.

Travel becomes a multidimensional experience of reality and primal to the eternal journey; so, get started now; practicing! It may be an imperative! In time, the travel circuits extend way beyond our capacity of understanding, into the infinity of space. It's easy; and is just a matter of <u>getting out the front door!</u>

The circuits are real physical <u>things</u> allowing us to get from point A to B and perhaps to A again, leading us from Brooklyn to the Seychelles Islands and back. We rode these circuits, sometimes walking in a bleak desert, riding bumpy buses over uninspiring lands, sharing crowded train coaches over multifarious lands of poor people; experiencing our deep love by the Taj Mahal, sometimes a passenger on silver planes flying through billowing clouds above the tallest mountains; even flowing in our own small world atop the timeless, endless, living, and serenely turbulent ocean waves.

We saw some of the heights of cultural civilization and the depths and depravity of humanity, of our brothers and sisters. Always there, enjoying the moment or saddened by man's inhumanity to man; but still there. These circuits are available to all, often temporarily short-circuited by the selfish cancer of partisanship or the perpetrators of war; religious or nationalistic.

But to be the first, to open a yet unridden circuit! That is what dreams are made of!

The <u>mind</u> circuits are different and difficult to understand and impossible to describe. But they are circuits, nonetheless, and about all we have a modicum of control. Sometimes these are <u>reflective</u> circuits of ideas, ideals, uncertainties, and hope. We dreamed of faraway places and unusual people but, with sincerity, we manifested these during this desirous quest for the unknown because we adjusted, and we adjusted, and we adjusted some more! Adjusting to the many and varied cultural variations, religions, and mores necessitated fluidity of thought as well as mastering of our tongues. The confusing monetary differences, food variances even within short distances evoked courageous temptations, while dress codes caused a showing of acceptance. But reflect we must.

These give a meaning to it all.

Rare, but truthful, were the joyful moments when experiencing the essence of the joining of minds and souls. What a thrill! Whether it was 2, 3, or more the emergence of a collective mind potential grew exponentially with each of our thoughts; somehow, someday we know it is destined to encompass every person in world unity, because God is in all of us.

So, what's the truth about the good life that transcends race, culture, nationality, and all human diversity? All people seemed the happiest when they experienced giving and receiving love of family and friends and had meaningful experiences and a valuable relationship with a loving God of their understanding. This is the unity that transcends the diversity and connects all of humanity. Loving God and serving each other is the very core of the truth about the good life!

A new circuit of creativity manifesting actuals from potentials when feeling oneness with Greek, Israeli, Afghani, Hindi, Nepalese, Thai, Balinese, or Ocean islanders; and hippies circuit riders everywhere. It wasn't about race, language, money, dress, or gender. It was about being <u>human</u> and alive, vital, and giving unselfishly; of being moral, ethical, and trying to live the highest levels of the Golden Rule.

We've always pursued peace and love, and now added TRUTH

to the mix.

For Kerouac the roads had opened, for us the circuits became vital and alive.

It does not matter if you go next door to a neighbor, friends in the next town, relatives in another state, or another country or around the world; just GO!!!

In the end, the lasting value of traveling these circuits was about the people.

Whether it be the young couple we crossed the Atlantic Ocean with, the Greek farmers inviting us to meal, the Israelis in the Kibbutz, the young American in Eilat, the German business man or the Turkish family on the train to Erzurum, the Goa family renting us their hut and the multitude of hippies by the beach, the Nepalese shop keeper, being picked-up by the wealthy Thai while hitchhiking, getting the monkey from the Canadian, the Balinese taxi driver, and of course our sailing companions, even the captain and wife on the boat in the Indian Ocean, and the Seychellois connections.

Then coming home being greeted by Arlene's parents, the Orlando students and friends, and our great commune group driving and living in Costa Rica, leading us back to Venice and engaging with our spiritual brothers and sisters; all leading to Pueblo, Colorado and a life of family love and community service.

Individual travelers can do more for world peace than all the other highfalutin supposed world peace organizations, with the inclusion of, perhaps, international traders. Getting out the front door leads to an inherent understanding of the goodness in human sameness, and this leads to tolerating differences, and this tolerance eventually leads to friendship and to love. One day this aroma of love will pervade the consciousness of all humanity, of every human being; and there will be peace on earth.

And since the very beginning of our parenthood, we no long use drugs. I recall sitting in our car looking at a sunset and agreeing that we no longer needed marijuana to help us relax, feel connected to others, and experience the peace that surpasses understanding. Our personal relationship with and our faith in God was a natural high that we could choose to experience at any moment anywhere in the world!

We have continued to travel to many countries while interacting with leaders and students of **"The Urantia Book",** to all the continents - Asia, Africa, Europe, North America, and South America, Australia – except Antarctica. Study Groups are a weekly regularity for us, and frequent national and international gatherings. Our musical tastes have changed; though we still listen to some rock n' roll, and also jazz, and lots of classical. Beethoven's 9th is a favorite.

Our relationships are eternal. Our personal love has continued to grow, but…the BIG unanswered question remains: did Arlene read Dostoevsky?

Yes, of course she did, and then some.

"The more you succeed in loving, the more you'll be convinced at the existence of God and the immortality of your soul." Fyodor Dostoevsky

Thanks. We hope you have enjoyed this ride.

And what of the *next* circuit?

Lightning Source UK Ltd.
Milton Keynes UK
UKHW021019280422
402163UK00005B/67